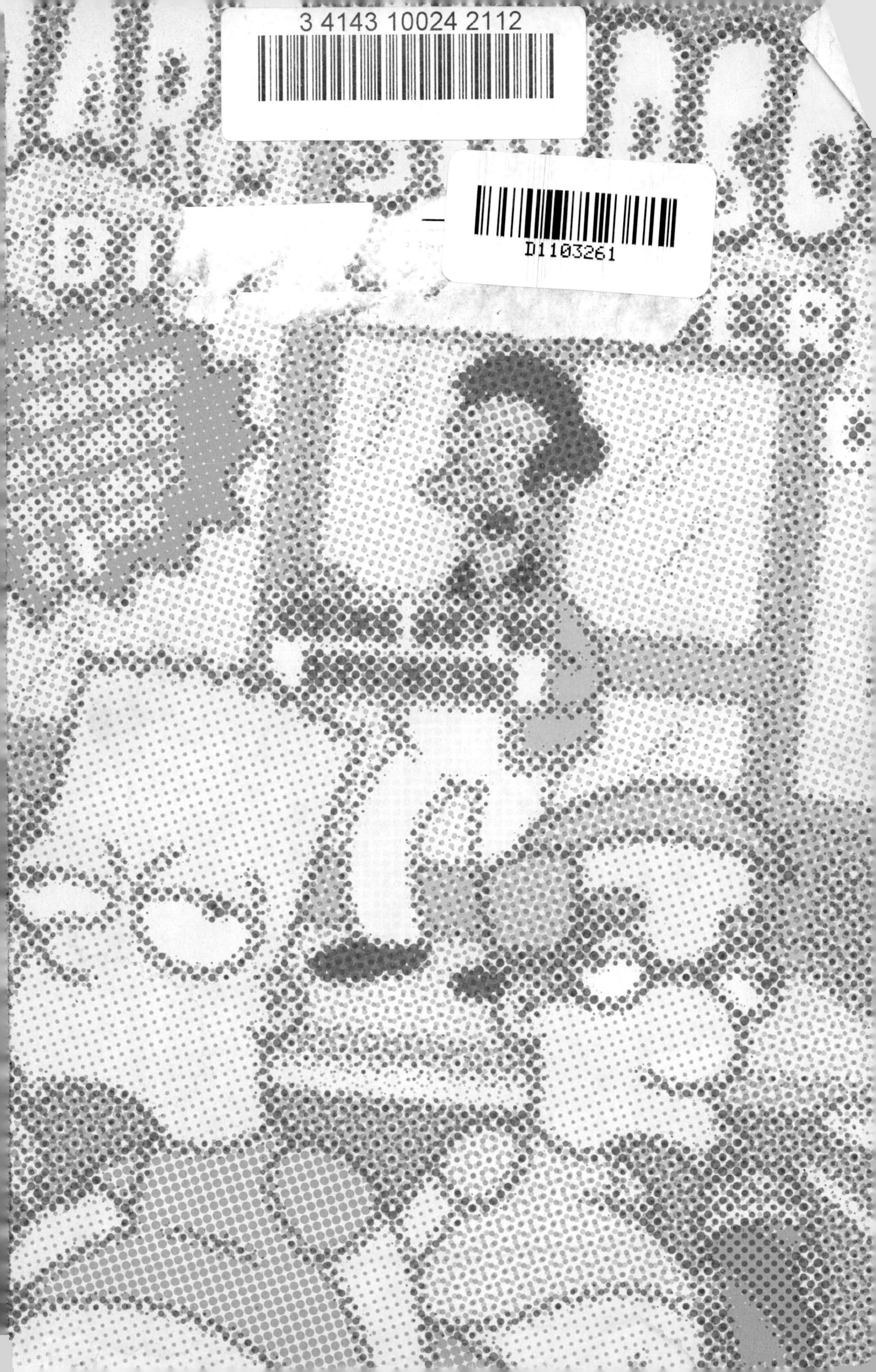

BIG BRILLIANT BOOK OF BART SIMPSON™

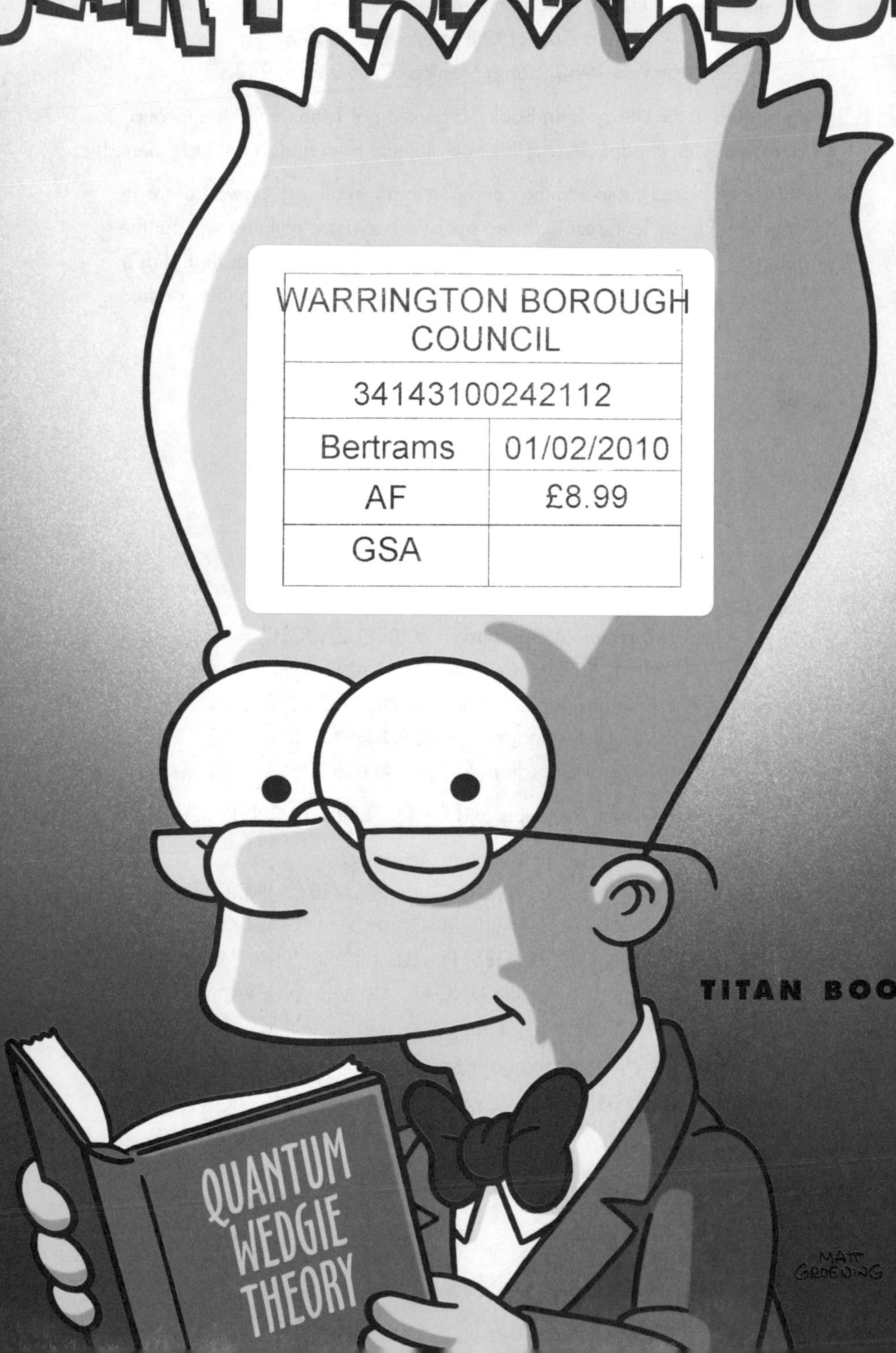
QUANTUM WEDGIE THEORY
MATT GROENING

TITAN BOOKS

BIG BRILLIANT BOOK OF BART SIMPSON

Copyright © 2005, 2006 & 2008 by
Bongo Entertainment, Inc. All rights reserved.
No part of this book may be used or reproduced in any manner whatsoever
without written permission except in the case of brief quotations
embodied in critical articles and reviews. For information address
Bongo Comics Group c/o Titan Books
P.O. Box 1963, Santa Monica, CA 90406-1963

Published in the UK by Titan Books, a division of Titan Publishing Group,
144 Southwark St., London SE1 0UP, under licence from Bongo Entertainment, Inc.

FIRST EDITION: MAY 2008

ISBN-10: 1 84576 752 7
ISBN-13: 9781845767525

2 4 6 8 10 9 7 5 3 1

Publisher: MATT GROENING
Creative Director: BILL MORRISON
Managing Editor: TERRY DELEGEANE
Director of Operations: ROBERT ZAUGH
Art Director: NATHAN KANE
Art Director Special Projects: SERBAN CRISTESCU
Production Manager: CHRISTOPHER UNGAR
Legal Guardian: SUSAN A. GRODE

Trade Paperback Concepts and Design: SERBAN CRISTESCU

Contributing Artists:
KAREN BATES, JOHN COSTANZA, JOHN DELANEY, MIKE DECARLO,
CLAY & SUSAN GRIFFITH, NATHAN HAMILL, JASON HO, NATHAN KANE, JAMES LLOYD,
JOEY MASON, BILL MORRISON, JOEY NILGES, PHYLLIS NOVIN, PHIL ORTIZ, ANDREW PEPOY,
MIKE ROTE, HOWARD SHUM, CHRIS UNGAR, ART VILLANUEVA, MIKE WORLEY

Contributing Writers:
JAMES W. BATES, CHUCK DIXON, EARL KRESS, JOHN JACKSON MILLER,
TOM PEYER, DAVID SEIDMAN, BRYAN UHLENBROCK, PATRIC VERRONE

PRINTED IN CANADA

TABLE OF CONTENTS

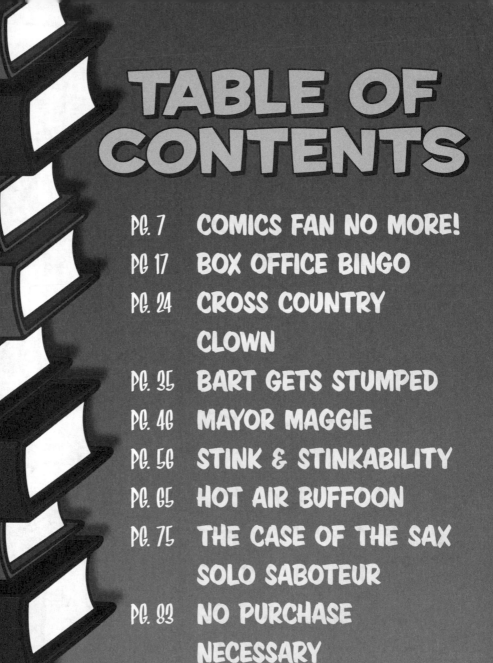

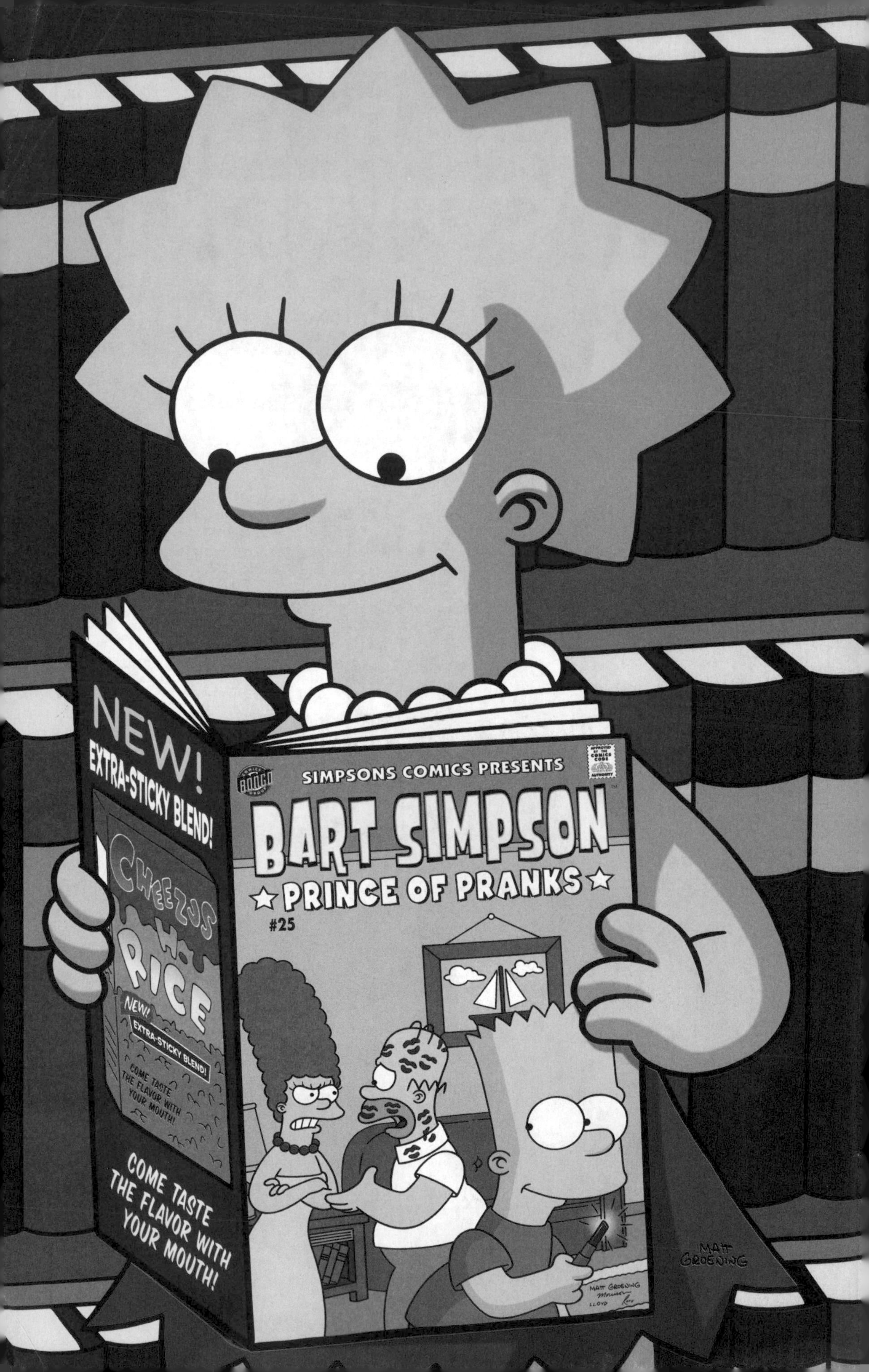
NEW!
EXTRA-STICKY BLEND!
CHEEZOS H-RICE
NEW!
EXTRA-STICKY BLEND!
COME TASTE THE FLAVOR WITH YOUR MOUTH!
COME TASTE THE FLAVOR WITH YOUR MOUTH!
SIMPSONS COMICS PRESENTS
BART SIMPSON
PRINCE OF PRANKS
#25
MATT GROENING
MATT GROENING

MATT GROENING PRESENTS

the UNDERACHIEVING BART SIMPSON

"COMICS FAN NO MORE!"

TOM PEYER	JOHN COSTANZA	HOWARD SHUM	JOEY MASON	KAREN BATES	BILL MORRISON
WRITER	PENCILS	INKS	COLORS	LETTERS	EDITOR

I AM A COMICS FAN *NO MORE*...

...SINCE WORKING FOR YOU AT THIS CONVENTION MAKES ME A *PRO*!

RIGHT, COMIC BOOK GUY? *RIGHT*?

SPRINGGRAPHNOVSEQARTCOMTRACARDCON
THE SPRINGFIELD GRAPHIC NOVEL, SEQUENTIAL ART, COMICS AND TRADING CARD CONVENTION
JUNE 7TH & 8TH

HARDLY, SIMPSON...

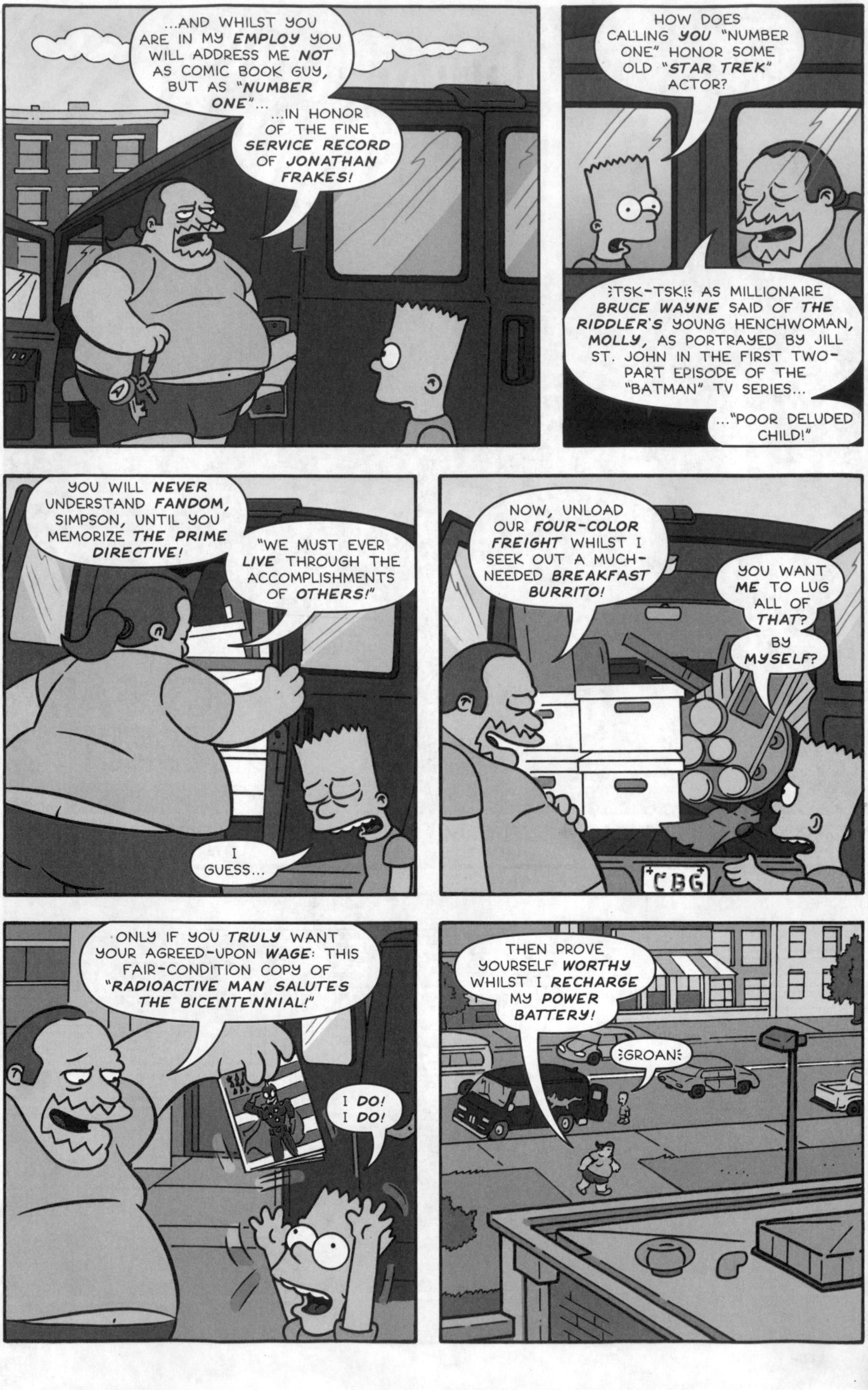
...AND WHILST YOU ARE IN MY EMPLOY YOU WILL ADDRESS ME NOT AS COMIC BOOK GUY, BUT AS "NUMBER ONE"...
...IN HONOR OF THE FINE SERVICE RECORD OF JONATHAN FRAKES!
HOW DOES CALLING YOU "NUMBER ONE" HONOR SOME OLD "STAR TREK" ACTOR?
⁝TSK-TSK!⁝ AS MILLIONAIRE BRUCE WAYNE SAID OF THE RIDDLER'S YOUNG HENCHWOMAN, MOLLY, AS PORTRAYED BY JILL ST. JOHN IN THE FIRST TWO-PART EPISODE OF THE "BATMAN" TV SERIES...
..."POOR DELUDED CHILD!"
YOU WILL NEVER UNDERSTAND FANDOM, SIMPSON, UNTIL YOU MEMORIZE THE PRIME DIRECTIVE!
"WE MUST EVER LIVE THROUGH THE ACCOMPLISHMENTS OF OTHERS!"
I GUESS...
NOW, UNLOAD OUR FOUR-COLOR FREIGHT WHILST I SEEK OUT A MUCH-NEEDED BREAKFAST BURRITO!
YOU WANT ME TO LUG ALL OF THAT? BY MYSELF?
CBG
ONLY IF YOU TRULY WANT YOUR AGREED-UPON WAGE: THIS FAIR-CONDITION COPY OF "RADIOACTIVE MAN SALUTES THE BICENTENNIAL!"
I DO! I DO!
THEN PROVE YOURSELF WORTHY WHILST I RECHARGE MY POWER BATTERY!
⁝GROAN⁝

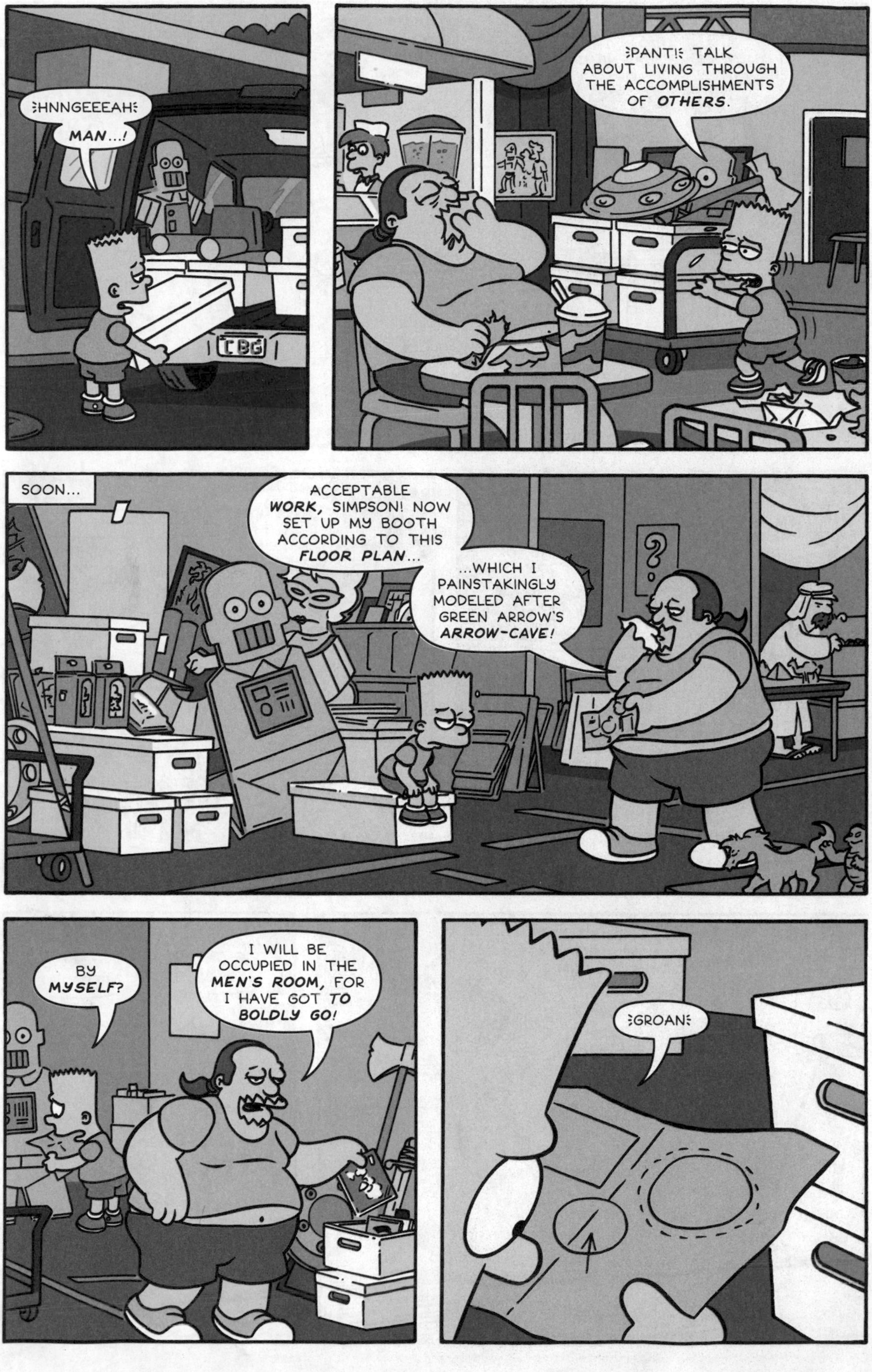
HNNGEEEAH
MAN...!
CBG
PANT! TALK ABOUT LIVING THROUGH THE ACCOMPLISHMENTS OF OTHERS.
SOON...
ACCEPTABLE WORK, SIMPSON! NOW SET UP MY BOOTH ACCORDING TO THIS FLOOR PLAN...
...WHICH I PAINSTAKINGLY MODELED AFTER GREEN ARROW'S ARROW-CAVE!
BY MYSELF?
I WILL BE OCCUPIED IN THE MEN'S ROOM, FOR I HAVE GOT TO BOLDLY GO!
GROAN

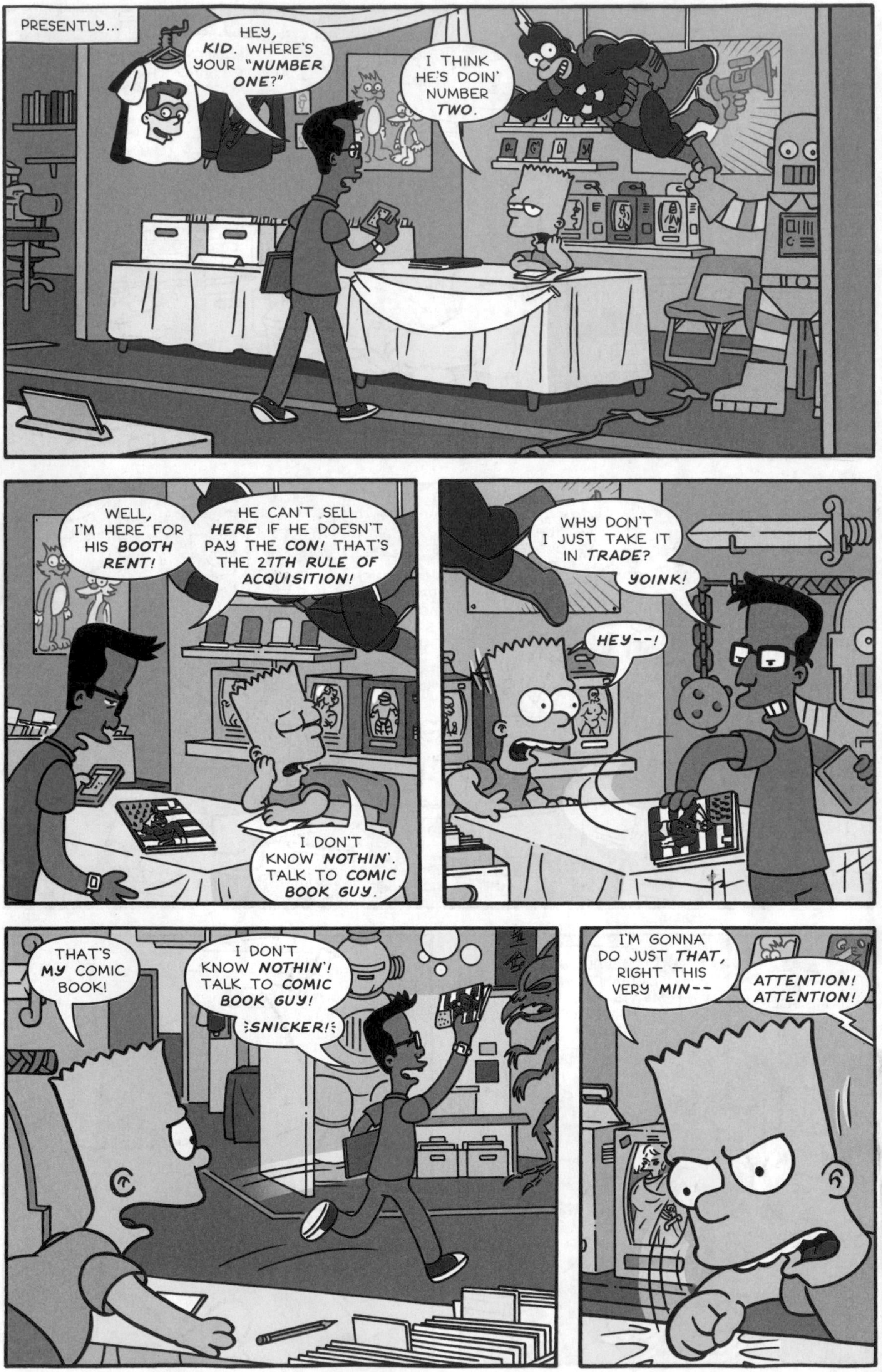
PRESENTLY...
HEY, KID. WHERE'S YOUR "NUMBER ONE?"
I THINK HE'S DOIN' NUMBER TWO.
WELL, I'M HERE FOR HIS BOOTH RENT!
HE CAN'T SELL HERE IF HE DOESN'T PAY THE CON! THAT'S THE 27TH RULE OF ACQUISITION!
I DON'T KNOW NOTHIN'. TALK TO COMIC BOOK GUY.
WHY DON'T I JUST TAKE IT IN TRADE?
YOINK!
HEY--!
THAT'S MY COMIC BOOK!
I DON'T KNOW NOTHIN'! TALK TO COMIC BOOK GUY!
SNICKER!
I'M GONNA DO JUST THAT, RIGHT THIS VERY MIN--
ATTENTION! ATTENTION!

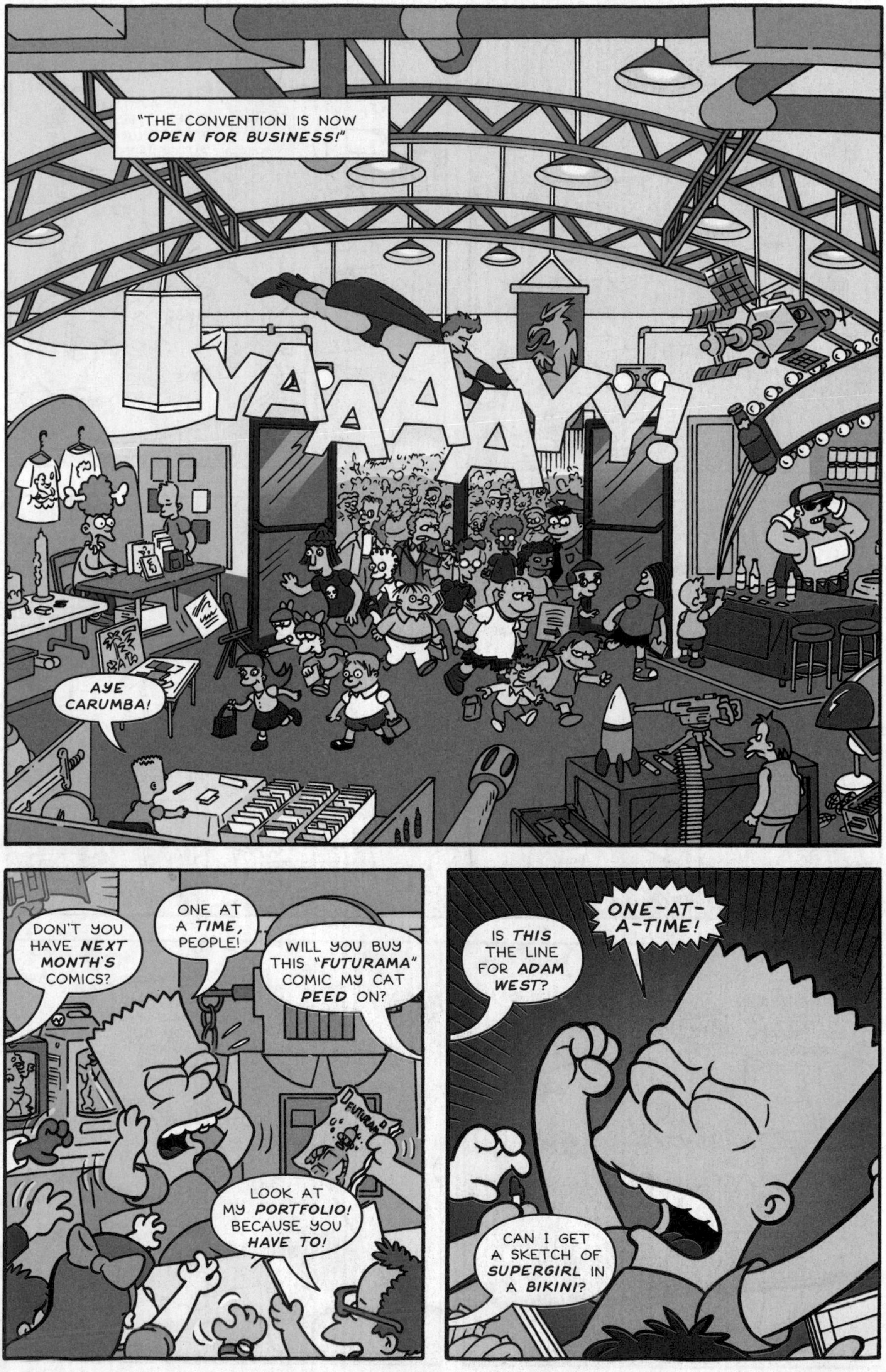
"THE CONVENTION IS NOW OPEN FOR BUSINESS!"
YAAAAY!
AYE CARUMBA!
DON'T YOU HAVE NEXT MONTH'S COMICS?
ONE AT A TIME, PEOPLE!
WILL YOU BUY THIS "FUTURAMA" COMIC MY CAT PEED ON?
LOOK AT MY PORTFOLIO! BECAUSE YOU HAVE TO!
IS THIS THE LINE FOR ADAM WEST?
ONE-AT-A-TIME!
CAN I GET A SKETCH OF SUPERGIRL IN A BIKINI?

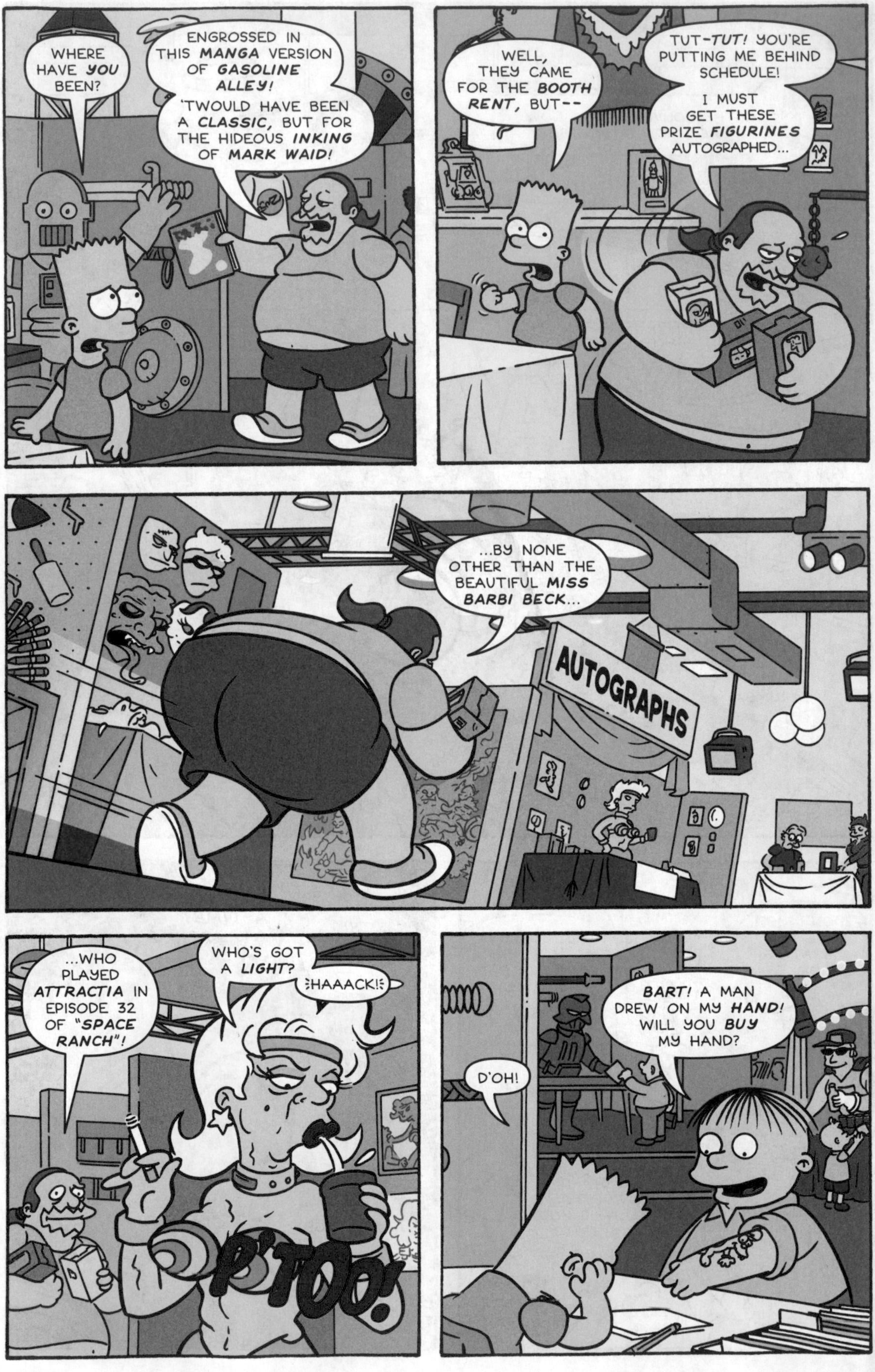

WHERE HAVE *YOU* BEEN?
ENGROSSED IN THIS *MANGA* VERSION OF *GASOLINE ALLEY!*
'TWOULD HAVE BEEN A *CLASSIC,* BUT FOR THE HIDEOUS *INKING* OF *MARK WAID!*
WELL, THEY CAME FOR THE *BOOTH RENT,* BUT--
TUT-*TUT!* YOU'RE PUTTING ME BEHIND SCHEDULE!
I MUST GET THESE PRIZE *FIGURINES* AUTOGRAPHED...
...BY NONE OTHER THAN THE BEAUTIFUL *MISS BARBI BECK*...
AUTOGRAPHS
...WHO PLAYED *ATTRACTIA* IN EPISODE 32 OF "*SPACE RANCH*"!
WHO'S GOT A *LIGHT?*
HAAACK!
P'TOO!
BART! A MAN DREW ON MY *HAND!* WILL YOU *BUY* MY HAND?
D'OH!

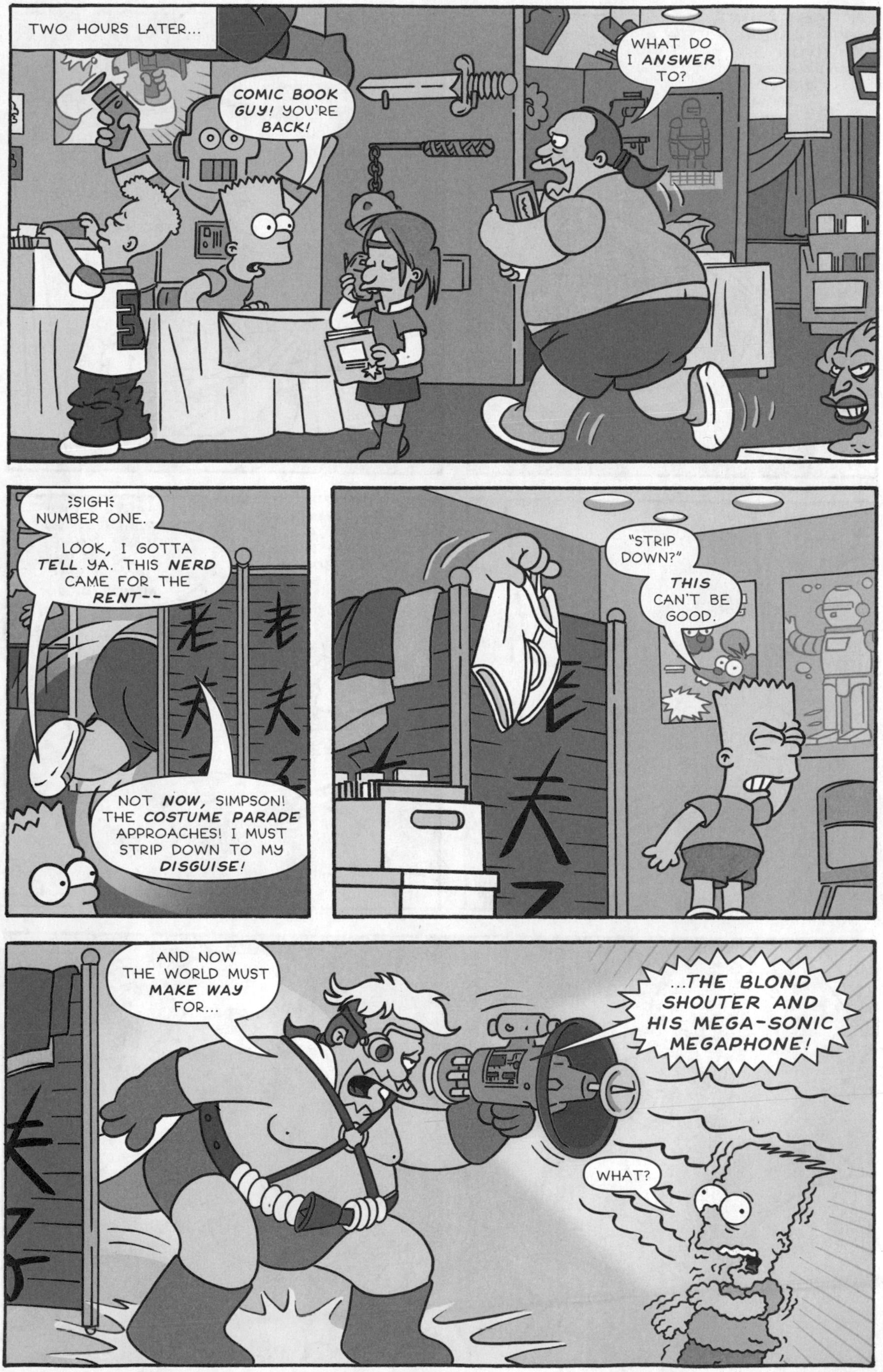
TWO HOURS LATER...
COMIC BOOK GUY! YOU'RE BACK!
WHAT DO I ANSWER TO?
:SIGH: NUMBER ONE.
LOOK, I GOTTA TELL YA. THIS NERD CAME FOR THE RENT--
NOT NOW, SIMPSON! THE COSTUME PARADE APPROACHES! I MUST STRIP DOWN TO MY DISGUISE!
"STRIP DOWN?"
THIS CAN'T BE GOOD.
AND NOW THE WORLD MUST MAKE WAY FOR...
...THE BLOND SHOUTER AND HIS MEGA-SONIC MEGAPHONE!
WHAT?

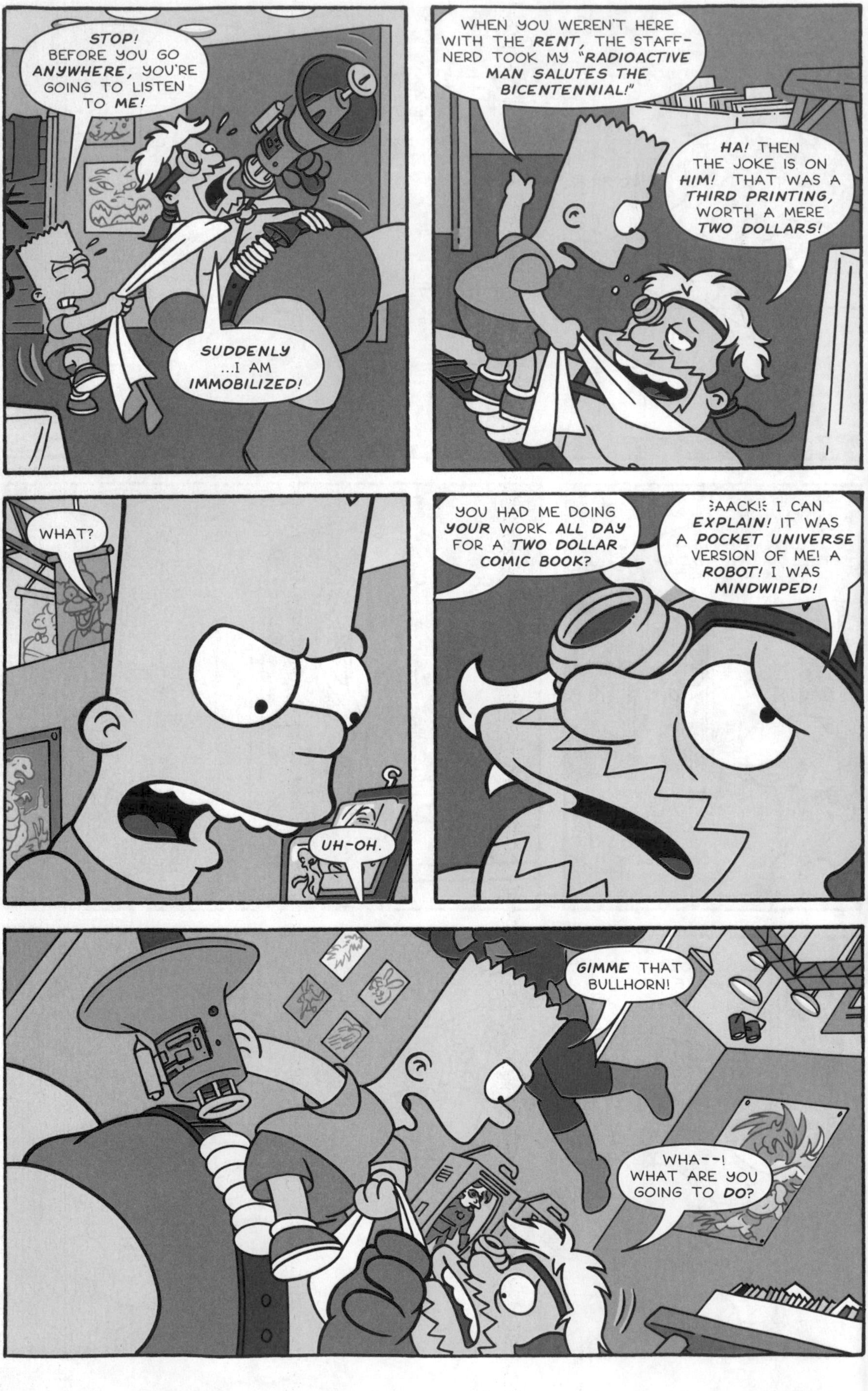

STOP! BEFORE YOU GO ANYWHERE, YOU'RE GOING TO LISTEN TO ME!
SUDDENLY ...I AM IMMOBILIZED!
WHEN YOU WEREN'T HERE WITH THE RENT, THE STAFF-NERD TOOK MY "RADIOACTIVE MAN SALUTES THE BICENTENNIAL!"
HA! THEN THE JOKE IS ON HIM! THAT WAS A THIRD PRINTING, WORTH A MERE TWO DOLLARS!
WHAT?
UH-OH.
YOU HAD ME DOING YOUR WORK ALL DAY FOR A TWO DOLLAR COMIC BOOK?
AACK!! I CAN EXPLAIN! IT WAS A POCKET UNIVERSE VERSION OF ME! A ROBOT! I WAS MINDWIPED!
GIMME THAT BULLHORN!
WHA--! WHAT ARE YOU GOING TO DO?

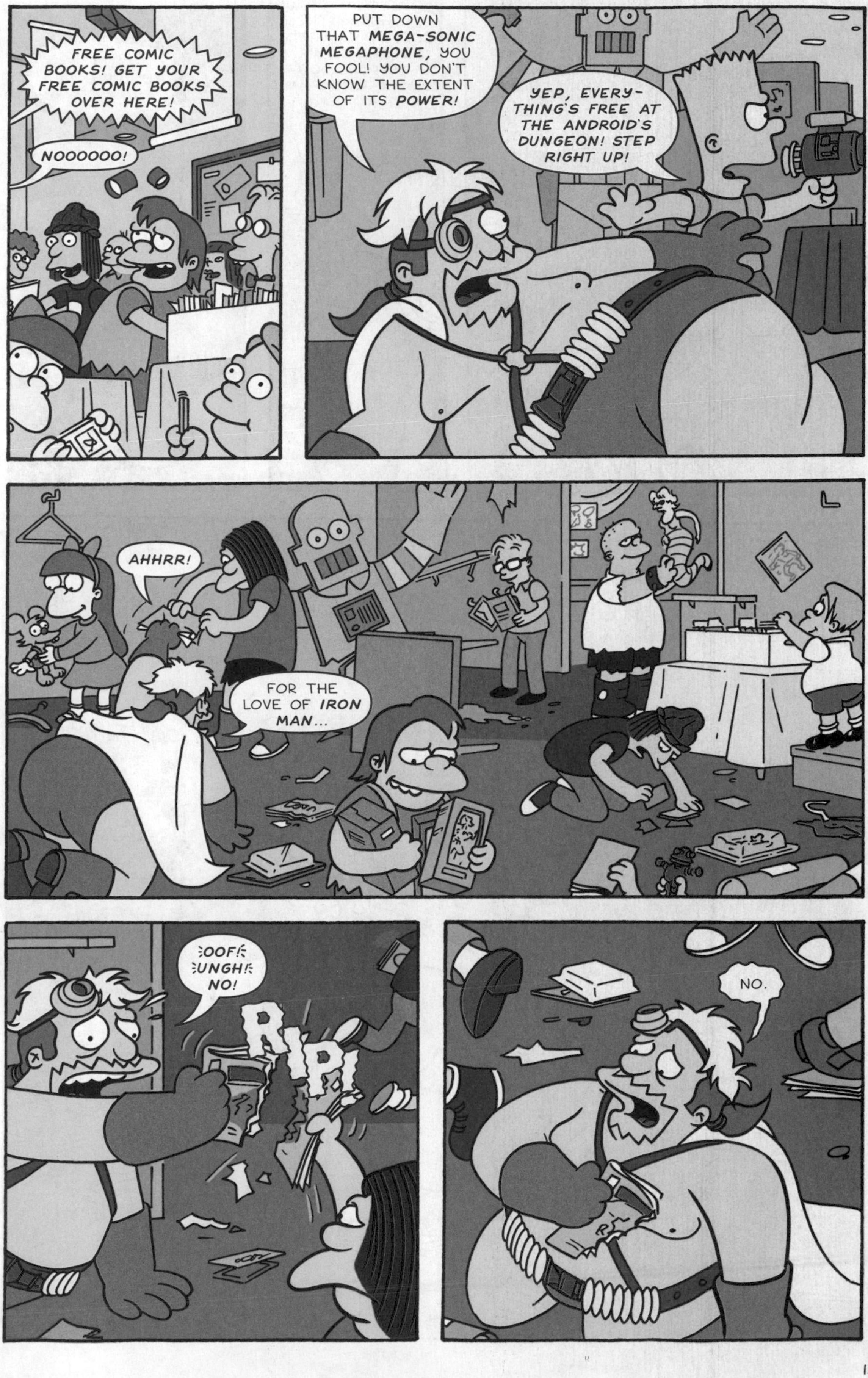

FREE COMIC BOOKS! GET YOUR FREE COMIC BOOKS OVER HERE!
NOOOOOO!
PUT DOWN THAT MEGA-SONIC MEGAPHONE, YOU FOOL! YOU DON'T KNOW THE EXTENT OF ITS POWER!
YEP, EVERY-THING'S FREE AT THE ANDROID'S DUNGEON! STEP RIGHT UP!
AHHRR!
FOR THE LOVE OF IRON MAN...
OOF! UNGH! NO!
RIP!
NO.

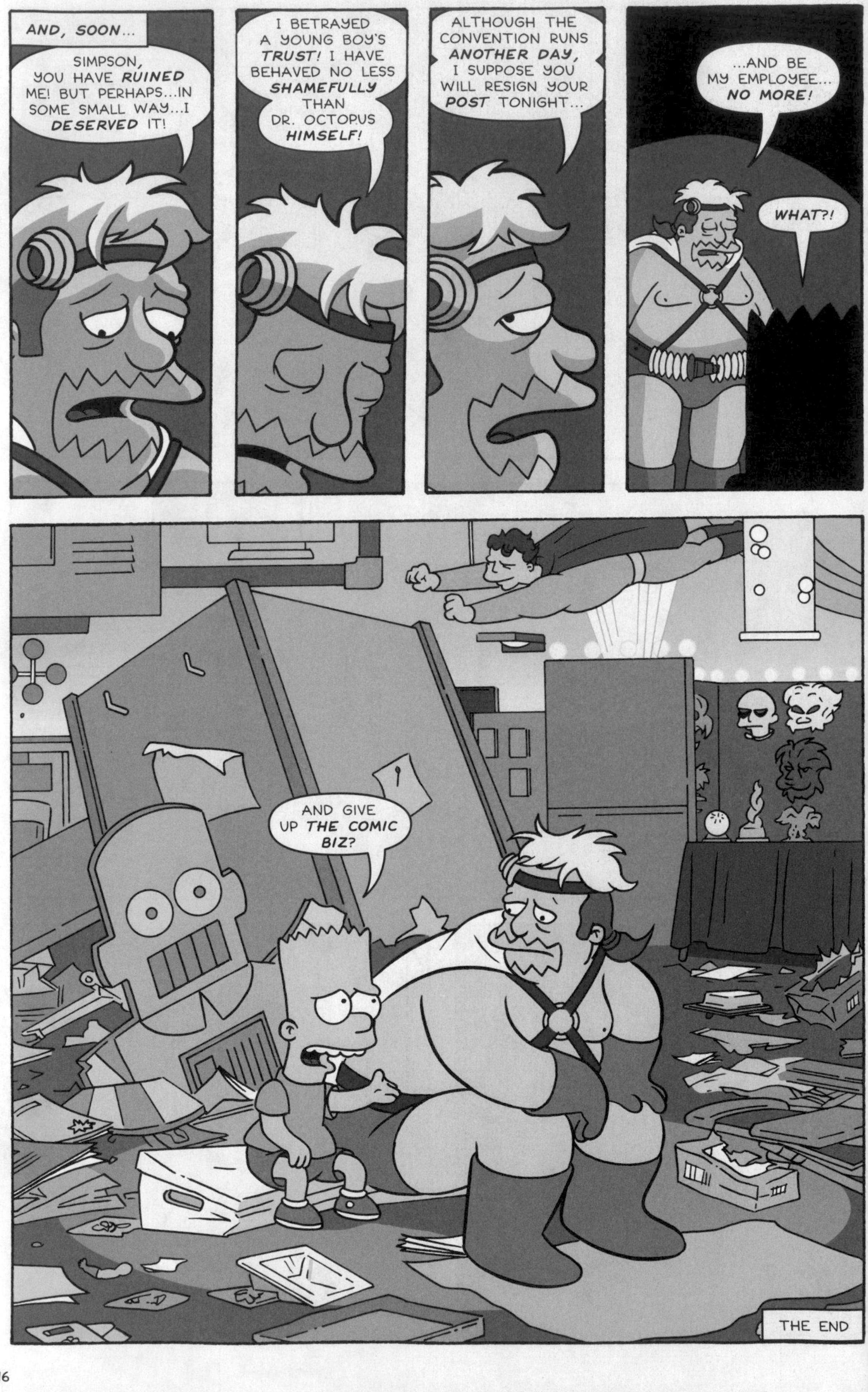
AND, SOON...
SIMPSON, YOU HAVE RUINED ME! BUT PERHAPS...IN SOME SMALL WAY...I DESERVED IT!
I BETRAYED A YOUNG BOY'S TRUST! I HAVE BEHAVED NO LESS SHAMEFULLY THAN DR. OCTOPUS HIMSELF!
ALTHOUGH THE CONVENTION RUNS ANOTHER DAY, I SUPPOSE YOU WILL RESIGN YOUR POST TONIGHT...
...AND BE MY EMPLOYEE... NO MORE!
WHAT?!
AND GIVE UP THE COMIC BIZ?
THE END

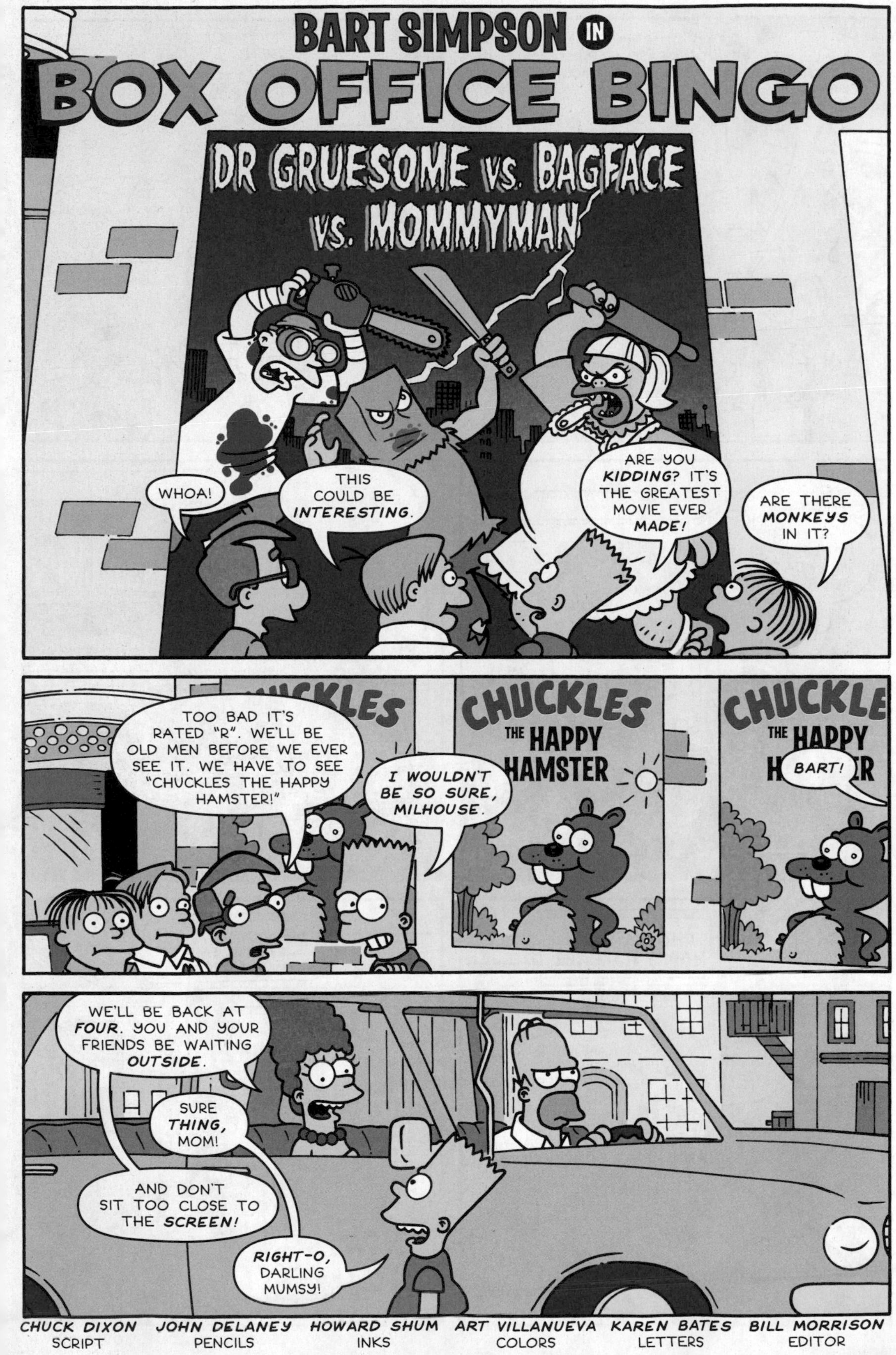
BART SIMPSON IN
BOX OFFICE BINGO
DR GRUESOME vs. BAGFACE vs. MOMMYMAN
WHOA!
THIS COULD BE *INTERESTING*.
ARE YOU *KIDDING*? IT'S THE GREATEST MOVIE EVER *MADE!*
ARE THERE *MONKEYS* IN IT?
CHUCKLES THE HAPPY HAMSTER
TOO BAD IT'S RATED "R". WE'LL BE OLD MEN BEFORE WE EVER SEE IT. WE HAVE TO SEE "CHUCKLES THE HAPPY HAMSTER!"
I WOULDN'T BE SO SURE, MILHOUSE.
BART!
WE'LL BE BACK AT *FOUR*. YOU AND YOUR FRIENDS BE WAITING *OUTSIDE*.
SURE *THING,* MOM!
AND DON'T SIT TOO CLOSE TO THE *SCREEN!*
RIGHT-O, DARLING MUMSY!

CHUCK DIXON SCRIPT *JOHN DELANEY* PENCILS *HOWARD SHUM* INKS *ART VILLANUEVA* COLORS *KAREN BATES* LETTERS *BILL MORRISON* EDITOR

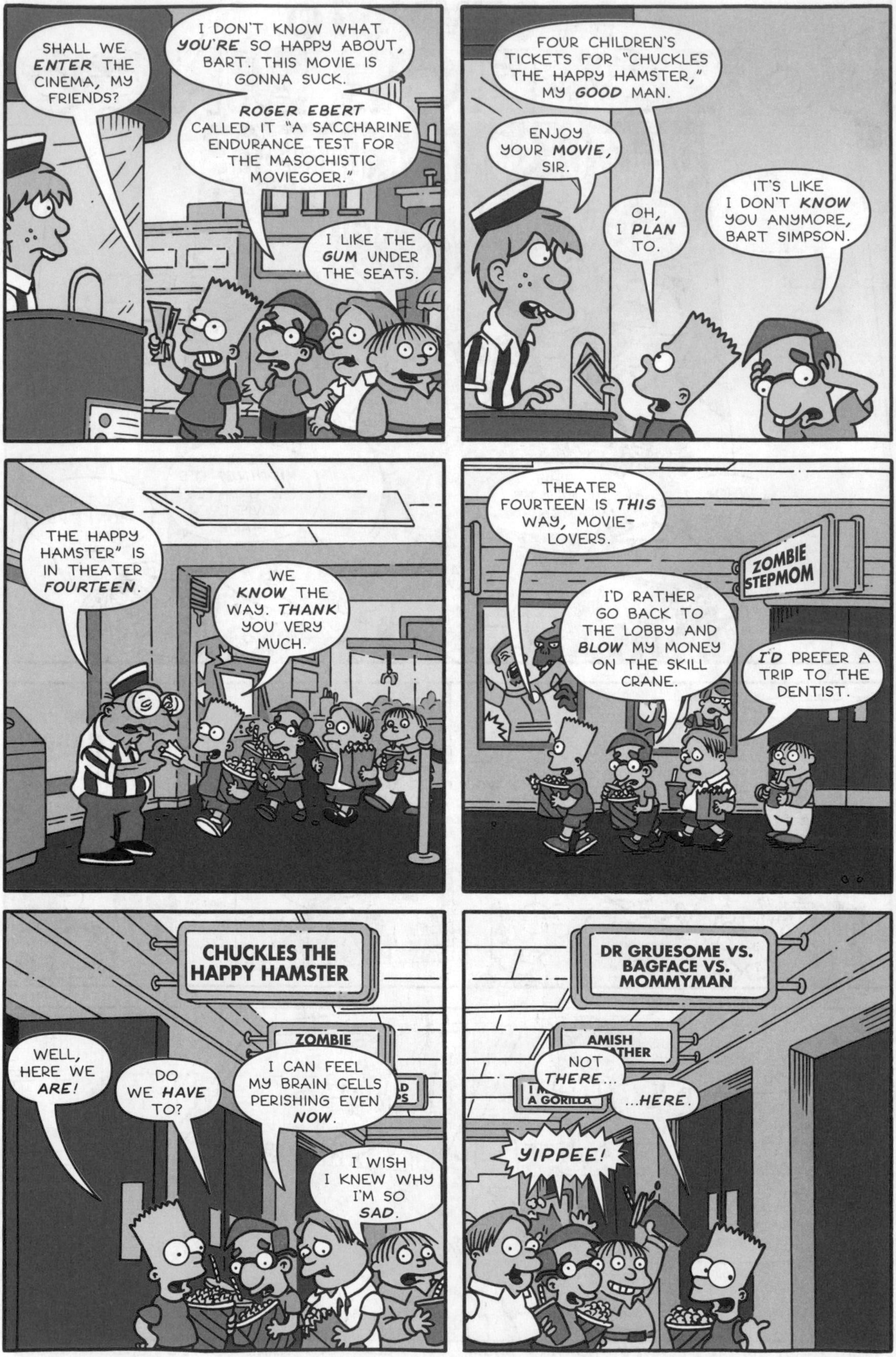
SHALL WE ENTER THE CINEMA, MY FRIENDS?
I DON'T KNOW WHAT YOU'RE SO HAPPY ABOUT, BART. THIS MOVIE IS GONNA SUCK.
ROGER EBERT CALLED IT "A SACCHARINE ENDURANCE TEST FOR THE MASOCHISTIC MOVIEGOER."
I LIKE THE GUM UNDER THE SEATS.
FOUR CHILDREN'S TICKETS FOR "CHUCKLES THE HAPPY HAMSTER," MY GOOD MAN.
ENJOY YOUR MOVIE, SIR.
OH, I PLAN TO.
IT'S LIKE I DON'T KNOW YOU ANYMORE, BART SIMPSON.
THE HAPPY HAMSTER" IS IN THEATER FOURTEEN.
WE KNOW THE WAY. THANK YOU VERY MUCH.
THEATER FOURTEEN IS THIS WAY, MOVIE-LOVERS.
ZOMBIE STEPMOM
I'D RATHER GO BACK TO THE LOBBY AND BLOW MY MONEY ON THE SKILL CRANE.
I'D PREFER A TRIP TO THE DENTIST.
CHUCKLES THE HAPPY HAMSTER
ZOMBIE
WELL, HERE WE ARE!
DO WE HAVE TO?
I CAN FEEL MY BRAIN CELLS PERISHING EVEN NOW.
I WISH I KNEW WHY I'M SO SAD.
DR GRUESOME VS. BAGFACE VS. MOMMYMAN
NOT THERE...
...HERE.
YIPPEE!

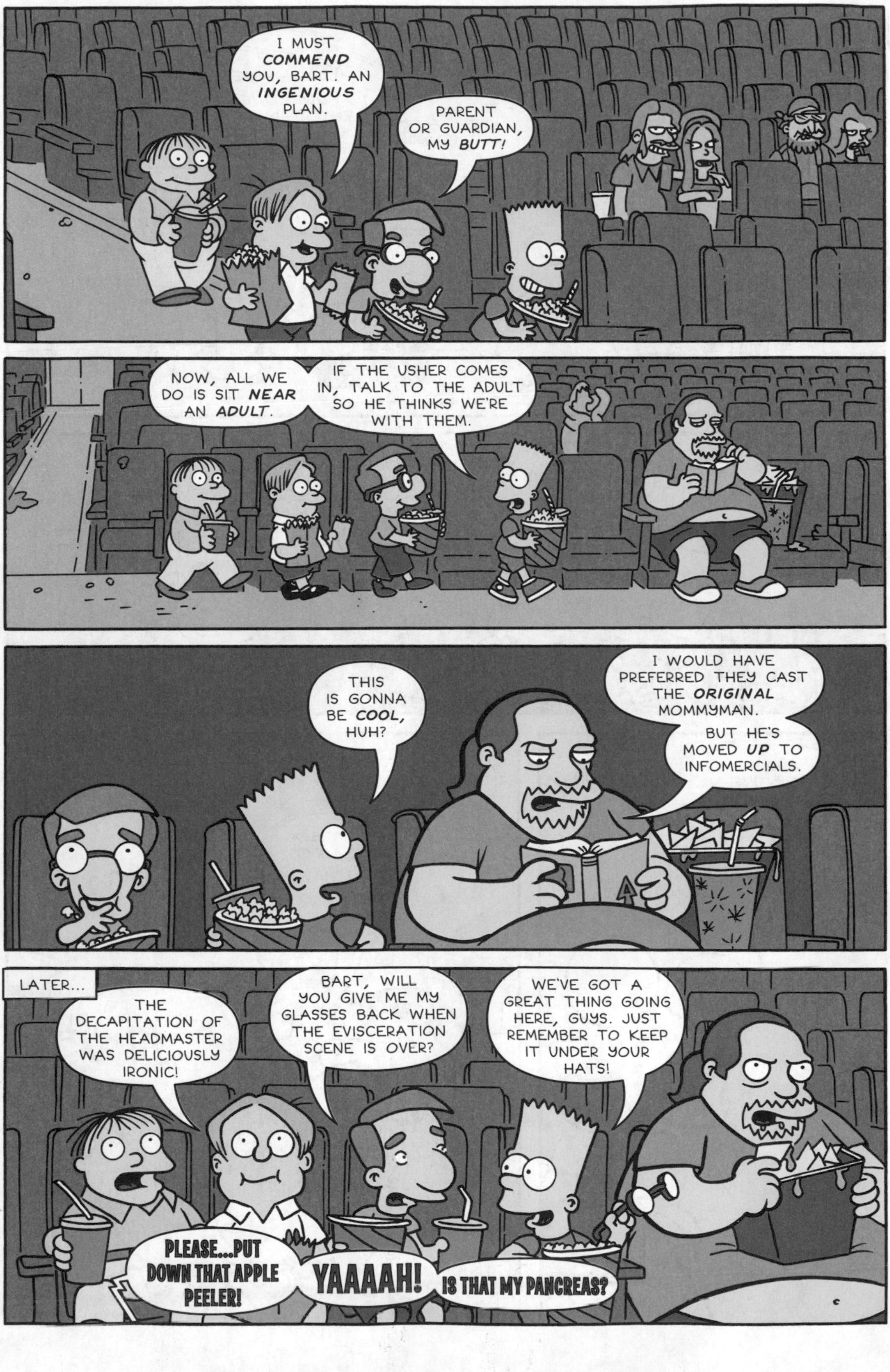
I MUST COMMEND YOU, BART. AN INGENIOUS PLAN.
PARENT OR GUARDIAN, MY BUTT!
NOW, ALL WE DO IS SIT NEAR AN ADULT.
IF THE USHER COMES IN, TALK TO THE ADULT SO HE THINKS WE'RE WITH THEM.
THIS IS GONNA BE COOL, HUH?
I WOULD HAVE PREFERRED THEY CAST THE ORIGINAL MOMMYMAN.
BUT HE'S MOVED UP TO INFOMERCIALS.
LATER...
THE DECAPITATION OF THE HEADMASTER WAS DELICIOUSLY IRONIC!
BART, WILL YOU GIVE ME MY GLASSES BACK WHEN THE EVISCERATION SCENE IS OVER?
WE'VE GOT A GREAT THING GOING HERE, GUYS. JUST REMEMBER TO KEEP IT UNDER YOUR HATS!
PLEASE...PUT DOWN THAT APPLE PEELER!
YAAAAH!
IS THAT MY PANCREAS?

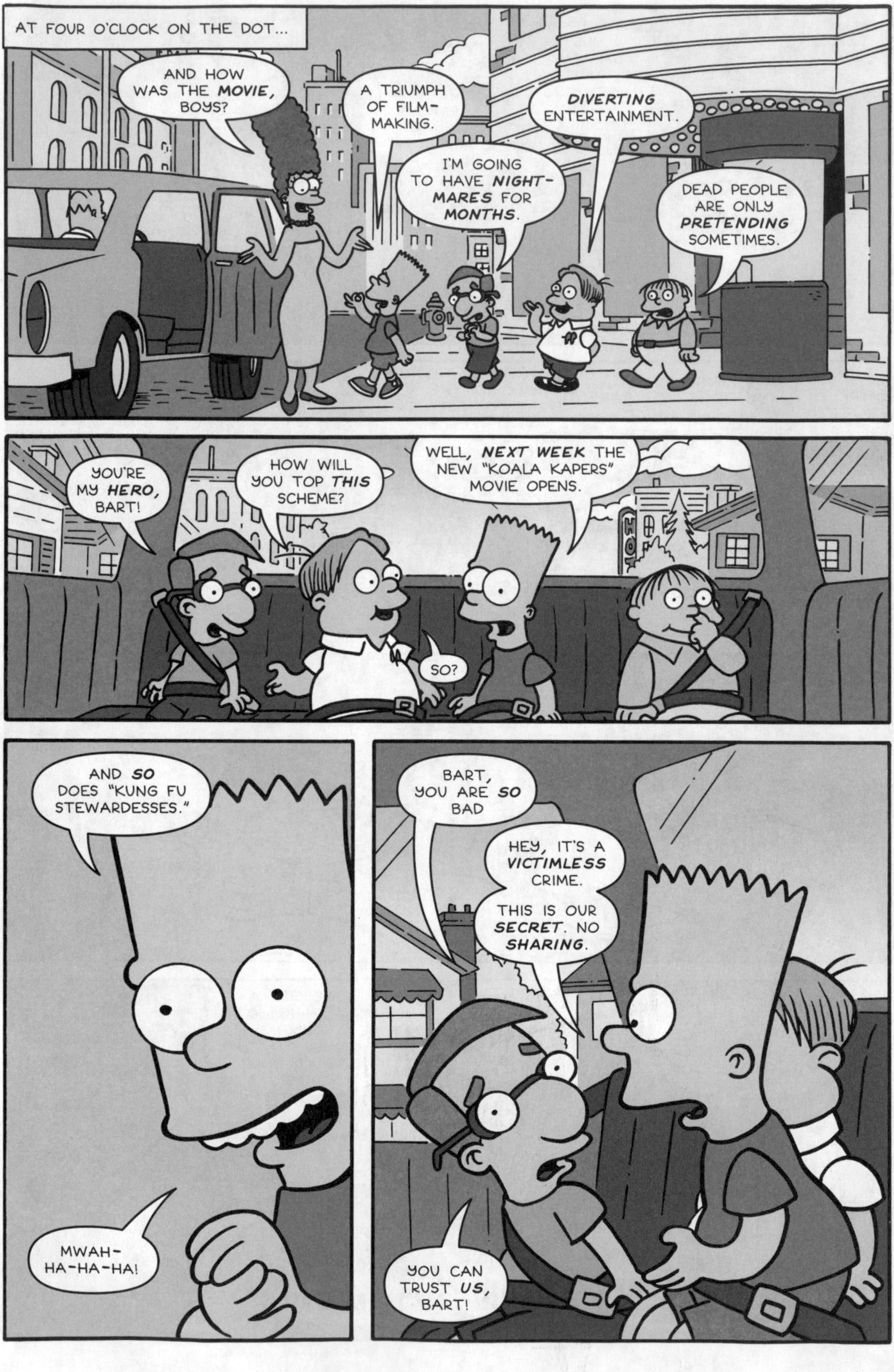
AT FOUR O'CLOCK ON THE DOT...
AND HOW WAS THE MOVIE, BOYS?
A TRIUMPH OF FILM-MAKING.
I'M GOING TO HAVE NIGHT-MARES FOR MONTHS.
DIVERTING ENTERTAINMENT.
DEAD PEOPLE ARE ONLY PRETENDING SOMETIMES.
YOU'RE MY HERO, BART!
HOW WILL YOU TOP THIS SCHEME?
WELL, NEXT WEEK THE NEW "KOALA KAPERS" MOVIE OPENS.
SO?
AND SO DOES "KUNG FU STEWARDESSES."
MWAH-HA-HA-HA!
BART, YOU ARE SO BAD
HEY, IT'S A VICTIMLESS CRIME.
THIS IS OUR SECRET. NO SHARING.
YOU CAN TRUST US, BART!

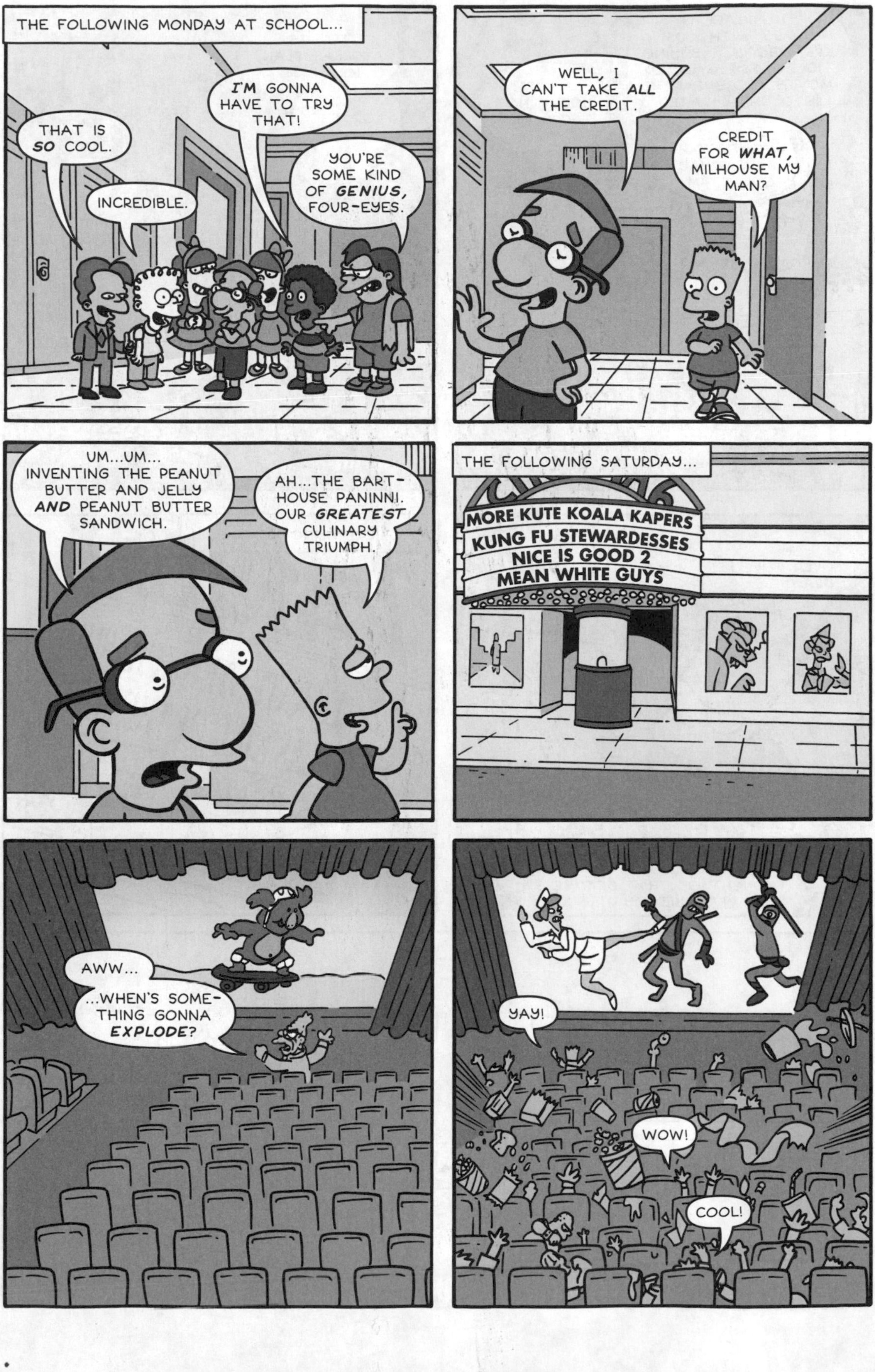
THE FOLLOWING MONDAY AT SCHOOL...
THAT IS SO COOL.
INCREDIBLE.
I'M GONNA HAVE TO TRY THAT!
YOU'RE SOME KIND OF GENIUS, FOUR-EYES.
WELL, I CAN'T TAKE ALL THE CREDIT.
CREDIT FOR WHAT, MILHOUSE MY MAN?
UM...UM... INVENTING THE PEANUT BUTTER AND JELLY AND PEANUT BUTTER SANDWICH.
AH...THE BART-HOUSE PANINNI. OUR GREATEST CULINARY TRIUMPH.
THE FOLLOWING SATURDAY...
MORE KUTE KOALA KAPERS
KUNG FU STEWARDESSES
NICE IS GOOD 2
MEAN WHITE GUYS
AWW...
...WHEN'S SOMETHING GONNA EXPLODE?
YAY!
WOW!
COOL!

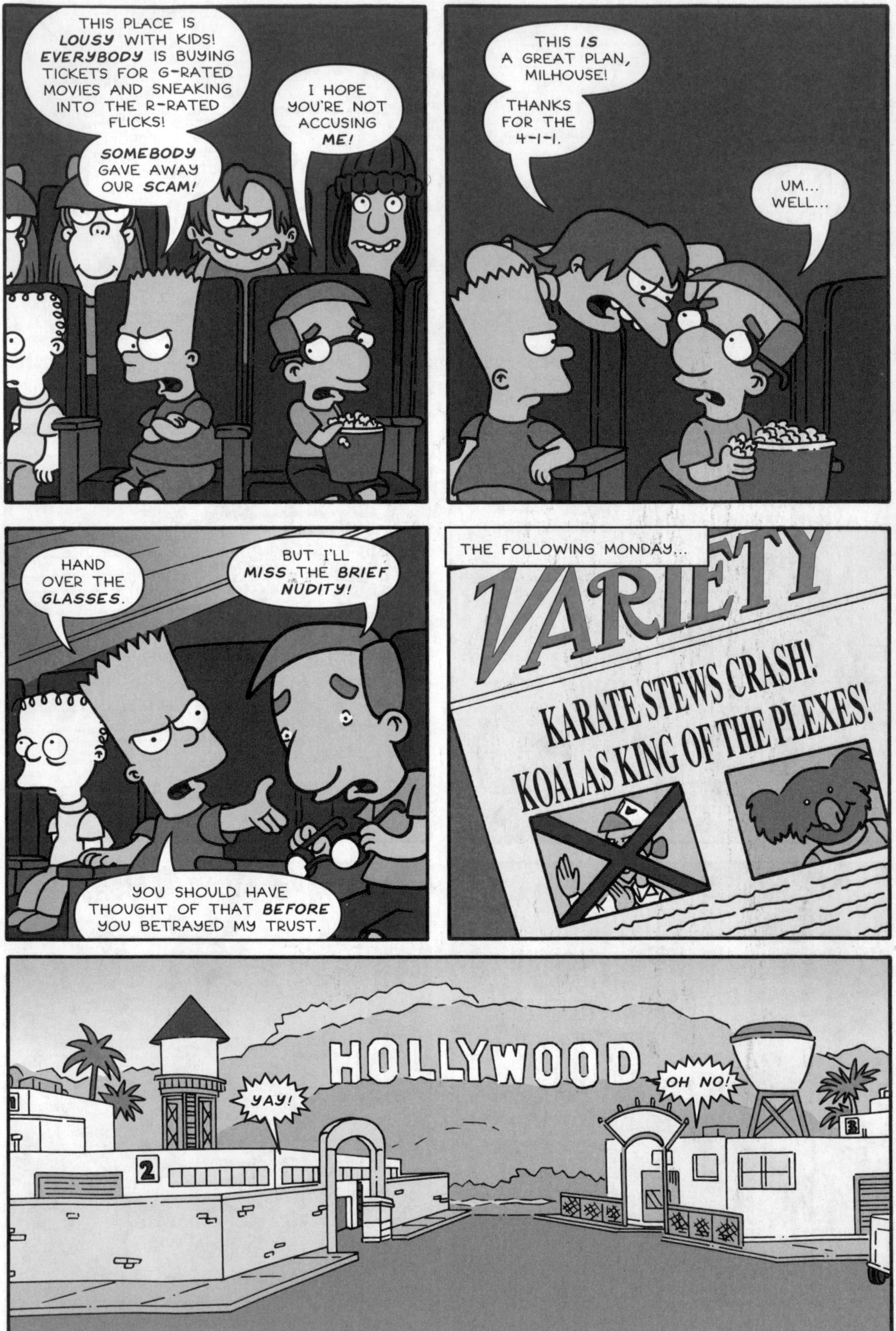

THIS PLACE IS LOUSY WITH KIDS! EVERYBODY IS BUYING TICKETS FOR G-RATED MOVIES AND SNEAKING INTO THE R-RATED FLICKS!
SOMEBODY GAVE AWAY OUR SCAM!
I HOPE YOU'RE NOT ACCUSING ME!
THIS IS A GREAT PLAN, MILHOUSE!
THANKS FOR THE 4-1-1.
UM... WELL...
HAND OVER THE GLASSES.
BUT I'LL MISS THE BRIEF NUDITY!
YOU SHOULD HAVE THOUGHT OF THAT BEFORE YOU BETRAYED MY TRUST.
THE FOLLOWING MONDAY...
VARIETY
KARATE STEWS CRASH!
KOALAS KING OF THE PLEXES!
HOLLYWOOD
YAY!
OH NO!
2
3

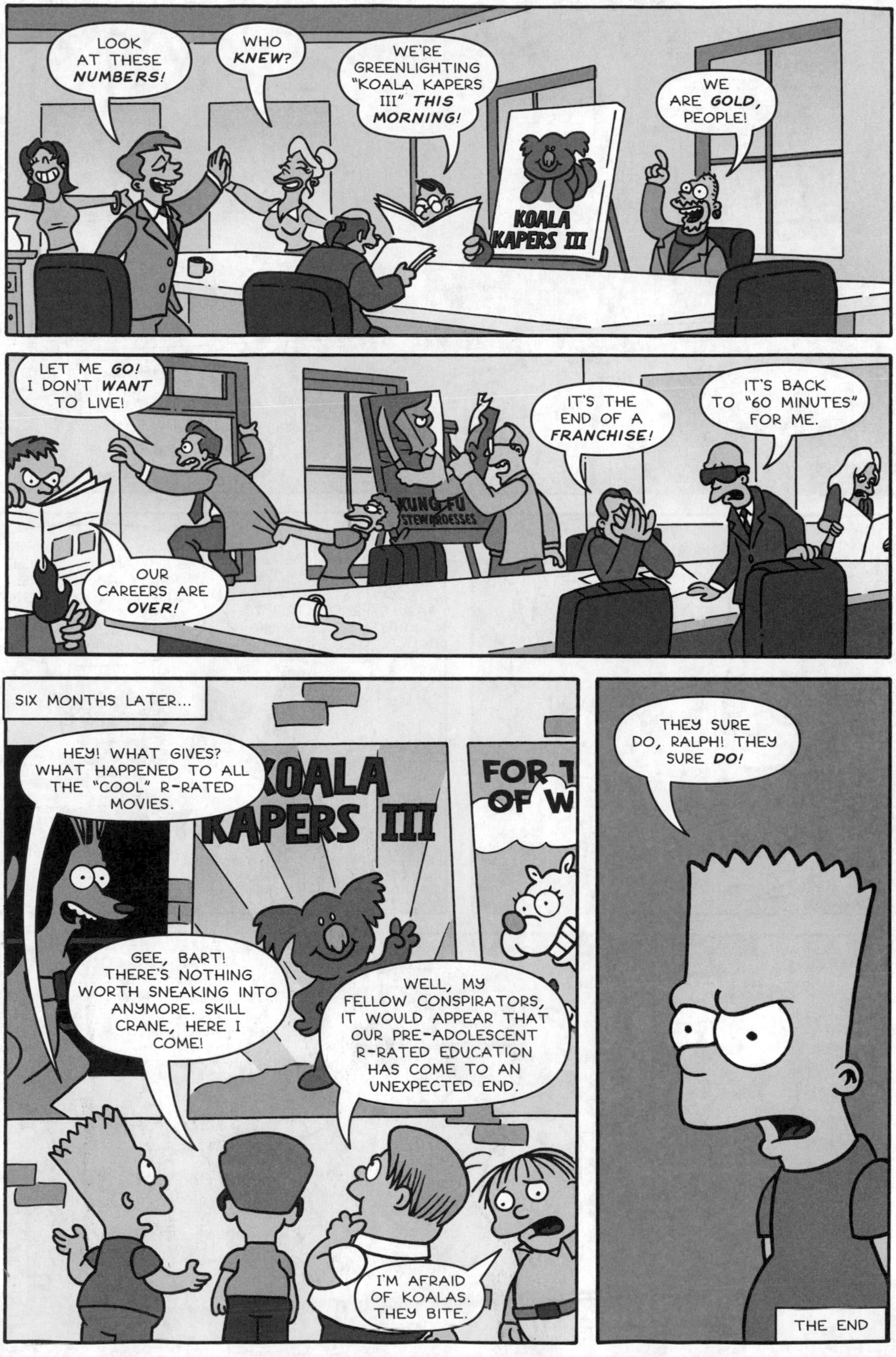
LOOK AT THESE NUMBERS!
WHO KNEW?
WE'RE GREENLIGHTING "KOALA KAPERS III" THIS MORNING!
KOALA KAPERS III
WE ARE GOLD, PEOPLE!
LET ME GO! I DON'T WANT TO LIVE!
KUNG FU STEWARDESSES
IT'S THE END OF A FRANCHISE!
IT'S BACK TO "60 MINUTES" FOR ME.
OUR CAREERS ARE OVER!
SIX MONTHS LATER...
HEY! WHAT GIVES? WHAT HAPPENED TO ALL THE "COOL" R-RATED MOVIES.
KOALA KAPERS III
GEE, BART! THERE'S NOTHING WORTH SNEAKING INTO ANYMORE. SKILL CRANE, HERE I COME!
WELL, MY FELLOW CONSPIRATORS, IT WOULD APPEAR THAT OUR PRE-ADOLESCENT R-RATED EDUCATION HAS COME TO AN UNEXPECTED END.
I'M AFRAID OF KOALAS. THEY BITE.
THEY SURE DO, RALPH! THEY SURE DO!
THE END

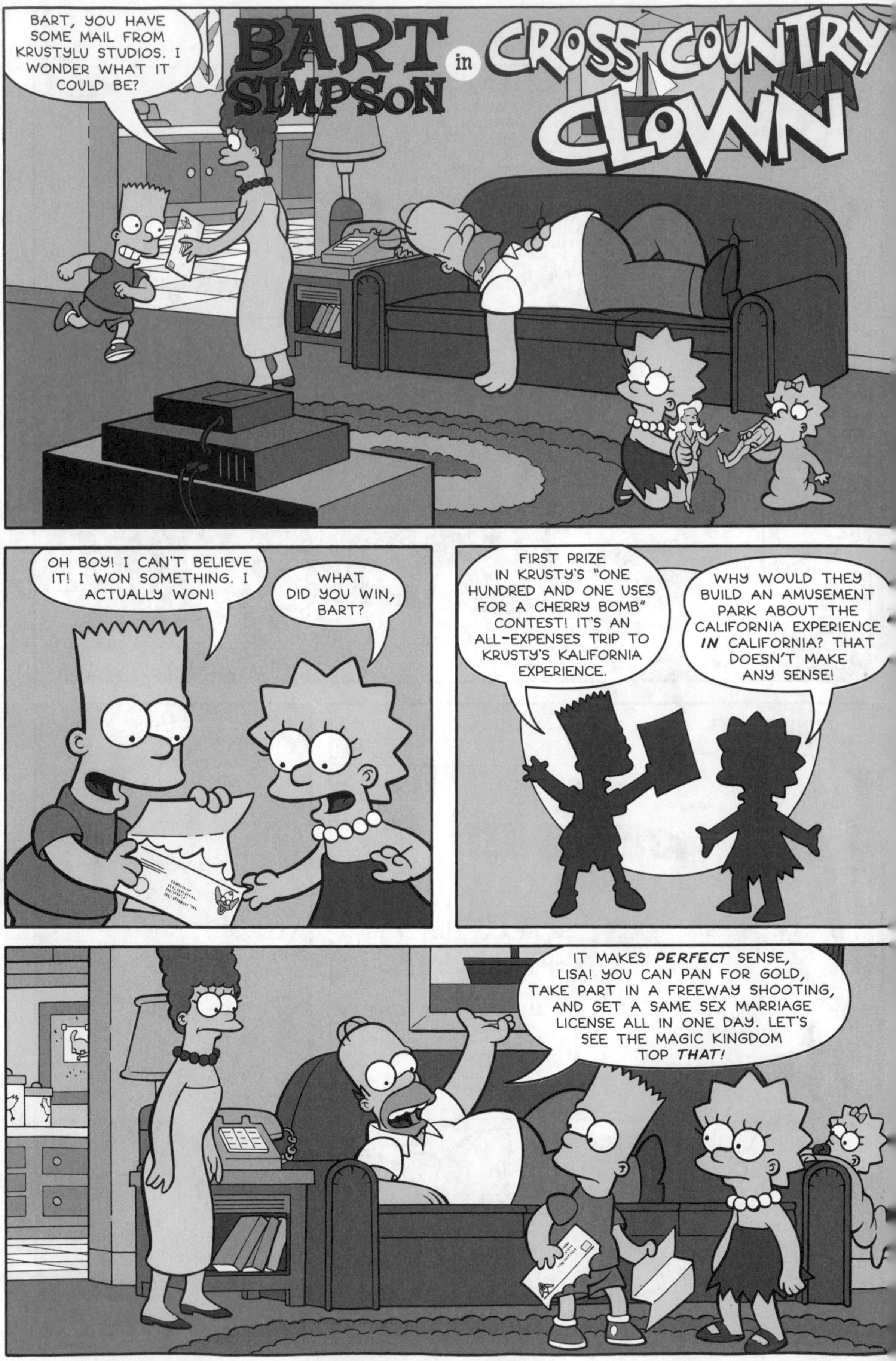
BART, YOU HAVE SOME MAIL FROM KRUSTYLU STUDIOS. I WONDER WHAT IT COULD BE?
BART SIMPSON in CROSS COUNTRY CLOWN
OH BOY! I CAN'T BELIEVE IT! I WON SOMETHING. I ACTUALLY WON!
WHAT DID YOU WIN, BART?
FIRST PRIZE IN KRUSTY'S "ONE HUNDRED AND ONE USES FOR A CHERRY BOMB" CONTEST! IT'S AN ALL-EXPENSES TRIP TO KRUSTY'S KALIFORNIA EXPERIENCE.
WHY WOULD THEY BUILD AN AMUSEMENT PARK ABOUT THE CALIFORNIA EXPERIENCE IN CALIFORNIA? THAT DOESN'T MAKE ANY SENSE!
IT MAKES PERFECT SENSE, LISA! YOU CAN PAN FOR GOLD, TAKE PART IN A FREEWAY SHOOTING, AND GET A SAME SEX MARRIAGE LICENSE ALL IN ONE DAY. LET'S SEE THE MAGIC KINGDOM TOP THAT!

EARL KRESS SCRIPT · **JAMES LLOYD** PENCILS · **ANDREW PEPOY** INKS · **ART VILLANUEVA** COLORS · **KAREN BATES** LETTERS · **BILL MORRISO[N]** EDITOR

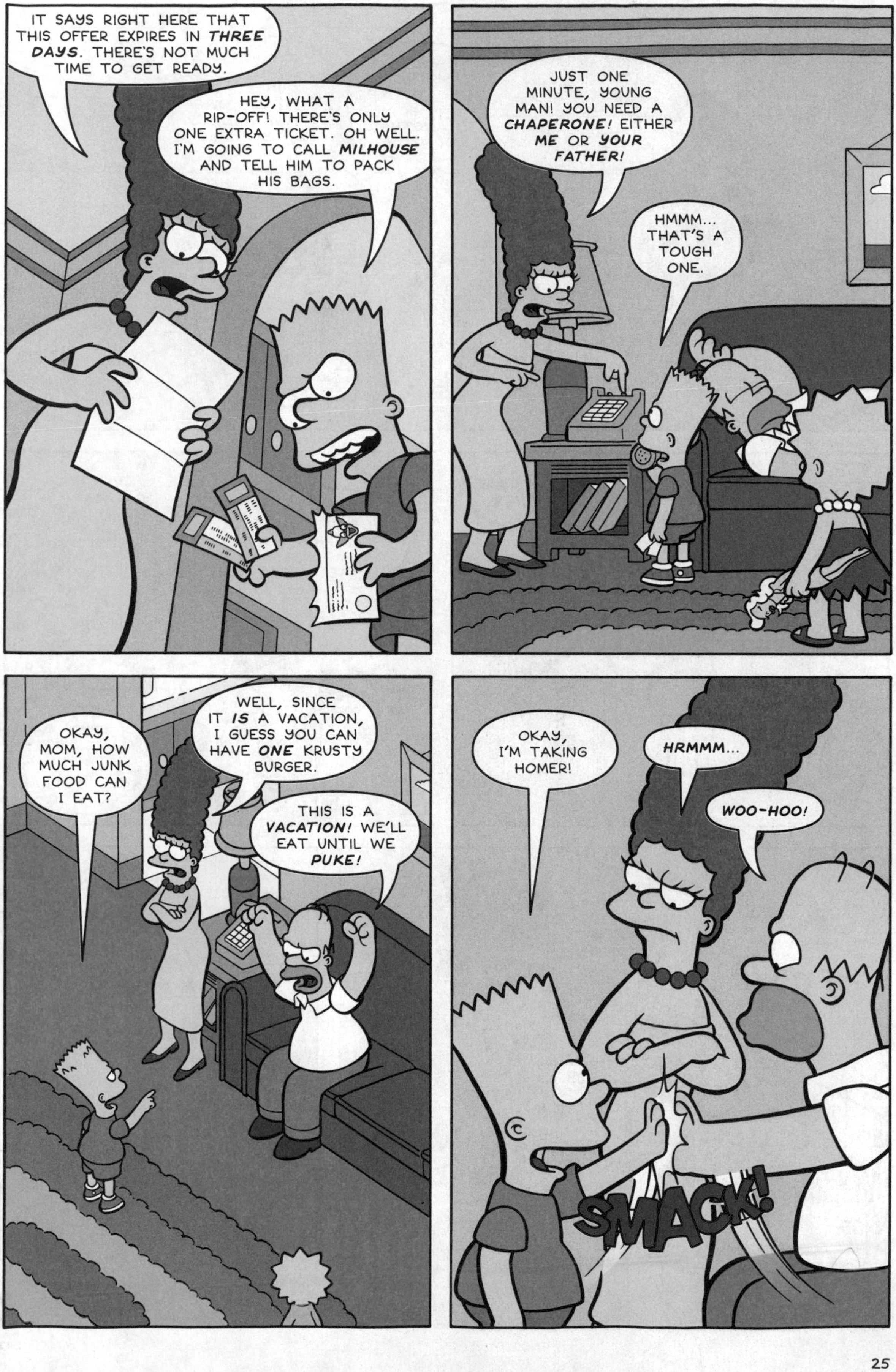
IT SAYS RIGHT HERE THAT THIS OFFER EXPIRES IN THREE DAYS. THERE'S NOT MUCH TIME TO GET READY.
HEY, WHAT A RIP-OFF! THERE'S ONLY ONE EXTRA TICKET. OH WELL. I'M GOING TO CALL MILHOUSE AND TELL HIM TO PACK HIS BAGS.
JUST ONE MINUTE, YOUNG MAN! YOU NEED A CHAPERONE! EITHER ME OR YOUR FATHER!
HMMM... THAT'S A TOUGH ONE.
OKAY, MOM, HOW MUCH JUNK FOOD CAN I EAT?
WELL, SINCE IT IS A VACATION, I GUESS YOU CAN HAVE ONE KRUSTY BURGER.
THIS IS A VACATION! WE'LL EAT UNTIL WE PUKE!
OKAY, I'M TAKING HOMER!
HRMMM...
WOO-HOO!
SMACK!

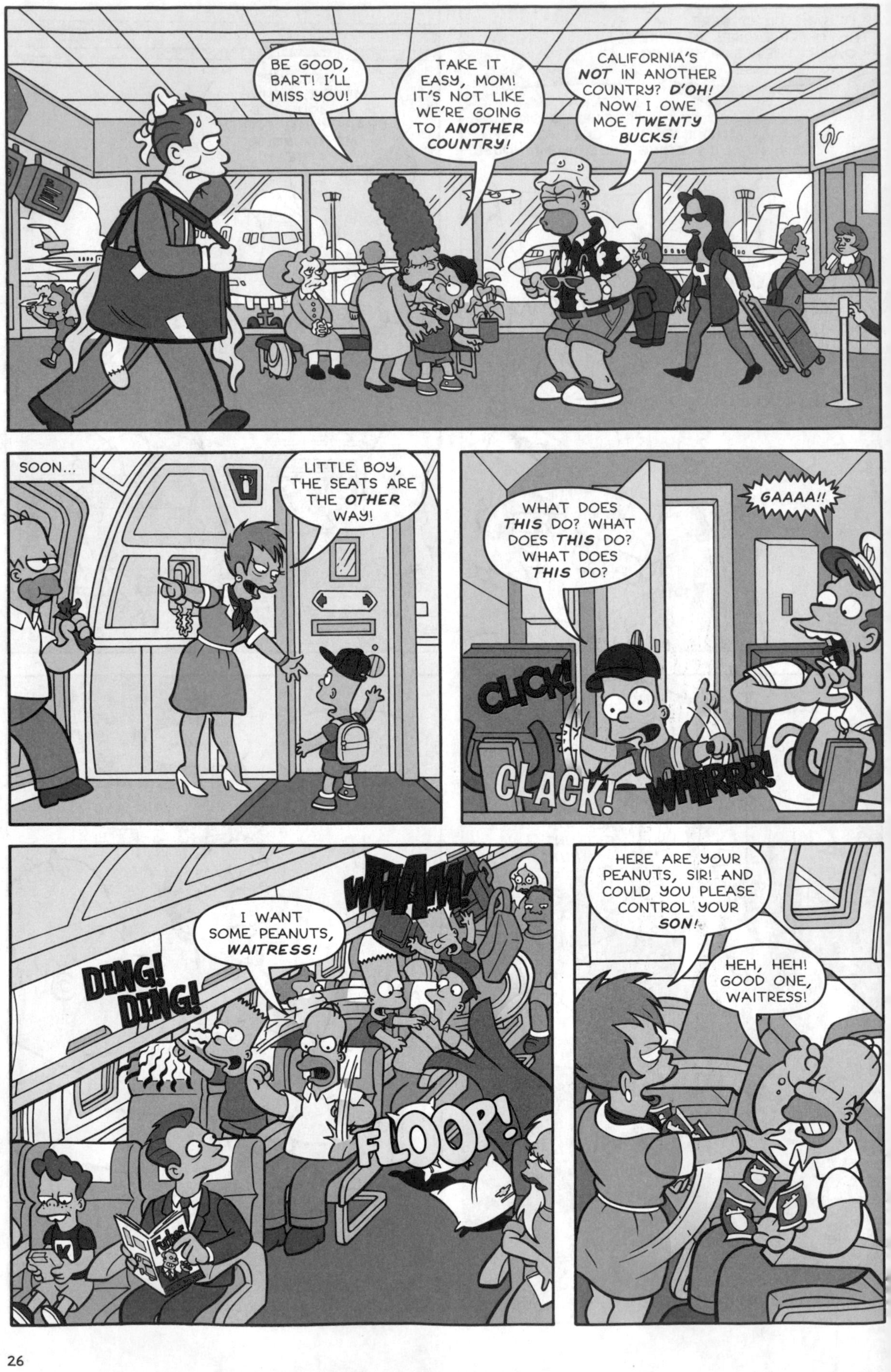
BE GOOD, BART! I'LL MISS YOU!
TAKE IT EASY, MOM! IT'S NOT LIKE WE'RE GOING TO ANOTHER COUNTRY!
CALIFORNIA'S NOT IN ANOTHER COUNTRY? D'OH! NOW I OWE MOE TWENTY BUCKS!
SOON...
LITTLE BOY, THE SEATS ARE THE OTHER WAY!
WHAT DOES THIS DO? WHAT DOES THIS DO? WHAT DOES THIS DO?
GAAAA!!
CLICK!
CLACK!
WHIRRR!
I WANT SOME PEANUTS, WAITRESS!
WHAM!
DING! DING!
FLOOP!
HERE ARE YOUR PEANUTS, SIR! AND COULD YOU PLEASE CONTROL YOUR SON!
HEH, HEH! GOOD ONE, WAITRESS!

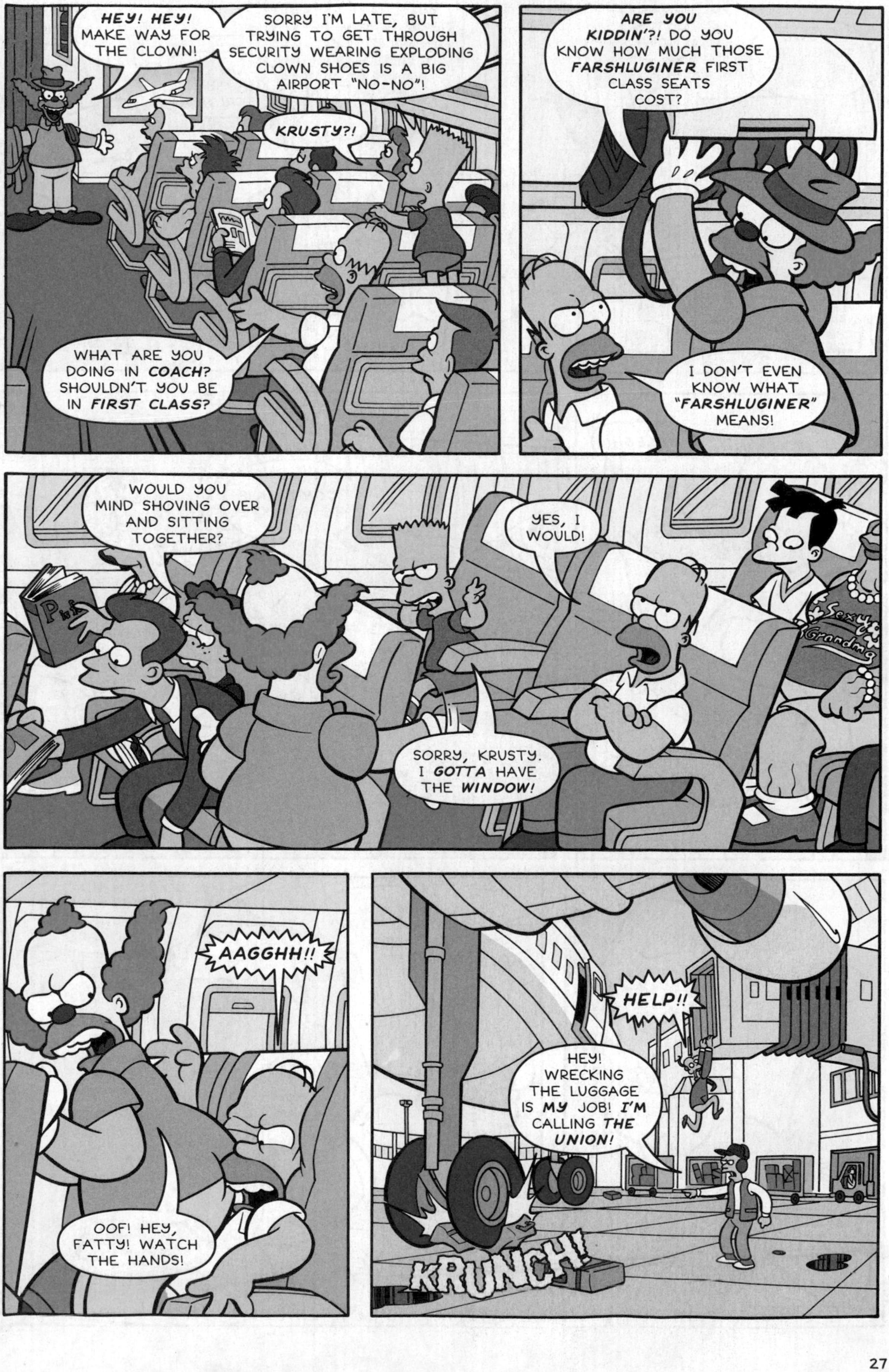
HEY! HEY! MAKE WAY FOR THE CLOWN!
SORRY I'M LATE, BUT TRYING TO GET THROUGH SECURITY WEARING EXPLODING CLOWN SHOES IS A BIG AIRPORT "NO-NO"!
KRUSTY?!
WHAT ARE YOU DOING IN COACH? SHOULDN'T YOU BE IN FIRST CLASS?
ARE YOU KIDDIN'?! DO YOU KNOW HOW MUCH THOSE FARSHLUGINER FIRST CLASS SEATS COST?
I DON'T EVEN KNOW WHAT "FARSHLUGINER" MEANS!
WOULD YOU MIND SHOVING OVER AND SITTING TOGETHER?
YES, I WOULD!
SORRY, KRUSTY. I GOTTA HAVE THE WINDOW!
Sexy Grandma
AAGGHH!!
OOF! HEY, FATTY! WATCH THE HANDS!
HELP!!
HEY! WRECKING THE LUGGAGE IS MY JOB! I'M CALLING THE UNION!
KRUNCH!

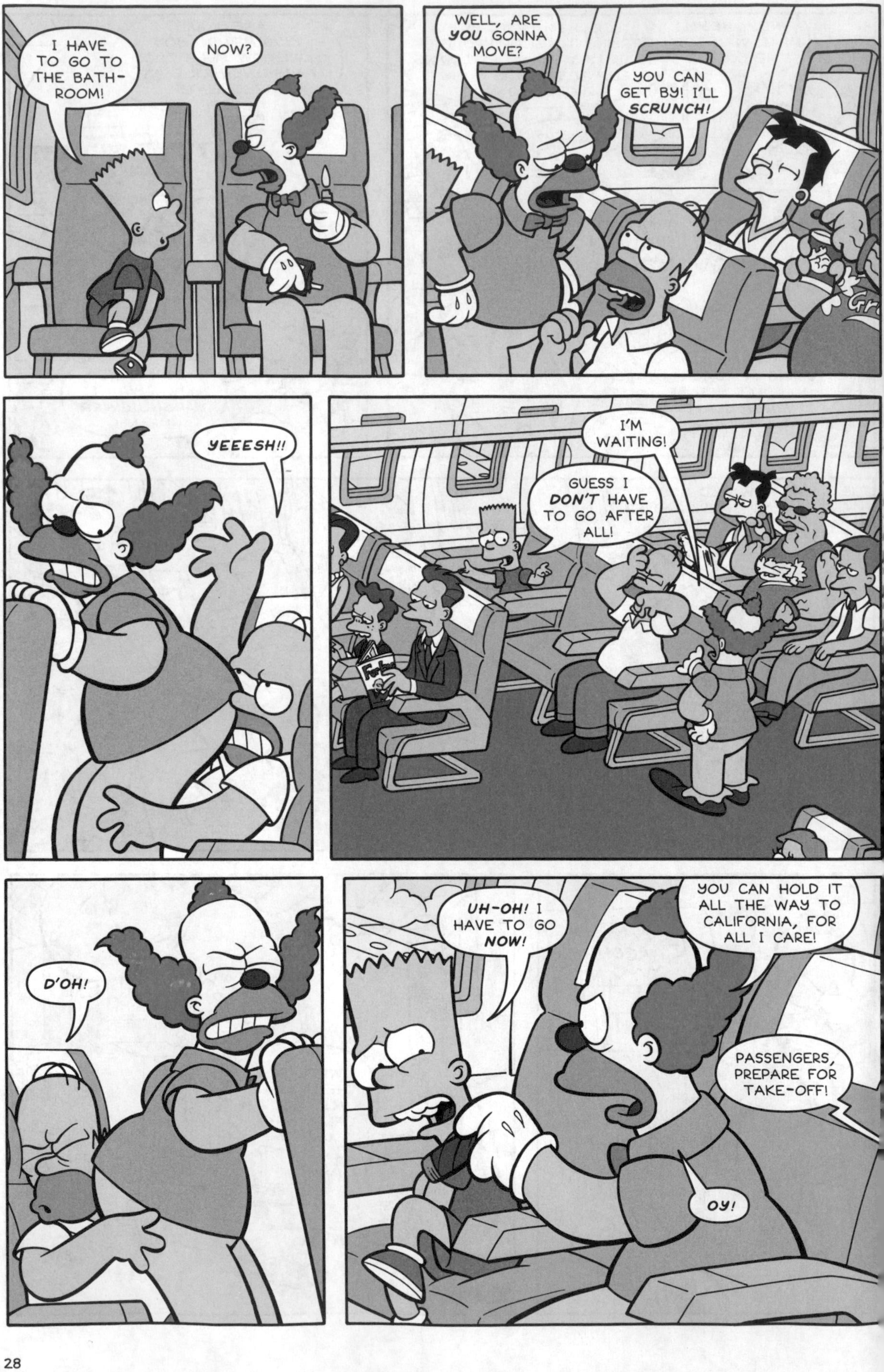
I HAVE TO GO TO THE BATH- ROOM!
NOW?
WELL, ARE YOU GONNA MOVE?
YOU CAN GET BY! I'LL SCRUNCH!
YEEESH!!
I'M WAITING!
GUESS I DON'T HAVE TO GO AFTER ALL!
D'OH!
UH-OH! I HAVE TO GO NOW!
YOU CAN HOLD IT ALL THE WAY TO CALIFORNIA, FOR ALL I CARE!
PASSENGERS, PREPARE FOR TAKE-OFF!
OY!

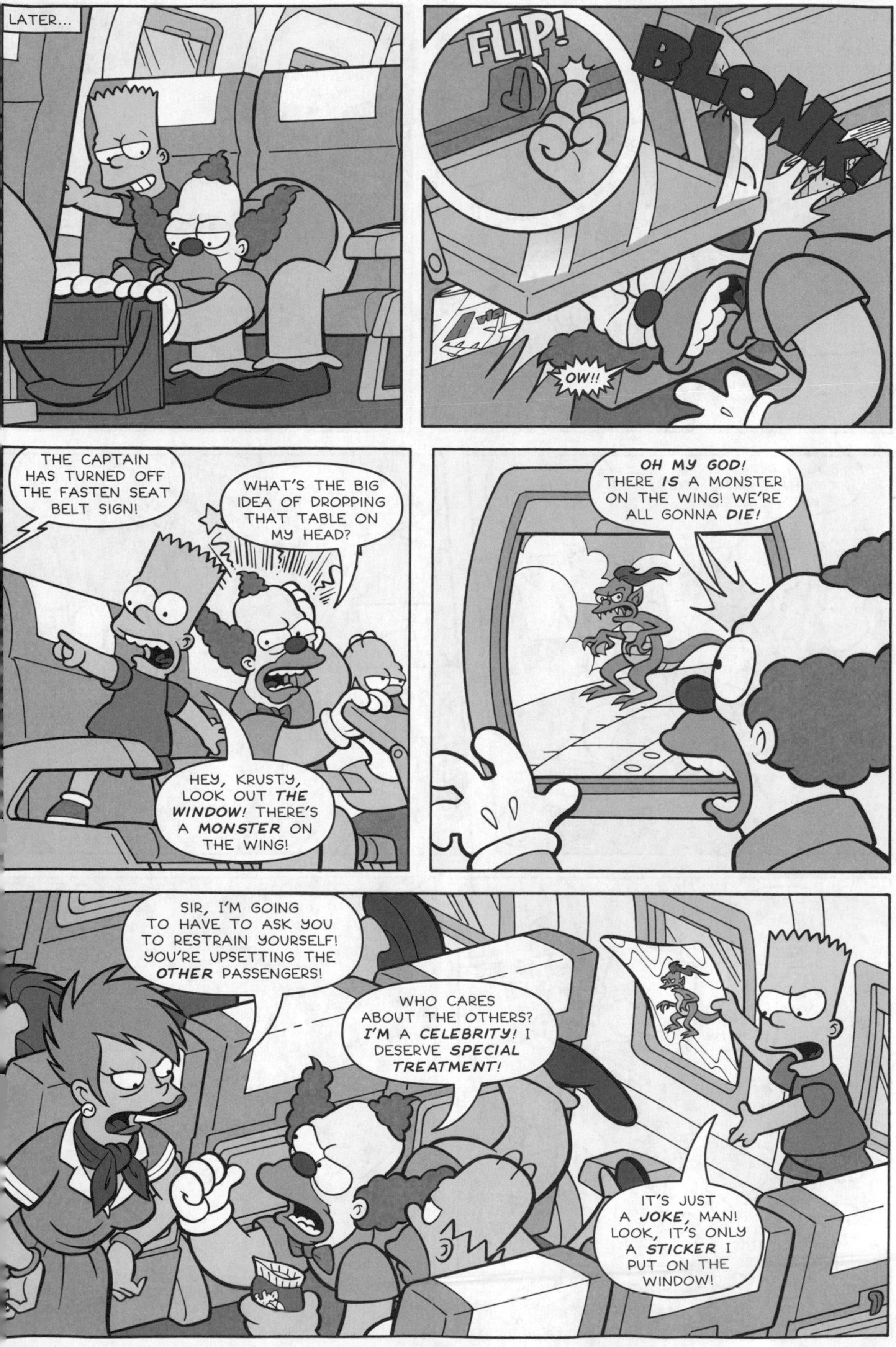
LATER...
FLIP!
BLONK!
OW!!
THE CAPTAIN HAS TURNED OFF THE FASTEN SEAT BELT SIGN!
WHAT'S THE BIG IDEA OF DROPPING THAT TABLE ON MY HEAD?
HEY, KRUSTY, LOOK OUT THE WINDOW! THERE'S A MONSTER ON THE WING!
OH MY GOD! THERE IS A MONSTER ON THE WING! WE'RE ALL GONNA DIE!
SIR, I'M GOING TO HAVE TO ASK YOU TO RESTRAIN YOURSELF! YOU'RE UPSETTING THE OTHER PASSENGERS!
WHO CARES ABOUT THE OTHERS? I'M A CELEBRITY! I DESERVE SPECIAL TREATMENT!
IT'S JUST A JOKE, MAN! LOOK, IT'S ONLY A STICKER I PUT ON THE WINDOW!

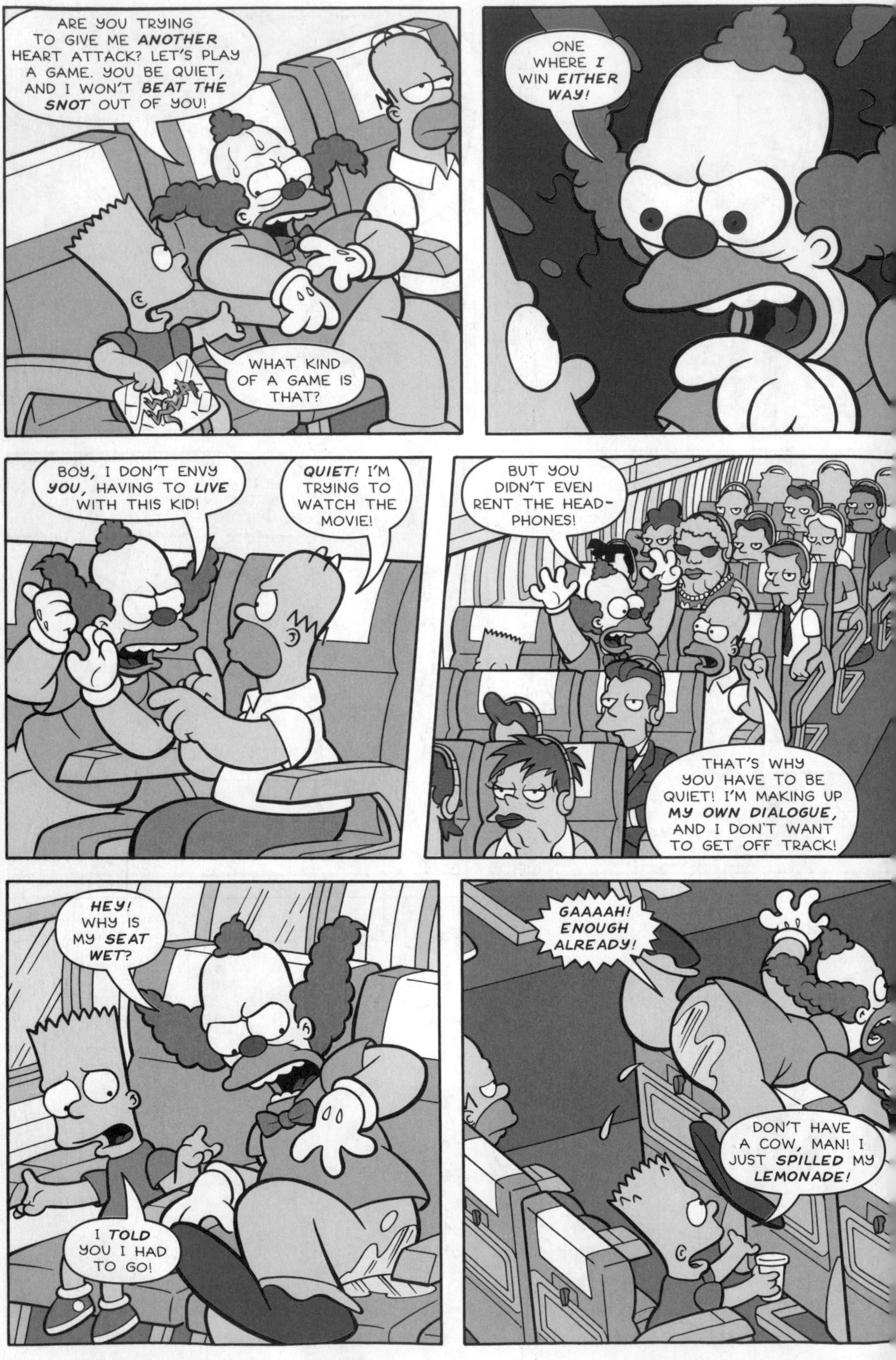
ARE YOU TRYING TO GIVE ME **ANOTHER** HEART ATTACK? LET'S PLAY A GAME. YOU BE QUIET, AND I WON'T **BEAT THE SNOT** OUT OF YOU!
WHAT KIND OF A GAME IS THAT?
ONE WHERE ***I*** WIN ***EITHER WAY!***
BOY, I DON'T ENVY ***YOU***, HAVING TO ***LIVE*** WITH THIS KID!
QUIET! I'M TRYING TO WATCH THE MOVIE!
BUT YOU DIDN'T EVEN RENT THE HEAD-PHONES!
THAT'S WHY YOU HAVE TO BE QUIET! I'M MAKING UP ***MY OWN DIALOGUE***, AND I DON'T WANT TO GET OFF TRACK!
HEY! WHY IS MY ***SEAT WET?***
I ***TOLD*** YOU I HAD TO GO!
GAAAAH! ENOUGH ALREADY!
DON'T HAVE A COW, MAN! I JUST ***SPILLED*** MY ***LEMONADE!***

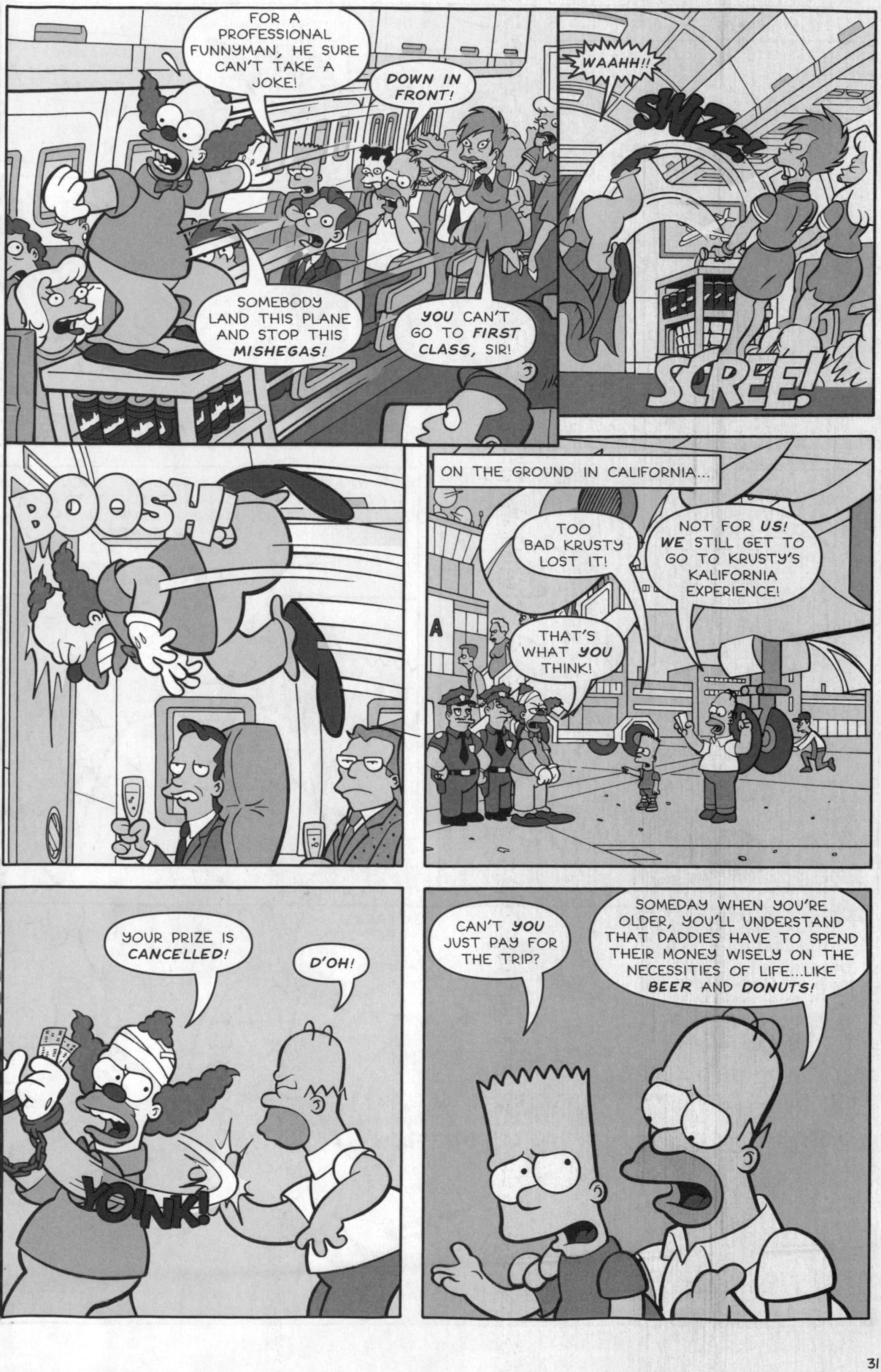

FOR A PROFESSIONAL FUNNYMAN, HE SURE CAN'T TAKE A JOKE!
DOWN IN FRONT!
SOMEBODY LAND THIS PLANE AND STOP THIS MISHEGAS!
YOU CAN'T GO TO FIRST CLASS, SIR!
WAAHH!!
SWIZZ!
SCREE!
BOOSH!
ON THE GROUND IN CALIFORNIA...
TOO BAD KRUSTY LOST IT!
NOT FOR US! WE STILL GET TO GO TO KRUSTY'S KALIFORNIA EXPERIENCE!
THAT'S WHAT YOU THINK!
YOUR PRIZE IS CANCELLED!
D'OH!
YOINK!
CAN'T YOU JUST PAY FOR THE TRIP?
SOMEDAY WHEN YOU'RE OLDER, YOU'LL UNDERSTAND THAT DADDIES HAVE TO SPEND THEIR MONEY WISELY ON THE NECESSITIES OF LIFE...LIKE BEER AND DONUTS!

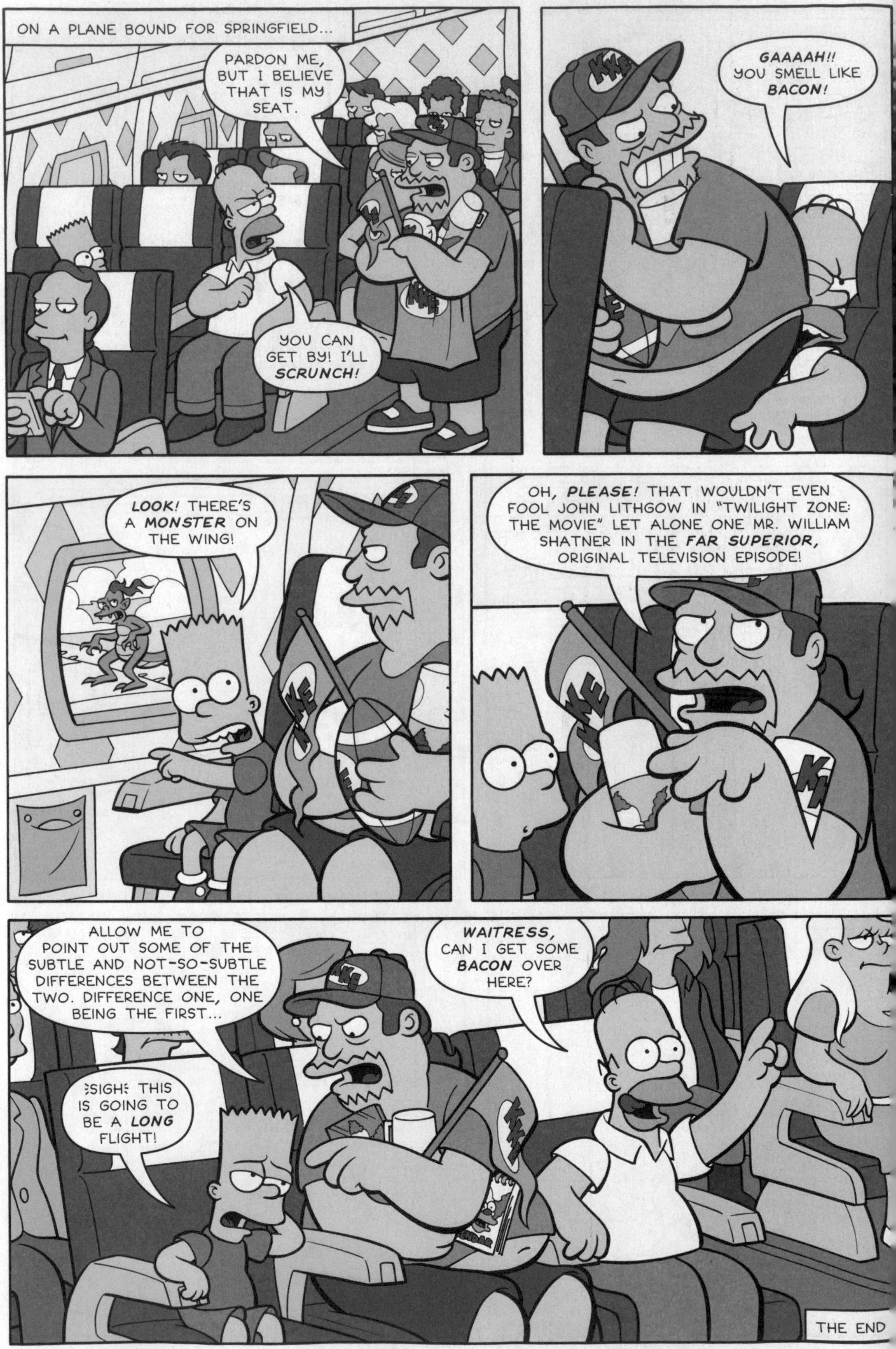
ON A PLANE BOUND FOR SPRINGFIELD...
PARDON ME, BUT I BELIEVE THAT IS MY SEAT.
YOU CAN GET BY! I'LL SCRUNCH!
GAAAAH!! YOU SMELL LIKE BACON!
LOOK! THERE'S A MONSTER ON THE WING!
OH, PLEASE! THAT WOULDN'T EVEN FOOL JOHN LITHGOW IN "TWILIGHT ZONE: THE MOVIE" LET ALONE ONE MR. WILLIAM SHATNER IN THE FAR SUPERIOR, ORIGINAL TELEVISION EPISODE!
ALLOW ME TO POINT OUT SOME OF THE SUBTLE AND NOT-SO-SUBTLE DIFFERENCES BETWEEN THE TWO. DIFFERENCE ONE, ONE BEING THE FIRST...
WAITRESS, CAN I GET SOME BACON OVER HERE?
:SIGH: THIS IS GOING TO BE A LONG FLIGHT!
THE END

WHAT'S ON BART'S MIND?

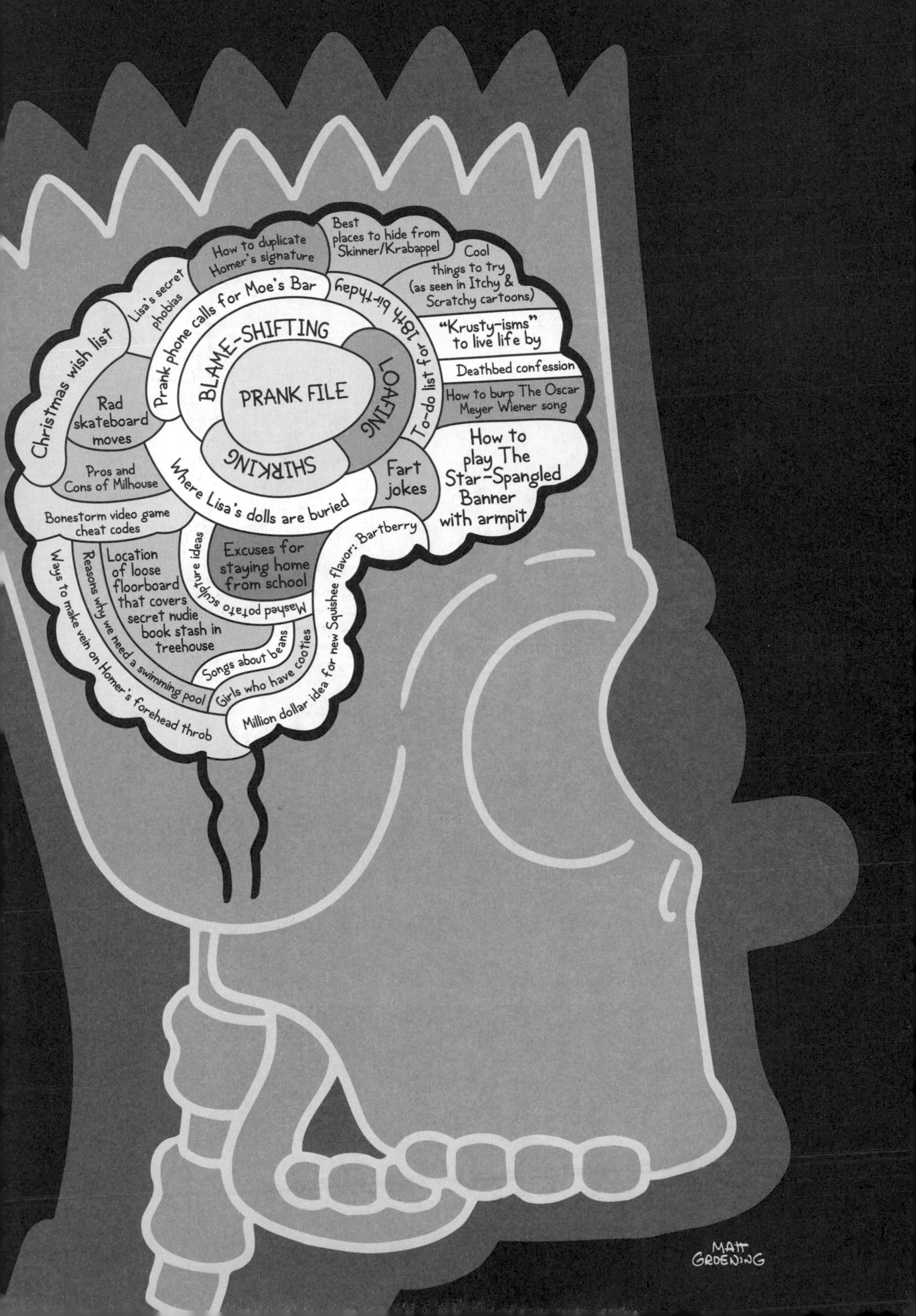

How to duplicate Homer's signature
Best places to hide from Skinner/Krabappel
Cool things to try (as seen in Itchy & Scratchy cartoons)
Lisa's secret phobias
Prank phone calls for Moe's Bar
To-do list for 18th bir-thday
Christmas wish list
BLAME-SHIFTING
PRANK FILE
LOAFING
SHIRKING
"Krusty-isms" to live life by
Deathbed confession
How to burp The Oscar Meyer Wiener song
Rad skateboard moves
How to play The Star-Spangled Banner with armpit
Fart jokes
Pros and Cons of Milhouse
Where Lisa's dolls are buried
Bonestorm video game cheat codes
Excuses for staying home from school
Mashed potato sculpture ideas
Location of loose floorboard that covers secret nudie book stash in treehouse
Ways to make vein on Homer's forehead throb
Reasons why we need a swimming pool
Songs about beans
Girls who have cooties
Million dollar idea for new Squishee flavor: Bartberry
MATT GROENING

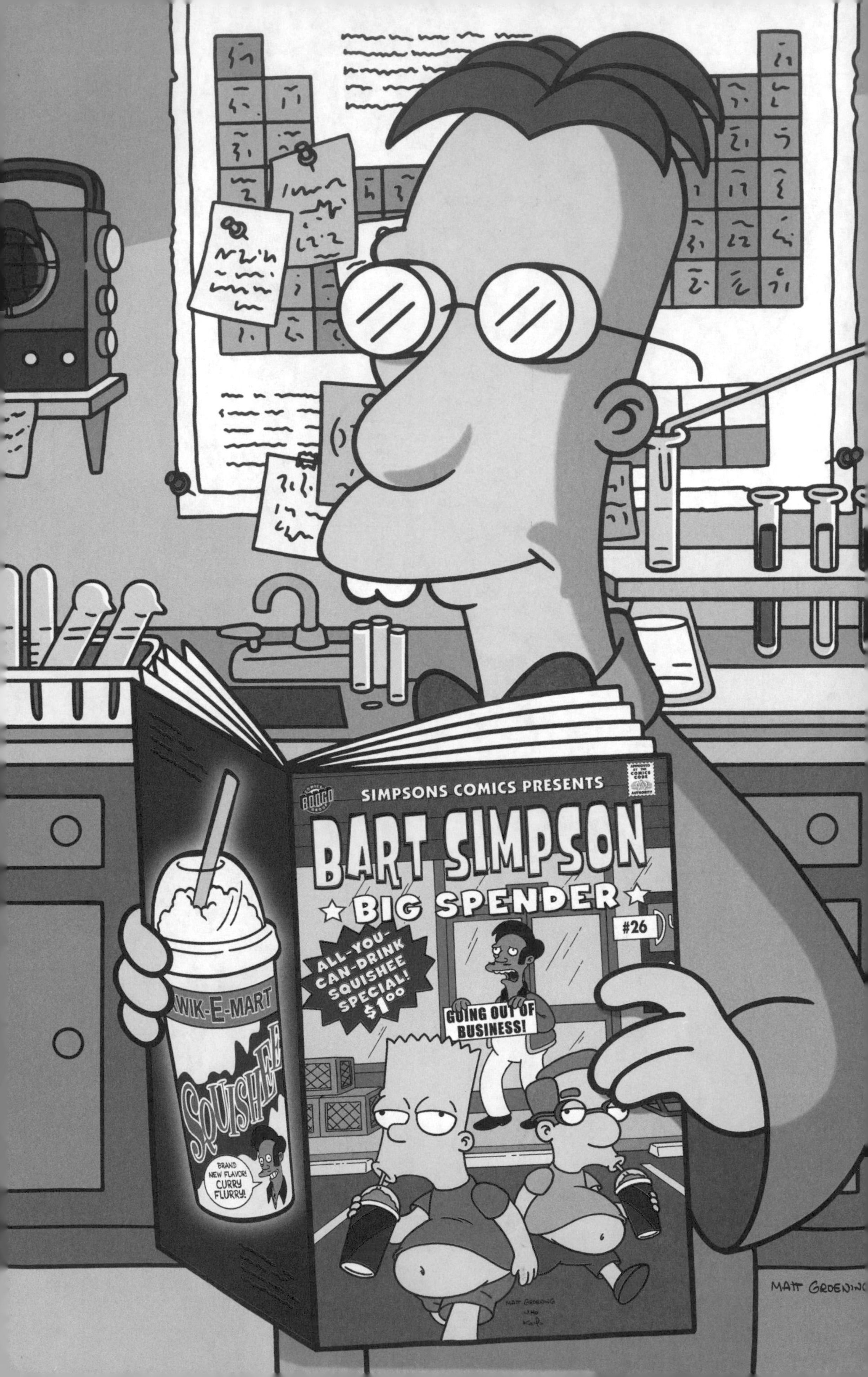
SIMPSONS COMICS PRESENTS
BART SIMPSON
BIG SPENDER
#26
ALL-YOU-CAN-DRINK SQUISHEE SPECIAL! $1.00
GOING OUT OF BUSINESS!
KWIK-E-MART
SQUISHEE
BRAND NEW FLAVOR! CURRY FLURRY!
MATT GROENING

MATT GROENING presents

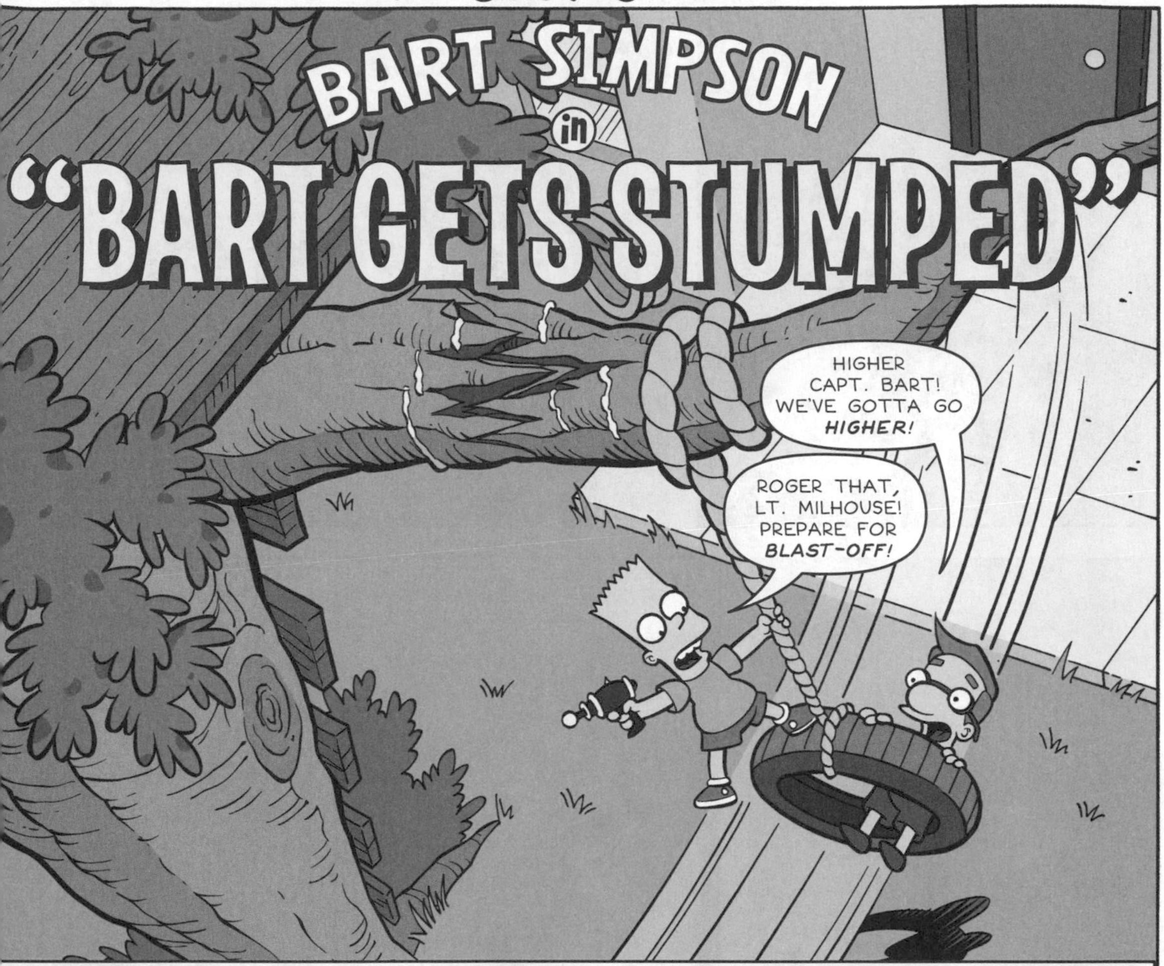
BART SIMPSON in
"BART GETS STUMPED"
HIGHER CAPT. BART! WE'VE GOTTA GO *HIGHER!*
ROGER THAT, LT. MILHOUSE! PREPARE FOR *BLAST-OFF!*

CLAY & SUSAN GRIFFITH	JAMES LLOYD	ANDREW PEPOY	NATHAN HAMILL	KAREN BATES	BILL MORRISON
SCRIPT	PENCILS	INKS	COLORS	LETTERS	EDITOR

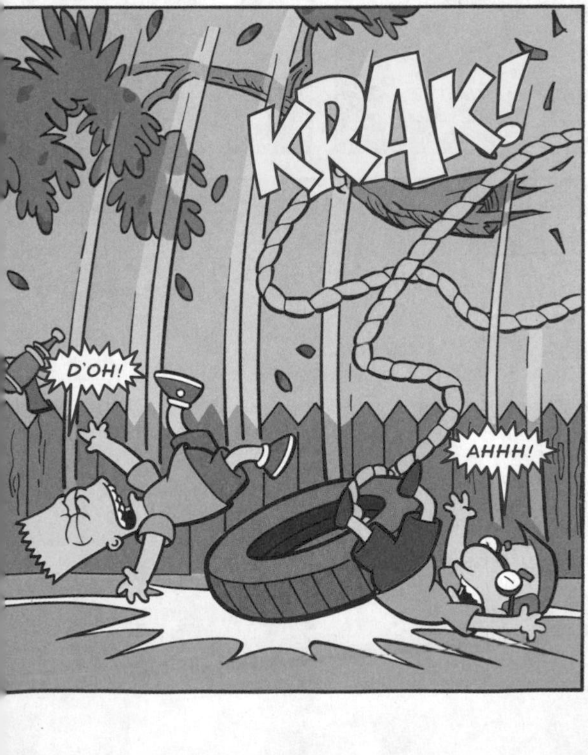
KRAK!
D'OH!
AHHH!

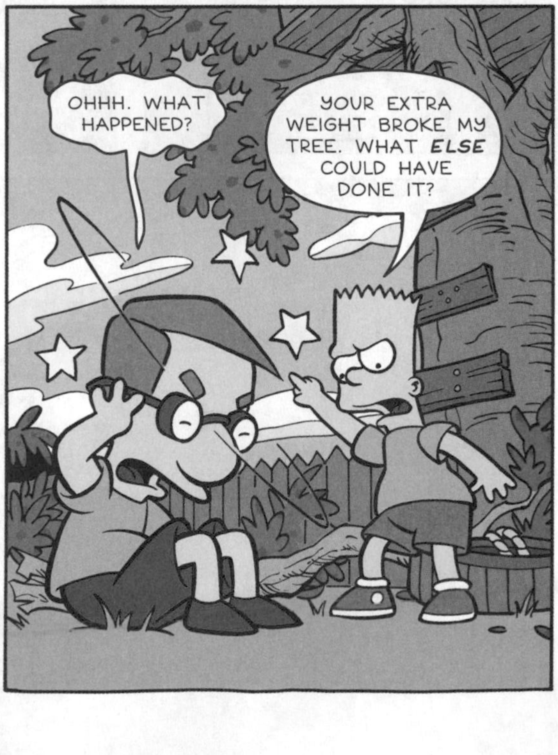
OHHH. WHAT HAPPENED?
YOUR EXTRA WEIGHT BROKE MY TREE. WHAT *ELSE* COULD HAVE DONE IT?

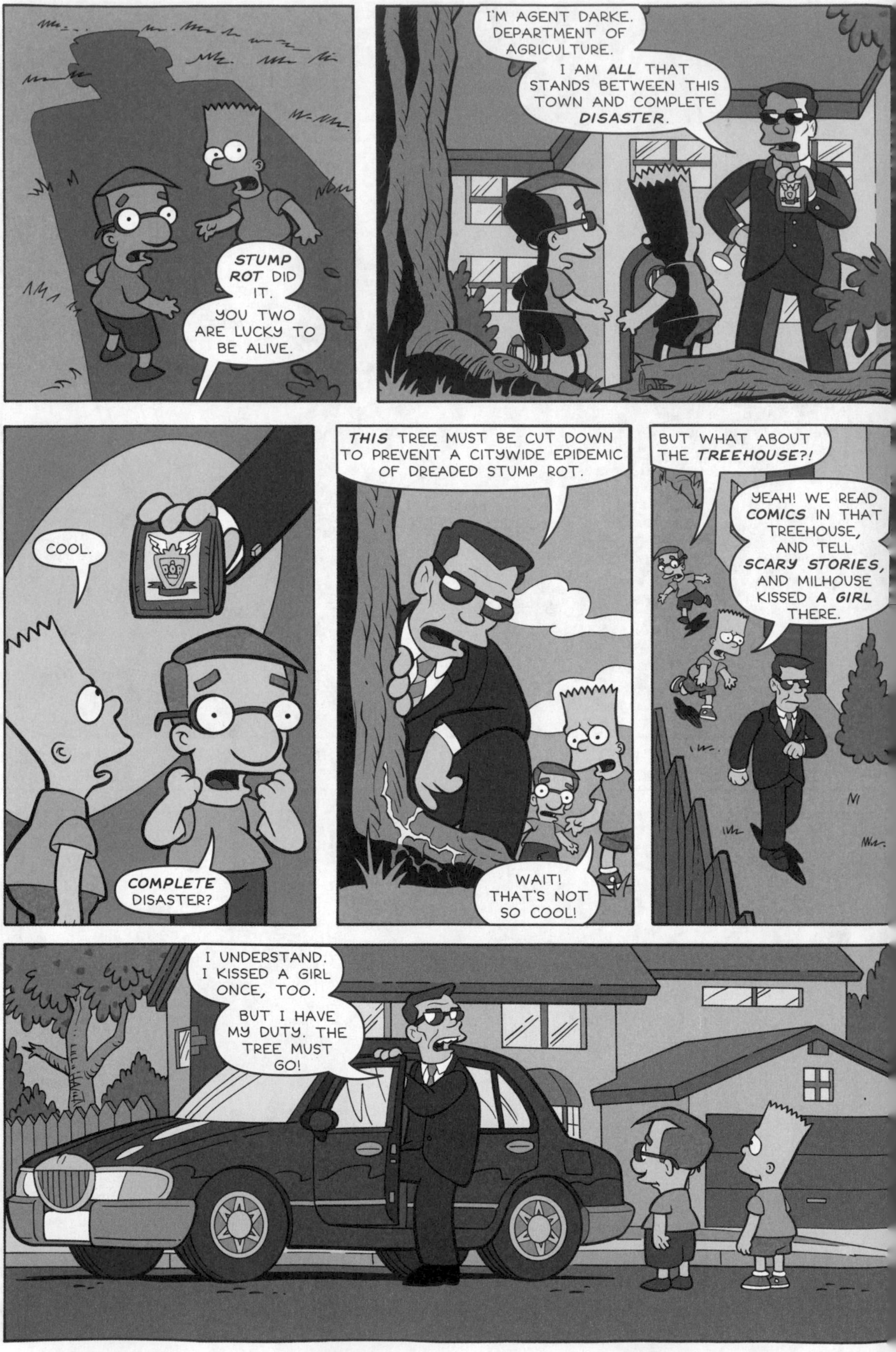
STUMP ROT DID IT.
YOU TWO ARE LUCKY TO BE ALIVE.
I'M AGENT DARKE. DEPARTMENT OF AGRICULTURE.
I AM ALL THAT STANDS BETWEEN THIS TOWN AND COMPLETE DISASTER.
COOL.
COMPLETE DISASTER?
THIS TREE MUST BE CUT DOWN TO PREVENT A CITYWIDE EPIDEMIC OF DREADED STUMP ROT.
WAIT! THAT'S NOT SO COOL!
BUT WHAT ABOUT THE TREEHOUSE?!
YEAH! WE READ COMICS IN THAT TREEHOUSE, AND TELL SCARY STORIES, AND MILHOUSE KISSED A GIRL THERE.
I UNDERSTAND. I KISSED A GIRL ONCE, TOO.
BUT I HAVE MY DUTY. THE TREE MUST GO!

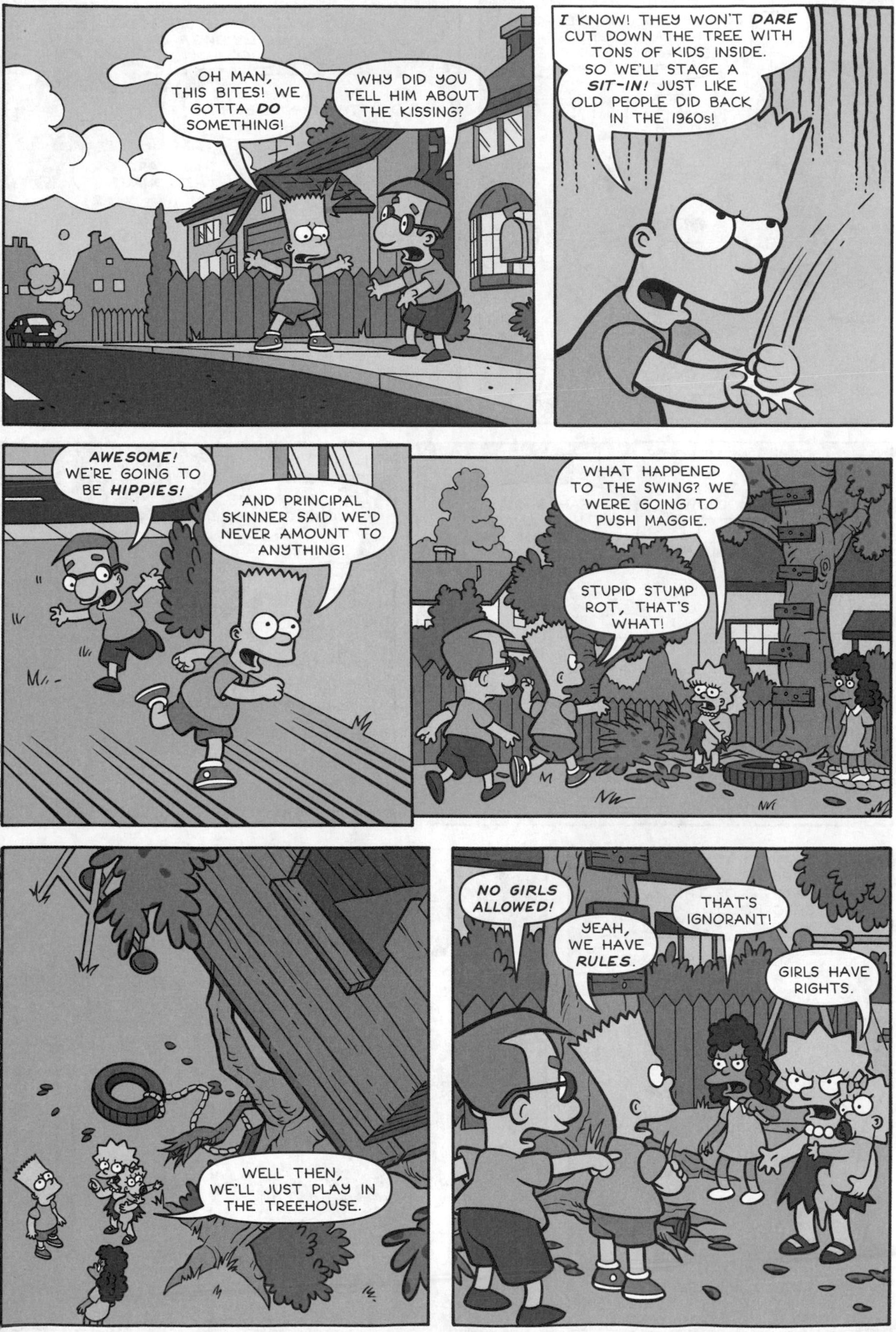
OH MAN, THIS BITES! WE GOTTA DO SOMETHING!
WHY DID YOU TELL HIM ABOUT THE KISSING?
I KNOW! THEY WON'T DARE CUT DOWN THE TREE WITH TONS OF KIDS INSIDE. SO WE'LL STAGE A SIT-IN! JUST LIKE OLD PEOPLE DID BACK IN THE 1960s!
AWESOME! WE'RE GOING TO BE HIPPIES!
AND PRINCIPAL SKINNER SAID WE'D NEVER AMOUNT TO ANYTHING!
WHAT HAPPENED TO THE SWING? WE WERE GOING TO PUSH MAGGIE.
STUPID STUMP ROT, THAT'S WHAT!
WELL THEN, WE'LL JUST PLAY IN THE TREEHOUSE.
NO GIRLS ALLOWED!
YEAH, WE HAVE RULES.
THAT'S IGNORANT!
GIRLS HAVE RIGHTS.

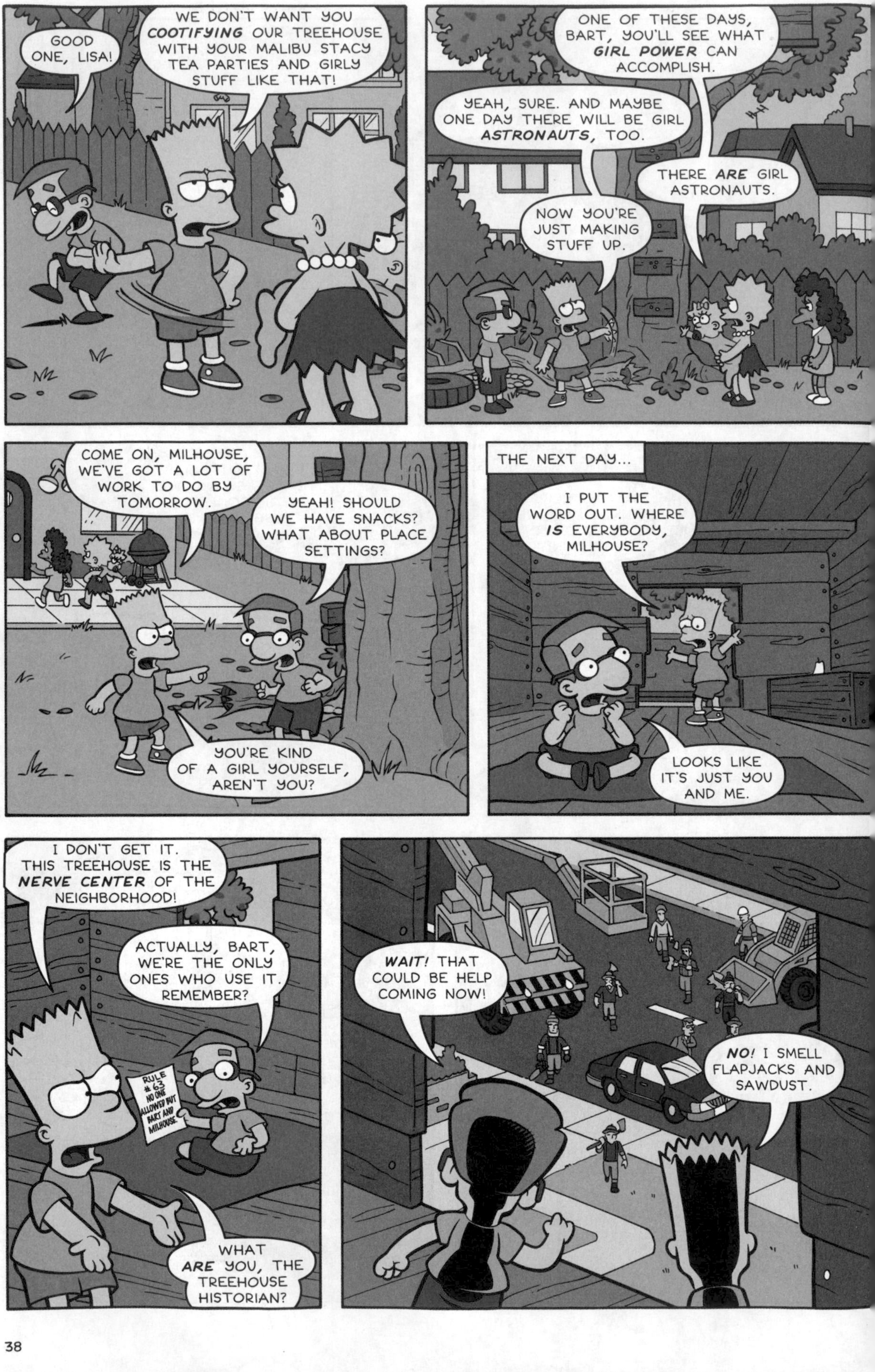
GOOD ONE, LISA!
WE DON'T WANT YOU COOTIFYING OUR TREEHOUSE WITH YOUR MALIBU STACY TEA PARTIES AND GIRLY STUFF LIKE THAT!
ONE OF THESE DAYS, BART, YOU'LL SEE WHAT GIRL POWER CAN ACCOMPLISH.
YEAH, SURE. AND MAYBE ONE DAY THERE WILL BE GIRL ASTRONAUTS, TOO.
THERE ARE GIRL ASTRONAUTS.
NOW YOU'RE JUST MAKING STUFF UP.
COME ON, MILHOUSE, WE'VE GOT A LOT OF WORK TO DO BY TOMORROW.
YEAH! SHOULD WE HAVE SNACKS? WHAT ABOUT PLACE SETTINGS?
YOU'RE KIND OF A GIRL YOURSELF, AREN'T YOU?
THE NEXT DAY...
I PUT THE WORD OUT. WHERE IS EVERYBODY, MILHOUSE?
LOOKS LIKE IT'S JUST YOU AND ME.
I DON'T GET IT. THIS TREEHOUSE IS THE NERVE CENTER OF THE NEIGHBORHOOD!
ACTUALLY, BART, WE'RE THE ONLY ONES WHO USE IT. REMEMBER?
RULE #63 NO ONE ALLOWED BUT BART AND MILHOUSE.
WHAT ARE YOU, THE TREEHOUSE HISTORIAN?
WAIT! THAT COULD BE HELP COMING NOW!
NO! I SMELL FLAPJACKS AND SAWDUST.

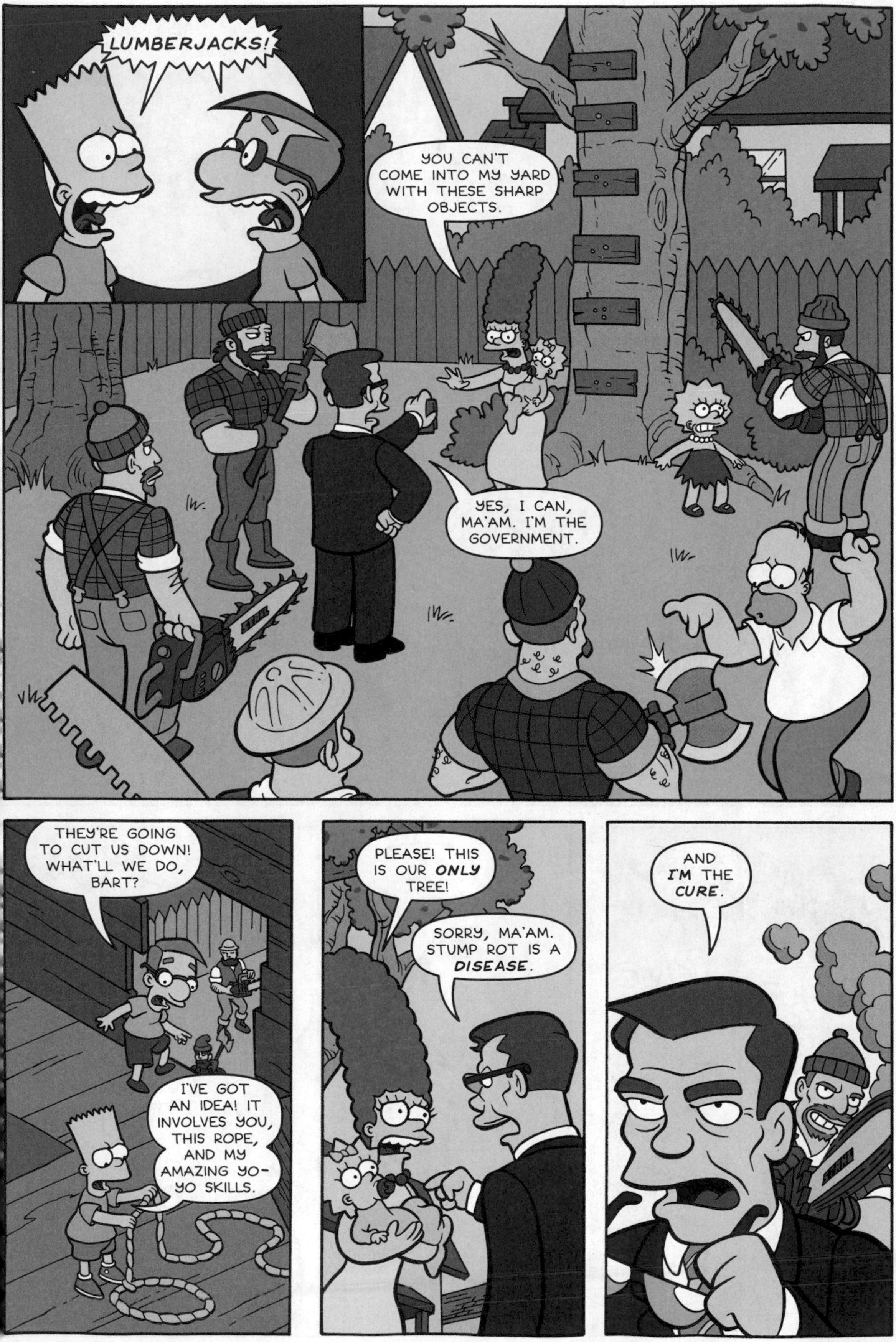
LUMBERJACKS!
YOU CAN'T COME INTO MY YARD WITH THESE SHARP OBJECTS.
YES, I CAN, MA'AM. I'M THE GOVERNMENT.
THEY'RE GOING TO CUT US DOWN! WHAT'LL WE DO, BART?
I'VE GOT AN IDEA! IT INVOLVES YOU, THIS ROPE, AND MY AMAZING YO-YO SKILLS.
PLEASE! THIS IS OUR ONLY TREE!
SORRY, MA'AM. STUMP ROT IS A DISEASE.
AND I'M THE CURE.

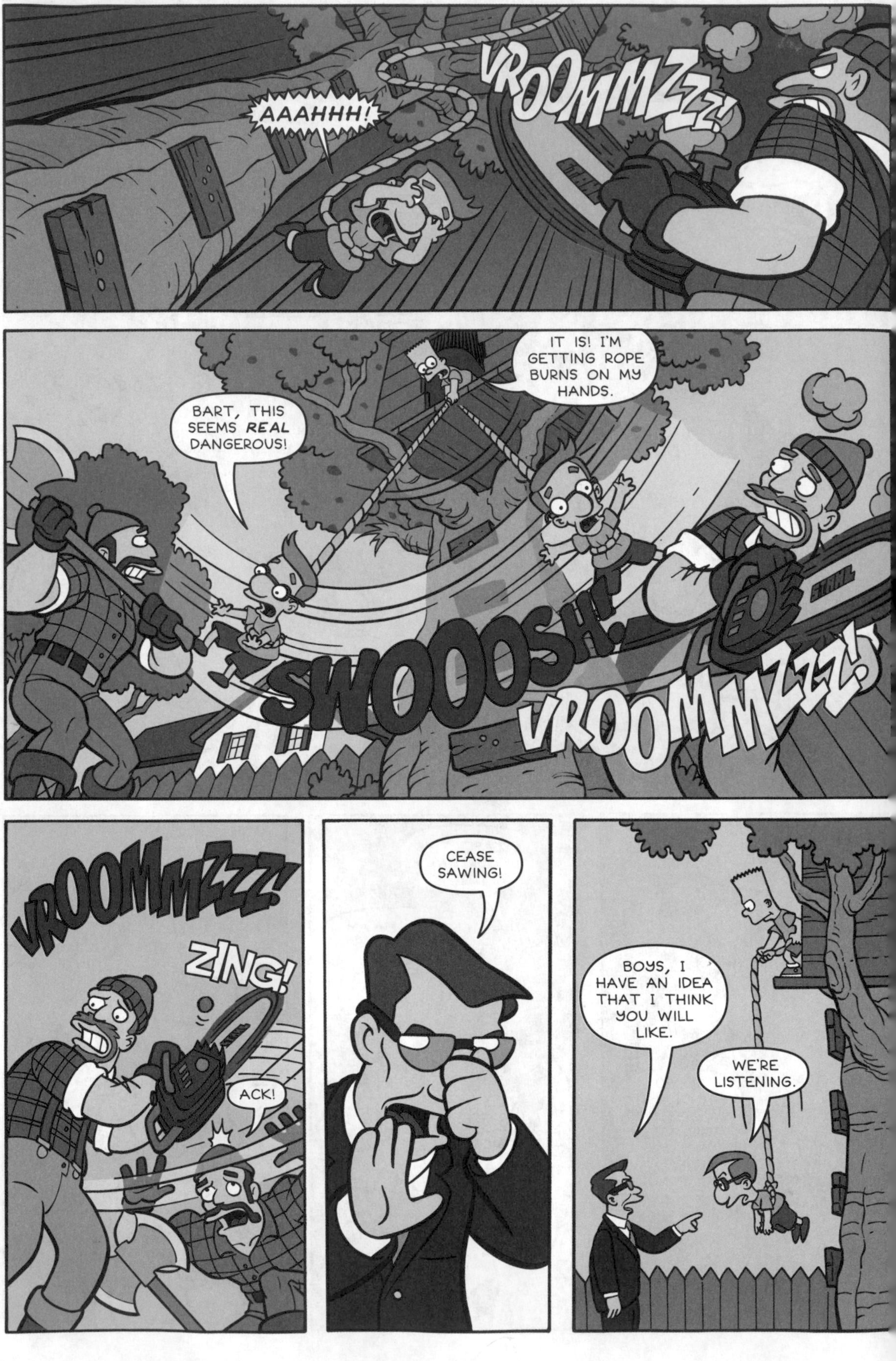
AAAHHH!
VROOMMZZZ!
IT IS! I'M GETTING ROPE BURNS ON MY HANDS.
BART, THIS SEEMS REAL DANGEROUS!
SWOOOSH!
VROOMMZZZ!
VROOMMZZZ!
ZING!
ACK!
CEASE SAWING!
BOYS, I HAVE AN IDEA THAT I THINK YOU WILL LIKE.
WE'RE LISTENING.

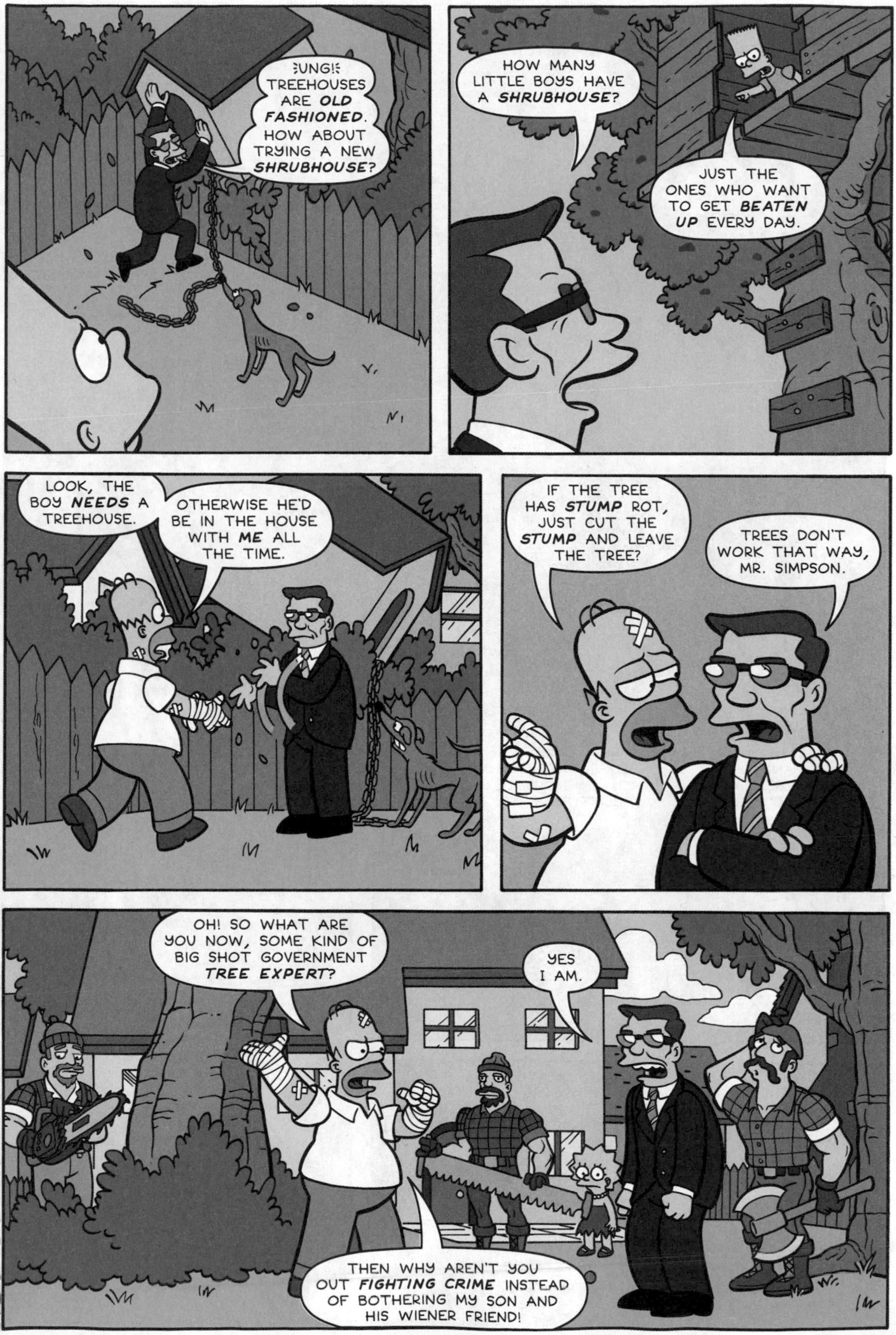

UNG! TREEHOUSES ARE OLD FASHIONED. HOW ABOUT TRYING A NEW SHRUBHOUSE?
HOW MANY LITTLE BOYS HAVE A SHRUBHOUSE?
JUST THE ONES WHO WANT TO GET BEATEN UP EVERY DAY.
LOOK, THE BOY NEEDS A TREEHOUSE.
OTHERWISE HE'D BE IN THE HOUSE WITH ME ALL THE TIME.
IF THE TREE HAS STUMP ROT, JUST CUT THE STUMP AND LEAVE THE TREE?
TREES DON'T WORK THAT WAY, MR. SIMPSON.
OH! SO WHAT ARE YOU NOW, SOME KIND OF BIG SHOT GOVERNMENT TREE EXPERT?
YES I AM.
THEN WHY AREN'T YOU OUT FIGHTING CRIME INSTEAD OF BOTHERING MY SON AND HIS WIENER FRIEND!

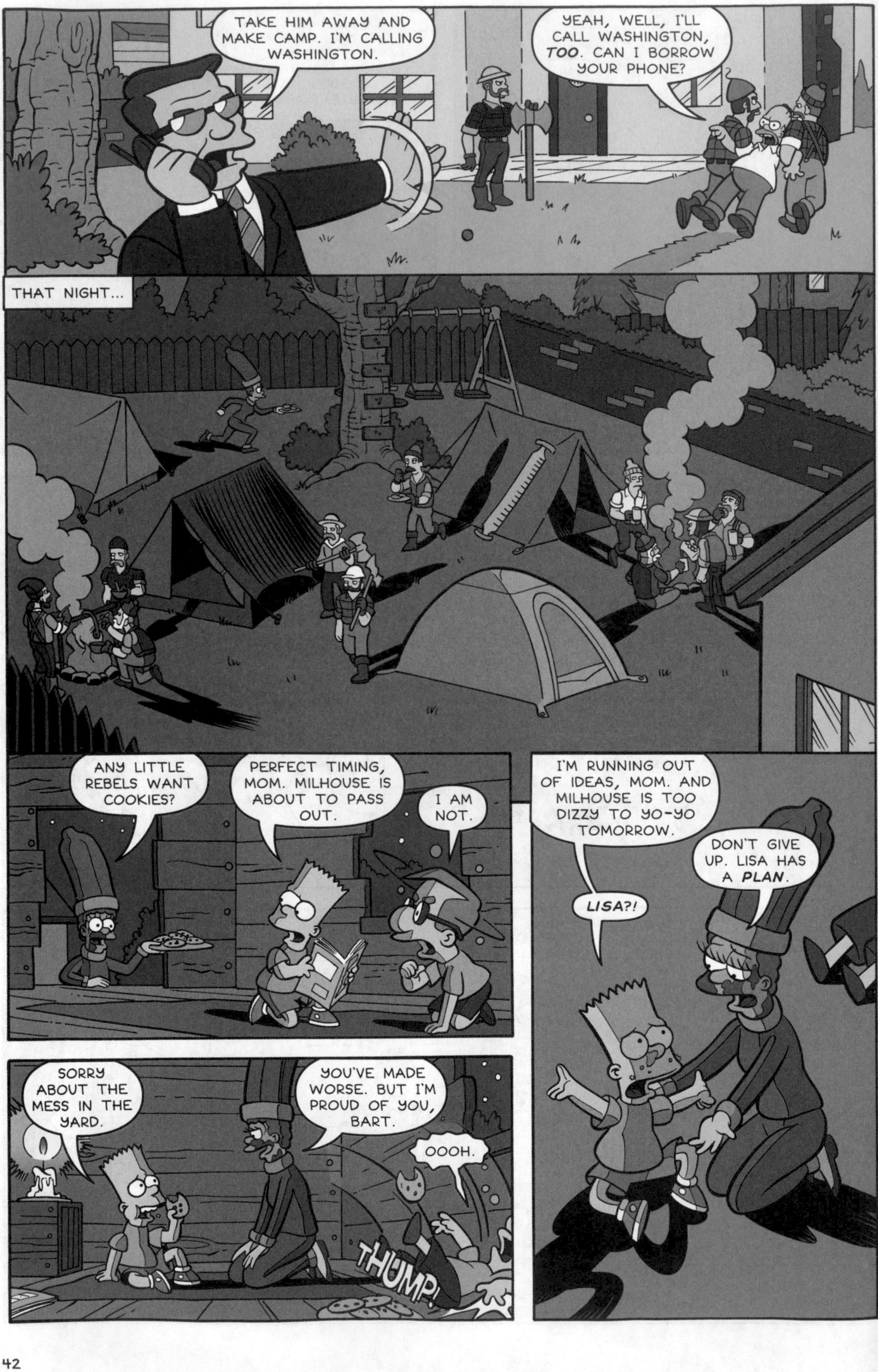
TAKE HIM AWAY AND MAKE CAMP. I'M CALLING WASHINGTON.
YEAH, WELL, I'LL CALL WASHINGTON, *TOO*. CAN I BORROW YOUR PHONE?
THAT NIGHT...
ANY LITTLE REBELS WANT COOKIES?
PERFECT TIMING, MOM. MILHOUSE IS ABOUT TO PASS OUT.
I AM NOT.
SORRY ABOUT THE MESS IN THE YARD.
YOU'VE MADE WORSE. BUT I'M PROUD OF YOU, BART.
OOOH.
THUMP!
I'M RUNNING OUT OF IDEAS, MOM. AND MILHOUSE IS TOO DIZZY TO YO-YO TOMORROW.
DON'T GIVE UP. LISA HAS A *PLAN*.
LISA?!

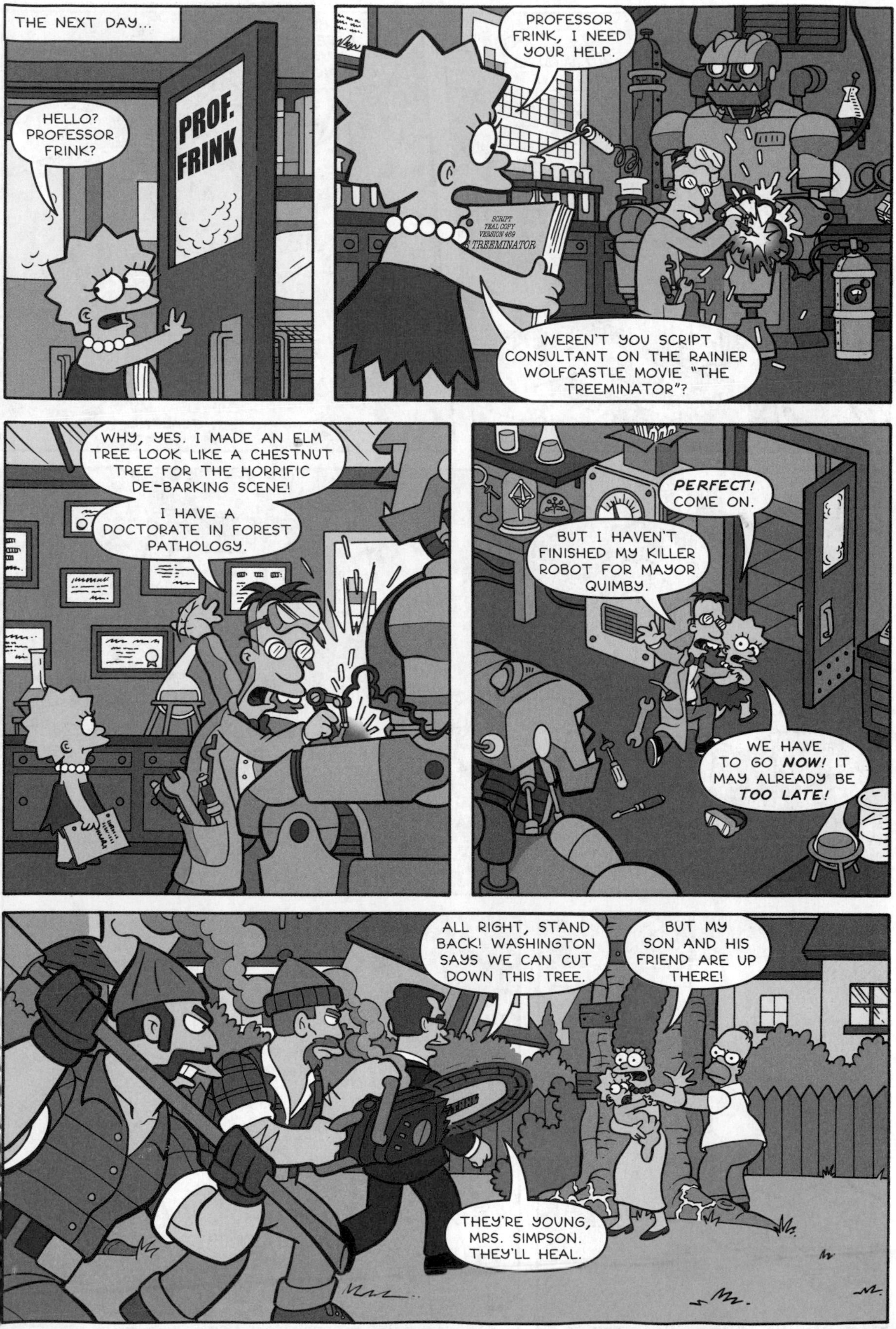
THE NEXT DAY...
HELLO? PROFESSOR FRINK?
PROF. FRINK
PROFESSOR FRINK, I NEED YOUR HELP.
SCRIPT TRIAL COPY VERSION 469 THE TREEMINATOR
WEREN'T YOU SCRIPT CONSULTANT ON THE RAINIER WOLFCASTLE MOVIE "THE TREEMINATOR"?
WHY, YES. I MADE AN ELM TREE LOOK LIKE A CHESTNUT TREE FOR THE HORRIFIC DE-BARKING SCENE!
I HAVE A DOCTORATE IN FOREST PATHOLOGY.
PERFECT! COME ON.
BUT I HAVEN'T FINISHED MY KILLER ROBOT FOR MAYOR QUIMBY.
WE HAVE TO GO ***NOW!*** IT MAY ALREADY BE ***TOO LATE!***
ALL RIGHT, STAND BACK! WASHINGTON SAYS WE CAN CUT DOWN THIS TREE.
BUT MY SON AND HIS FRIEND ARE UP THERE!
THEY'RE YOUNG, MRS. SIMPSON. THEY'LL HEAL.

JUST A *GLAVIN* MINUTE! I CAN *SAVE* THIS TREE!

BUT THE TREE IS *DISEASED*. IT *MUST* BE *ERADICATED*.

HE'S QUITE THE DRAMA QUEEN. ꓕNG-HOOEY!ꓕ LISA, MY *SCALPEL*.

VROOMMMZZ!

I NEED ABSOLUTE SILENCE FOR THIS DELICATE PROCEDURE WITH THE PERSPIRING AND THE STICKY SAP ON THE FIN-GERS!

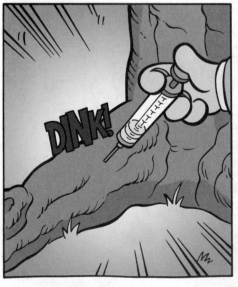

DINK!

ꓕNG-HEY!ꓕ I DECLARE THIS TREE *HEALTHY*!

IN YOUR FACE, GOVERNMENT TREE EXPERT!

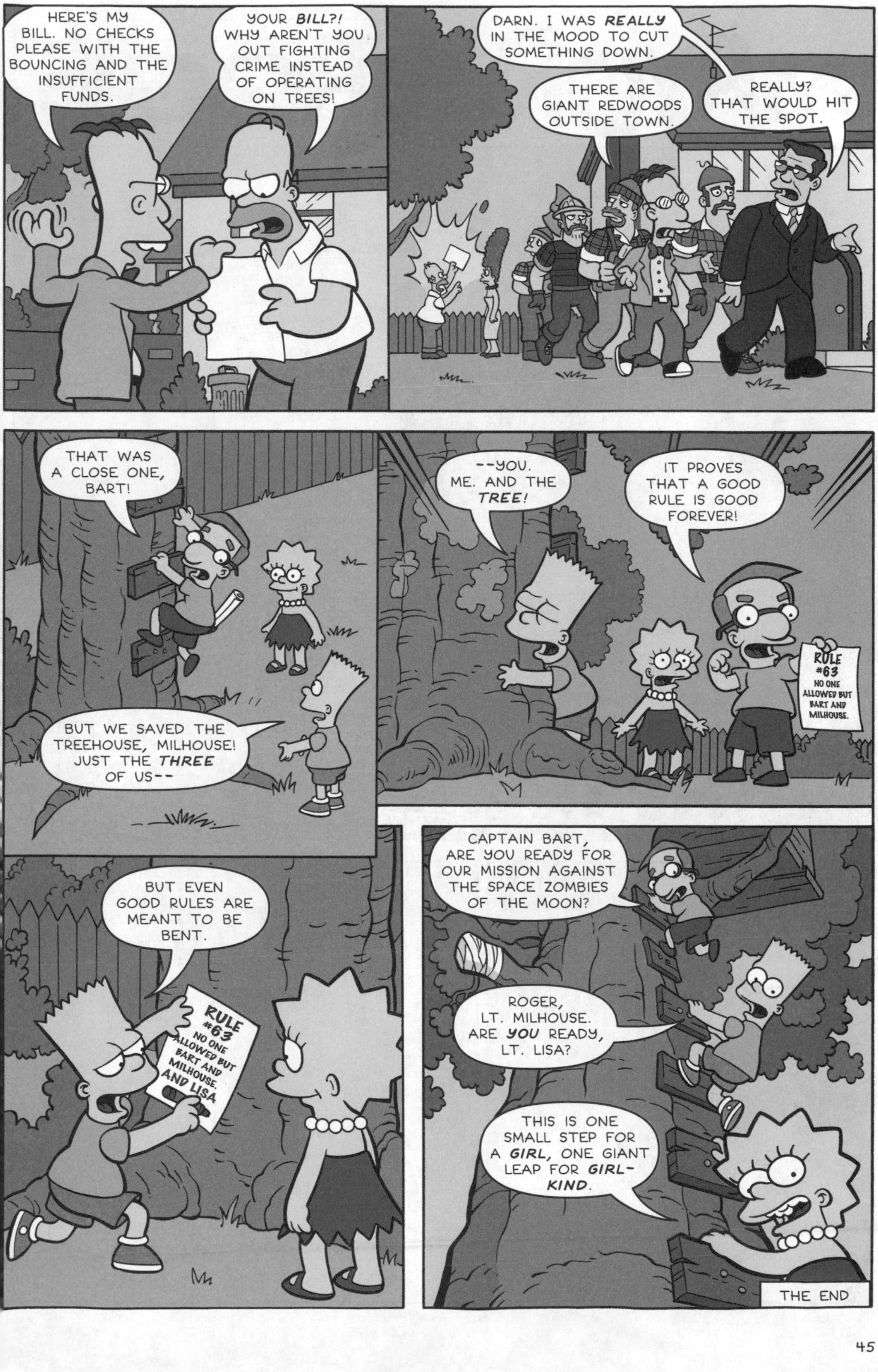
HERE'S MY BILL. NO CHECKS PLEASE WITH THE BOUNCING AND THE INSUFFICIENT FUNDS.
YOUR BILL?! WHY AREN'T YOU OUT FIGHTING CRIME INSTEAD OF OPERATING ON TREES!
DARN. I WAS REALLY IN THE MOOD TO CUT SOMETHING DOWN.
THERE ARE GIANT REDWOODS OUTSIDE TOWN.
REALLY? THAT WOULD HIT THE SPOT.
THAT WAS A CLOSE ONE, BART!
BUT WE SAVED THE TREEHOUSE, MILHOUSE! JUST THE THREE OF US--
--YOU. ME. AND THE TREE!
IT PROVES THAT A GOOD RULE IS GOOD FOREVER!
RULE #63 NO ONE ALLOWED BUT BART AND MILHOUSE.
BUT EVEN GOOD RULES ARE MEANT TO BE BENT.
RULE #63 NO ONE ALLOWED BUT BART AND MILHOUSE. AND LISA
CAPTAIN BART, ARE YOU READY FOR OUR MISSION AGAINST THE SPACE ZOMBIES OF THE MOON?
ROGER, LT. MILHOUSE. ARE YOU READY, LT. LISA?
THIS IS ONE SMALL STEP FOR A GIRL, ONE GIANT LEAP FOR GIRL-KIND.
THE END

MAYOR MAGGIE

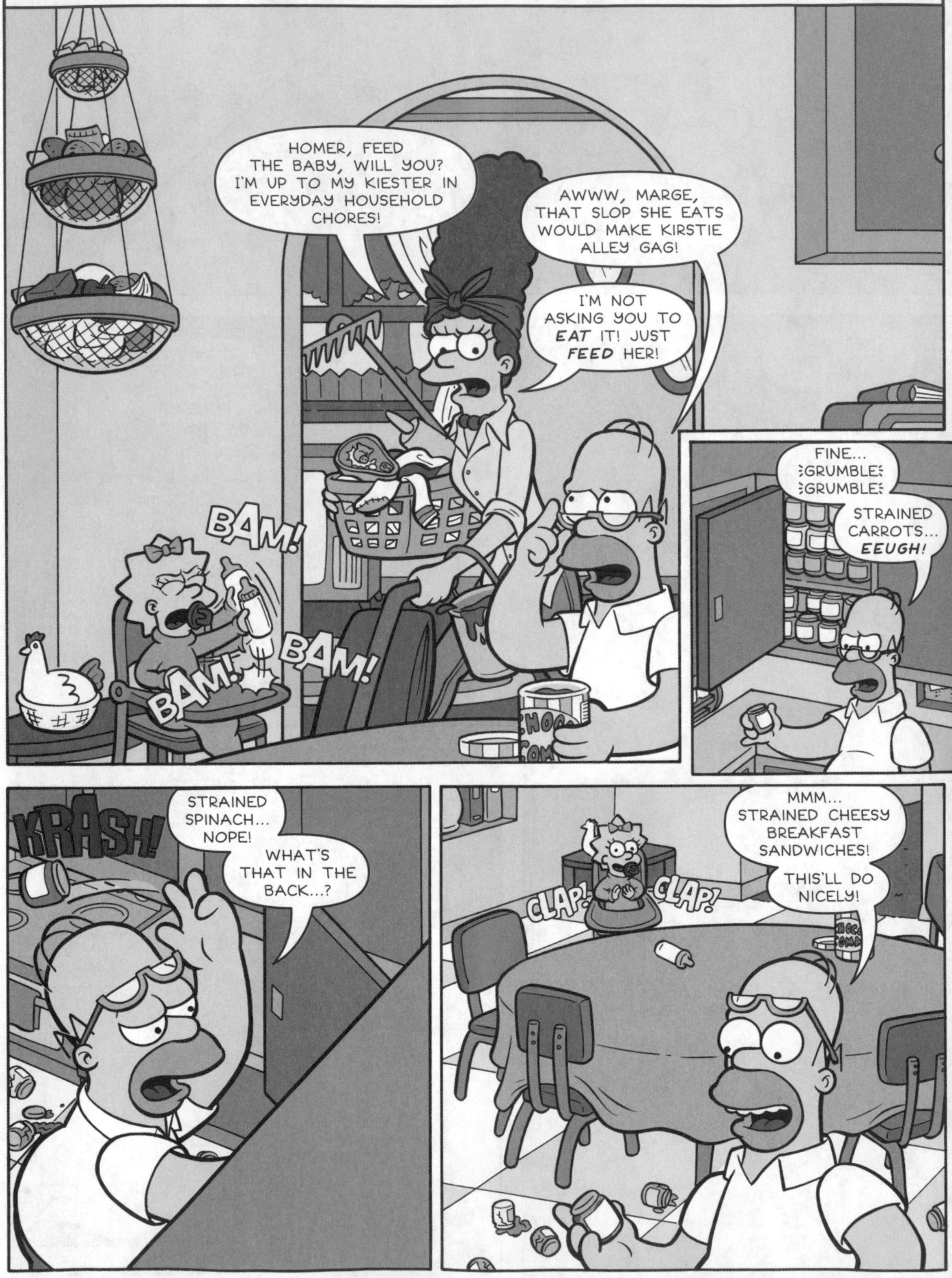
HOMER, FEED THE BABY, WILL YOU? I'M UP TO MY KIESTER IN EVERYDAY HOUSEHOLD CHORES!
AWWW, MARGE, THAT SLOP SHE EATS WOULD MAKE KIRSTIE ALLEY GAG!
I'M NOT ASKING YOU TO *EAT* IT! JUST *FEED* HER!
BAM!
BAM!
BAM!
FINE... GRUMBLE GRUMBLE
STRAINED CARROTS... **EEUGH!**
KRASH!
STRAINED SPINACH... NOPE!
WHAT'S THAT IN THE BACK...?
CLAP! CLAP!
MMM... STRAINED CHEESY BREAKFAST SANDWICHES!
THIS'LL DO NICELY!

TOM PEYER SCRIPT — JASON HO PENCILS — ANDREW PEPOY INKS — NATHAN HAMILL COLORS — KAREN BATES LETTERS — BILL MORRISON EDITOR

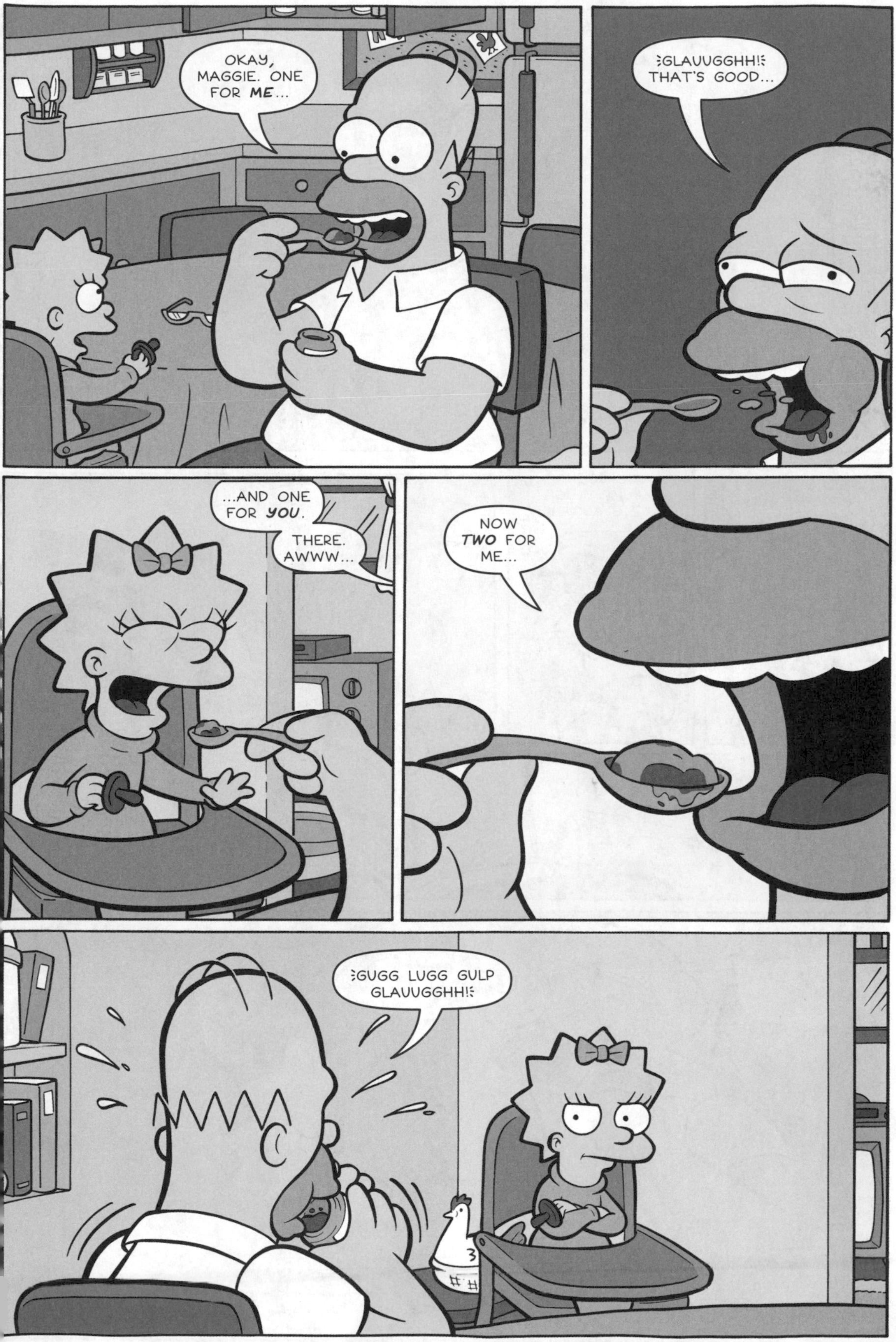
OKAY, MAGGIE. ONE FOR ME...
⁝GLAUUGGHH!⁝ THAT'S GOOD...
...AND ONE FOR YOU.
THERE. AWWW...
NOW TWO FOR ME...
⁝GUGG LUGG GULP GLAUUGGHH!⁝

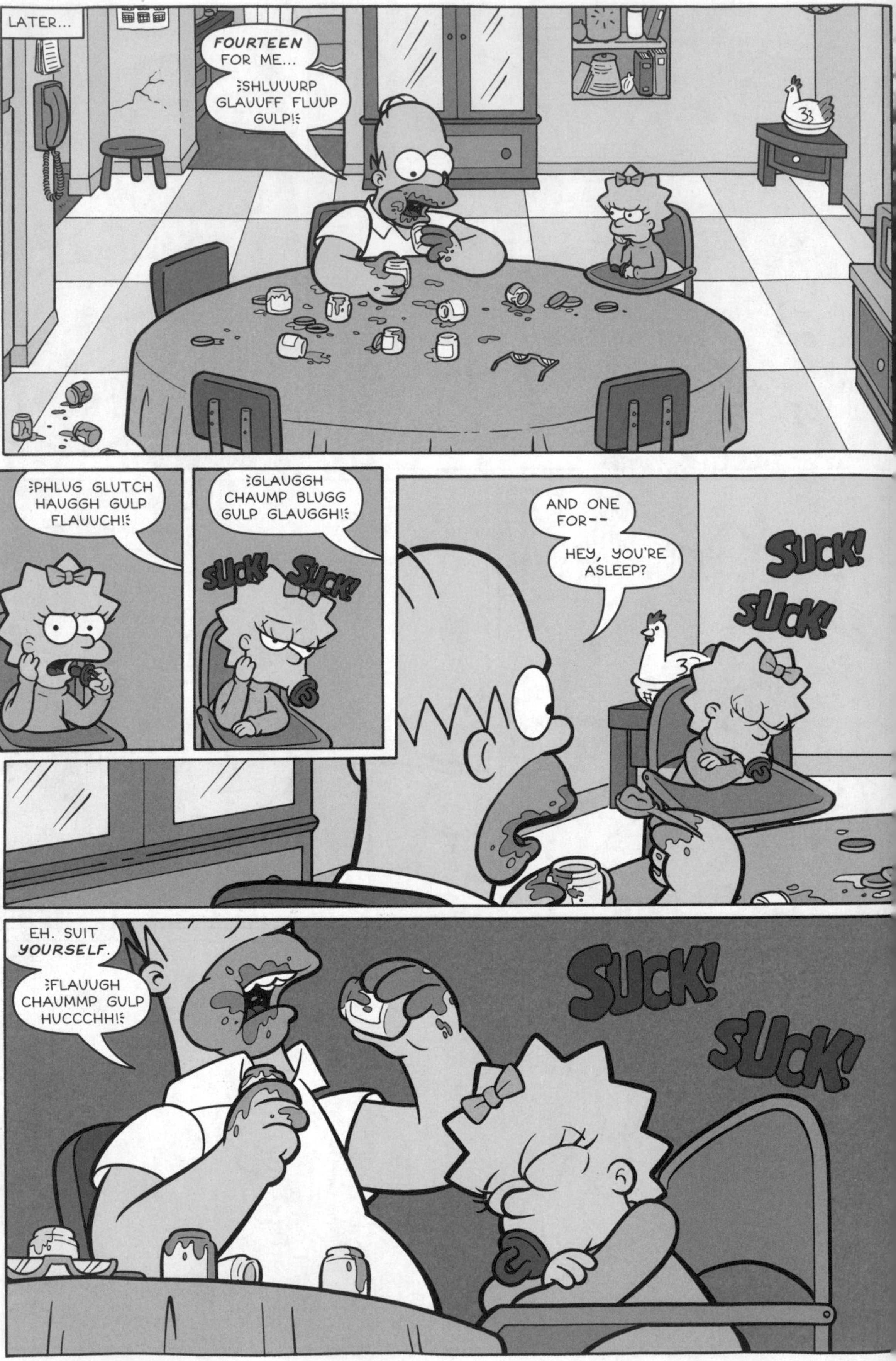
LATER...
FOURTEEN FOR ME...
SHLUUURP GLAUUFF FLUUP GULP!
PHLUG GLUTCH HAUGGH GULP FLAUUCH!
GLAUGGH CHAUMP BLUGG GULP GLAUGGH!
SUCK! SUCK!
AND ONE FOR--
HEY, YOU'RE ASLEEP?
SUCK!
SUCK!
EH. SUIT YOURSELF.
FLAUUGH CHAUMMP GULP HUCCCHH!
SUCK!
SUCK!

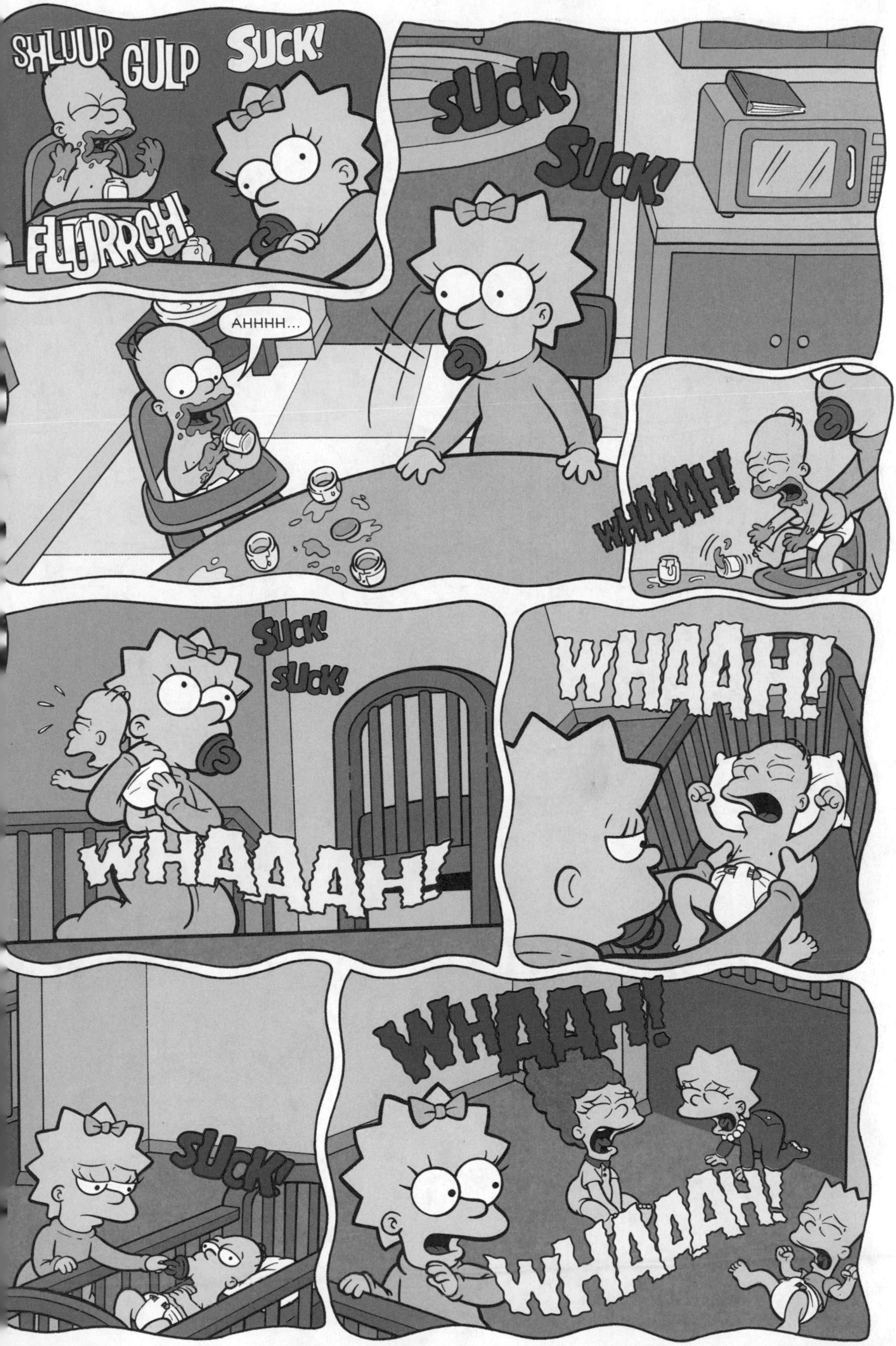
SHLUUP
GULP
SUCK!
FLURRCH!
SUCK!
SUCK!
AHHHH...
WHAAAH!
SUCK!
SUCK!
WHAAAH!
WHAAH!
SUCK!
WHAAH!
WHAAAH!

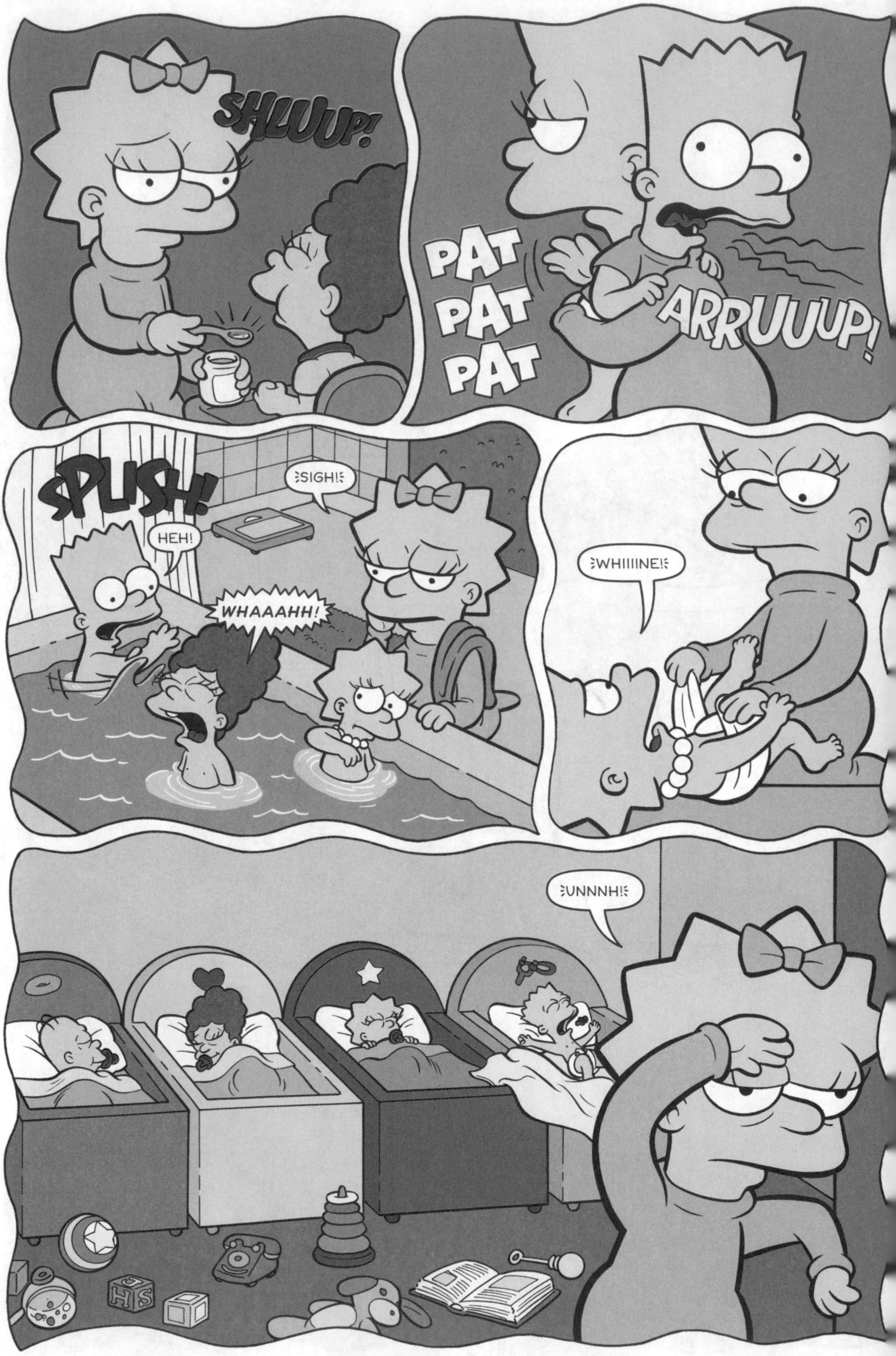
SHLUUP!
PAT PAT PAT
ARRUUUP!
SPLISH!
HEH!
SIGH!
WHAAAHH!
WHIIIINE!
UNNNH!

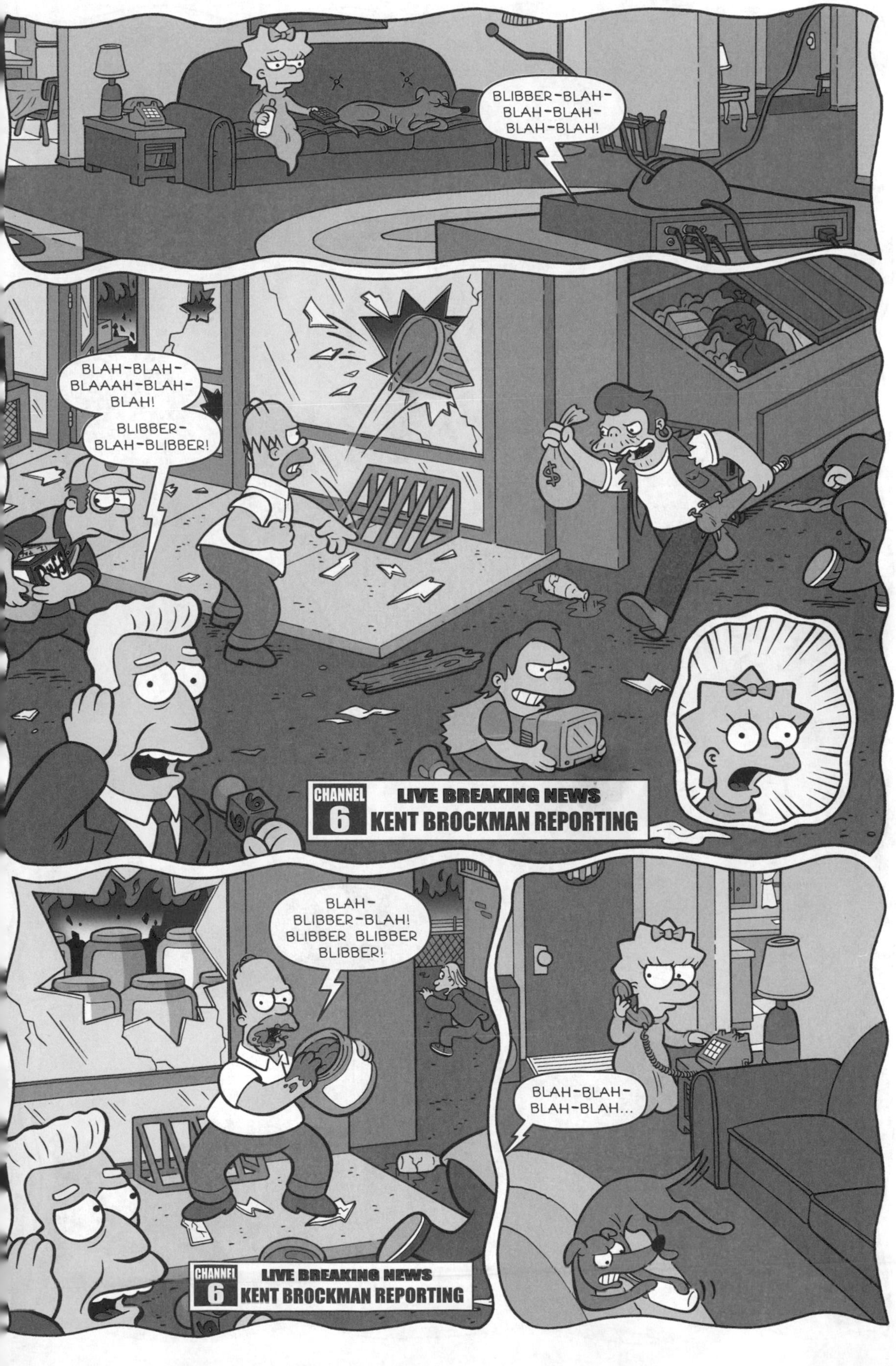
BLIBBER-BLAH-BLAH-BLAH-BLAH-BLAH!
BLAH-BLAH-BLAAAH-BLAH-BLAH!
BLIBBER-BLAH-BLIBBER!
CHANNEL 6 LIVE BREAKING NEWS KENT BROCKMAN REPORTING
BLAH-BLIBBER-BLAH! BLIBBER BLIBBER BLIBBER!
CHANNEL 6 LIVE BREAKING NEWS KENT BROCKMAN REPORTING
BLAH-BLAH-BLAH-BLAH...

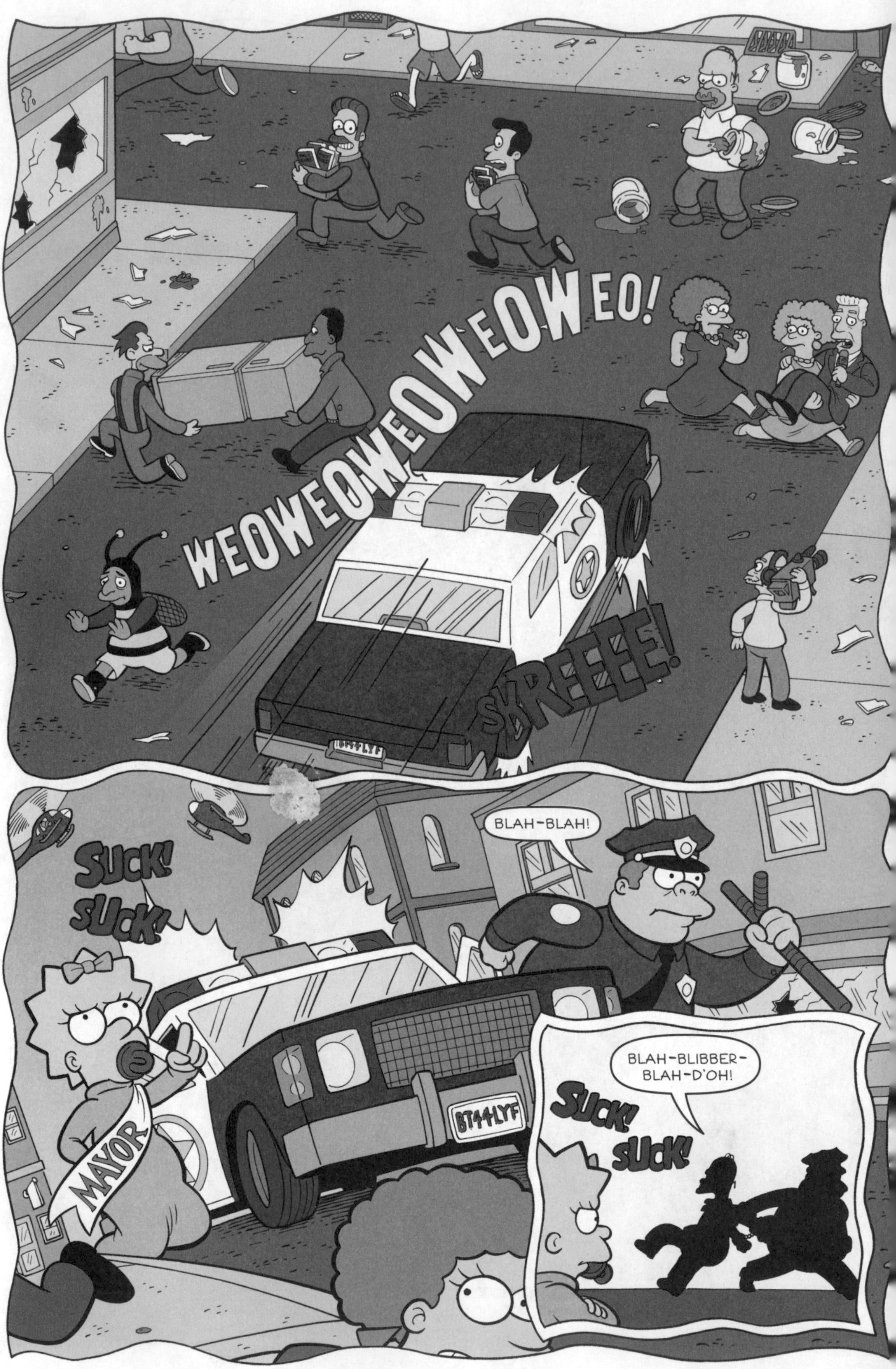
WEOWEOWEOWEOWEOWEO!
SKREEEE!
SUCK!
SUCK!
BLAH-BLAH!
MAYOR
BT44LYF
BLAH-BLIBBER-BLAH-D'OH!
SUCK!
SUCK!

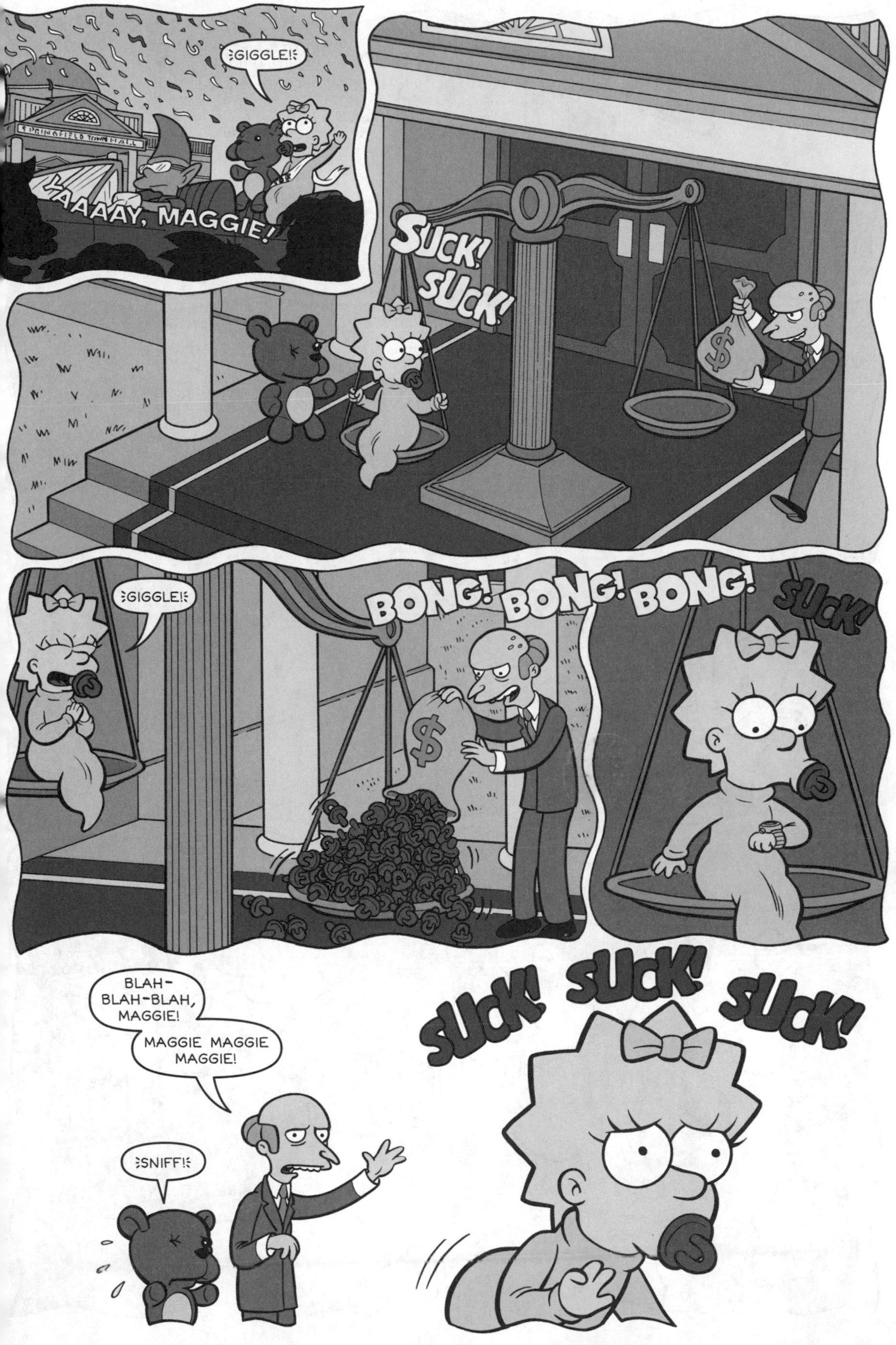
GIGGLE!
SPRINGFIELD TOWN HALL
YAAAAY, MAGGIE!
SUCK! SUCK!
GIGGLE!
BONG! BONG! BONG!
SUCK!
BLAH-BLAH-BLAH, MAGGIE!
MAGGIE MAGGIE MAGGIE!
SNIFF!
SUCK! SUCK! SUCK!

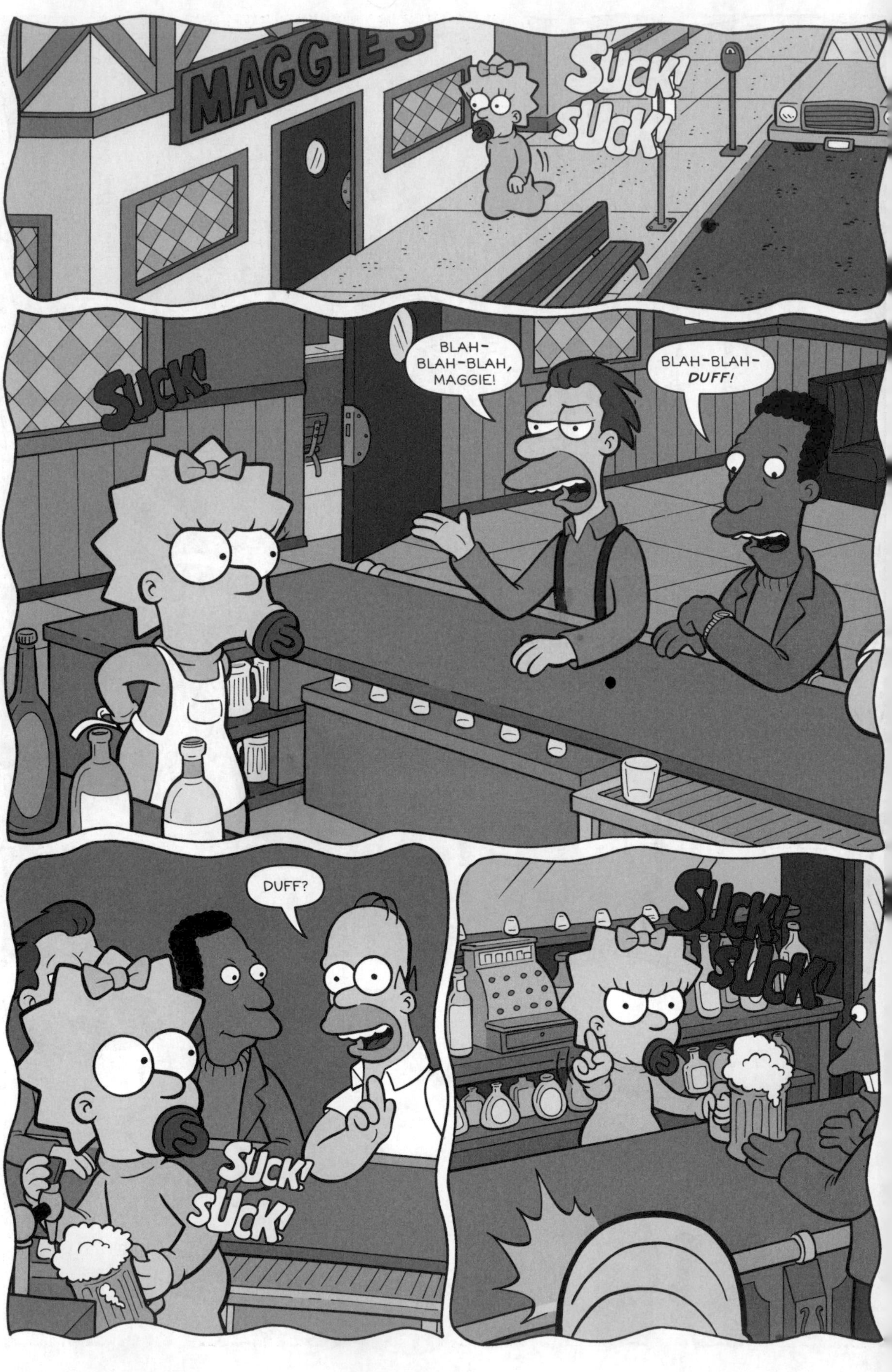
MAGGIE'S
SUCK! SUCK!
SUCK!
BLAH-BLAH-BLAH, MAGGIE!
BLAH-BLAH-DUFF!
DUFF?
SUCK! SUCK!
SUCK! SUCK!

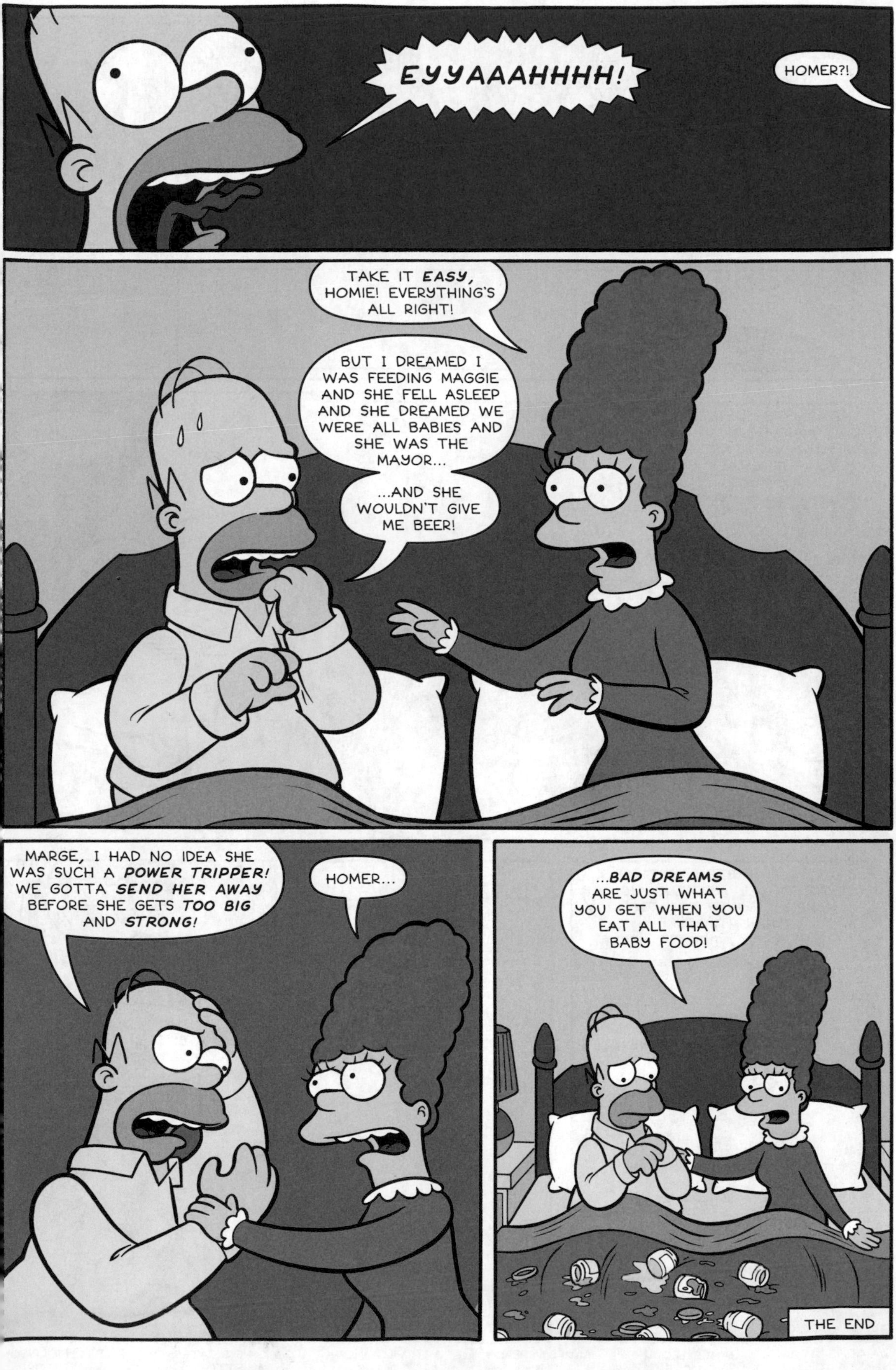
EYYAAAHHHH!
HOMER?!
TAKE IT EASY, HOMIE! EVERYTHING'S ALL RIGHT!
BUT I DREAMED I WAS FEEDING MAGGIE AND SHE FELL ASLEEP AND SHE DREAMED WE WERE ALL BABIES AND SHE WAS THE MAYOR...
...AND SHE WOULDN'T GIVE ME BEER!
MARGE, I HAD NO IDEA SHE WAS SUCH A POWER TRIPPER! WE GOTTA SEND HER AWAY BEFORE SHE GETS TOO BIG AND STRONG!
HOMER...
...BAD DREAMS ARE JUST WHAT YOU GET WHEN YOU EAT ALL THAT BABY FOOD!
THE END

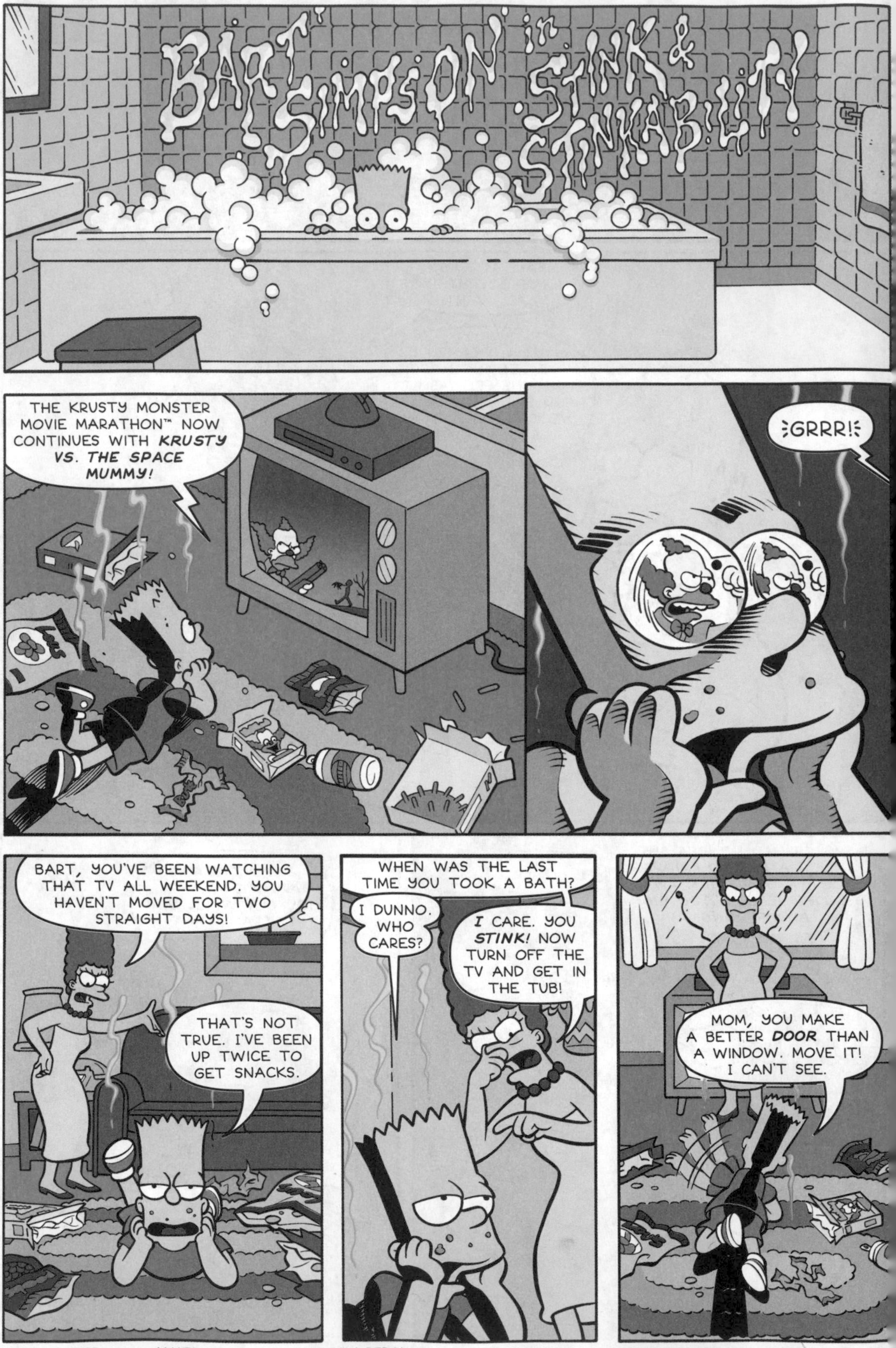
BART SIMPSON in STINK & STINKABILITY!
THE KRUSTY MONSTER MOVIE MARATHON™ NOW CONTINUES WITH KRUSTY VS. THE SPACE MUMMY!
GRRR!
BART, YOU'VE BEEN WATCHING THAT TV ALL WEEKEND. YOU HAVEN'T MOVED FOR TWO STRAIGHT DAYS!
THAT'S NOT TRUE. I'VE BEEN UP TWICE TO GET SNACKS.
WHEN WAS THE LAST TIME YOU TOOK A BATH?
I DUNNO. WHO CARES?
I CARE. YOU STINK! NOW TURN OFF THE TV AND GET IN THE TUB!
MOM, YOU MAKE A BETTER DOOR THAN A WINDOW. MOVE IT! I CAN'T SEE.

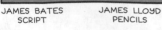

JAMES BATES SCRIPT — JAMES LLOYD PENCILS — ANDREW PEPOY INKS — ART VILLANUEVA COLORS — KAREN BATES LETTERS — BILL MORRISON EDITOR

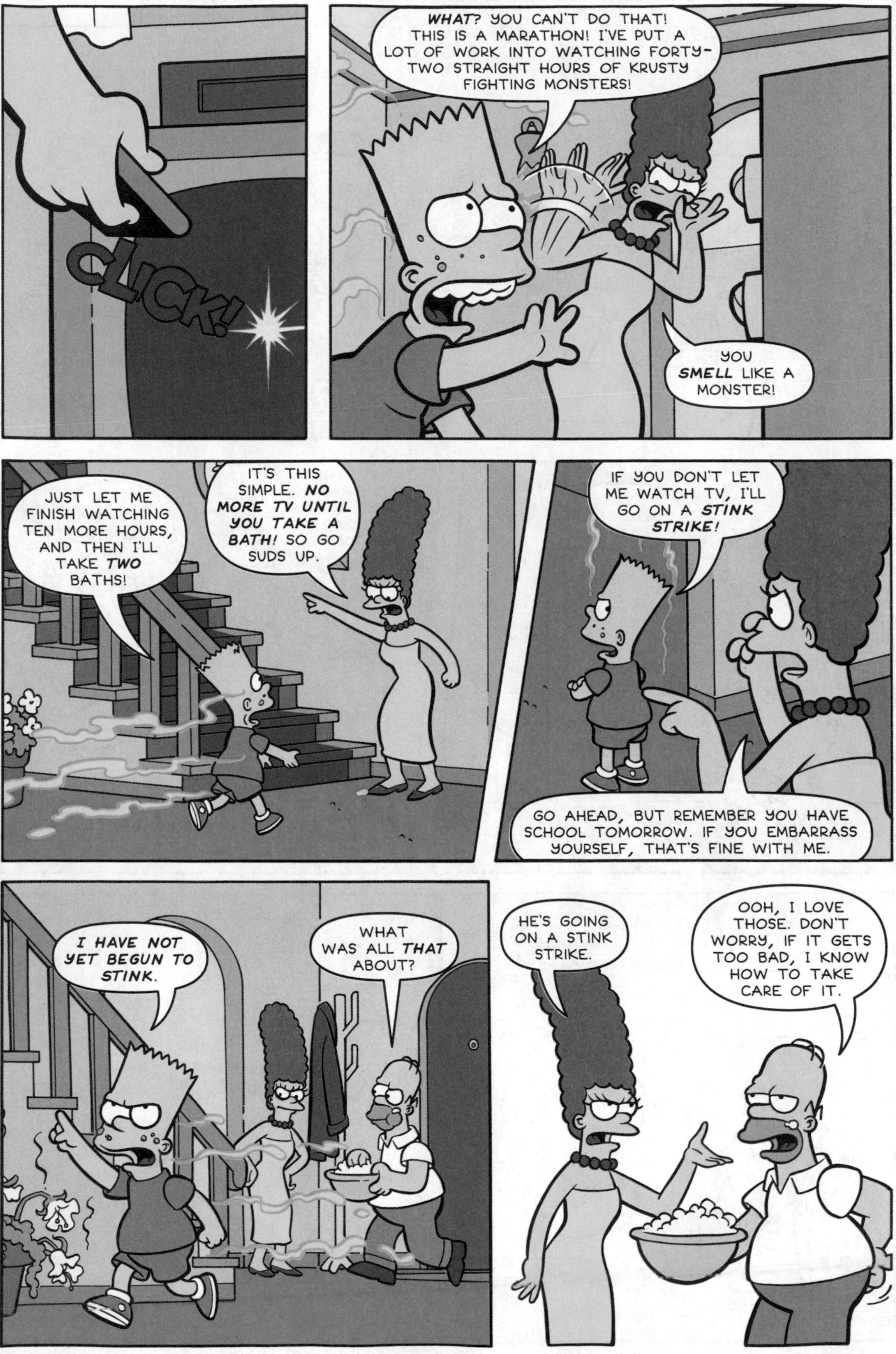
CLICK!
WHAT? YOU CAN'T DO THAT! THIS IS A MARATHON! I'VE PUT A LOT OF WORK INTO WATCHING FORTY-TWO STRAIGHT HOURS OF KRUSTY FIGHTING MONSTERS!
YOU SMELL LIKE A MONSTER!
JUST LET ME FINISH WATCHING TEN MORE HOURS, AND THEN I'LL TAKE TWO BATHS!
IT'S THIS SIMPLE. NO MORE TV UNTIL YOU TAKE A BATH! SO GO SUDS UP.
IF YOU DON'T LET ME WATCH TV, I'LL GO ON A STINK STRIKE!
GO AHEAD, BUT REMEMBER YOU HAVE SCHOOL TOMORROW. IF YOU EMBARRASS YOURSELF, THAT'S FINE WITH ME.
I HAVE NOT YET BEGUN TO STINK.
WHAT WAS ALL THAT ABOUT?
HE'S GOING ON A STINK STRIKE.
OOH, I LOVE THOSE. DON'T WORRY, IF IT GETS TOO BAD, I KNOW HOW TO TAKE CARE OF IT.

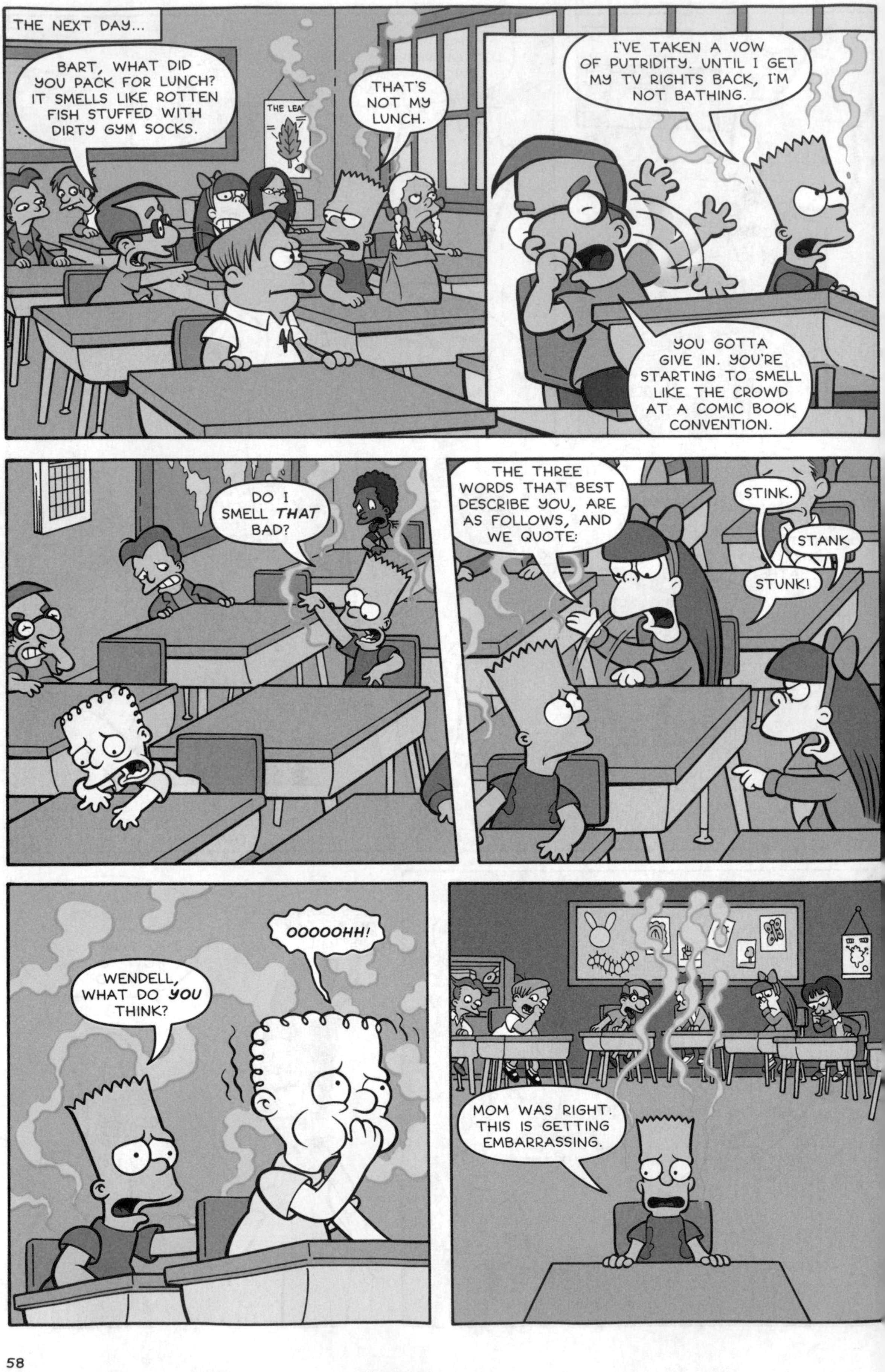
THE NEXT DAY...
BART, WHAT DID YOU PACK FOR LUNCH? IT SMELLS LIKE ROTTEN FISH STUFFED WITH DIRTY GYM SOCKS.
THAT'S NOT MY LUNCH.
I'VE TAKEN A VOW OF PUTRIDITY. UNTIL I GET MY TV RIGHTS BACK, I'M NOT BATHING.
YOU GOTTA GIVE IN. YOU'RE STARTING TO SMELL LIKE THE CROWD AT A COMIC BOOK CONVENTION.
DO I SMELL *THAT* BAD?
THE THREE WORDS THAT BEST DESCRIBE YOU, ARE AS FOLLOWS, AND WE QUOTE:
STINK.
STANK
STUNK!
WENDELL, WHAT DO *YOU* THINK?
OOOOOHH!
MOM WAS RIGHT. THIS IS GETTING EMBARRASSING.

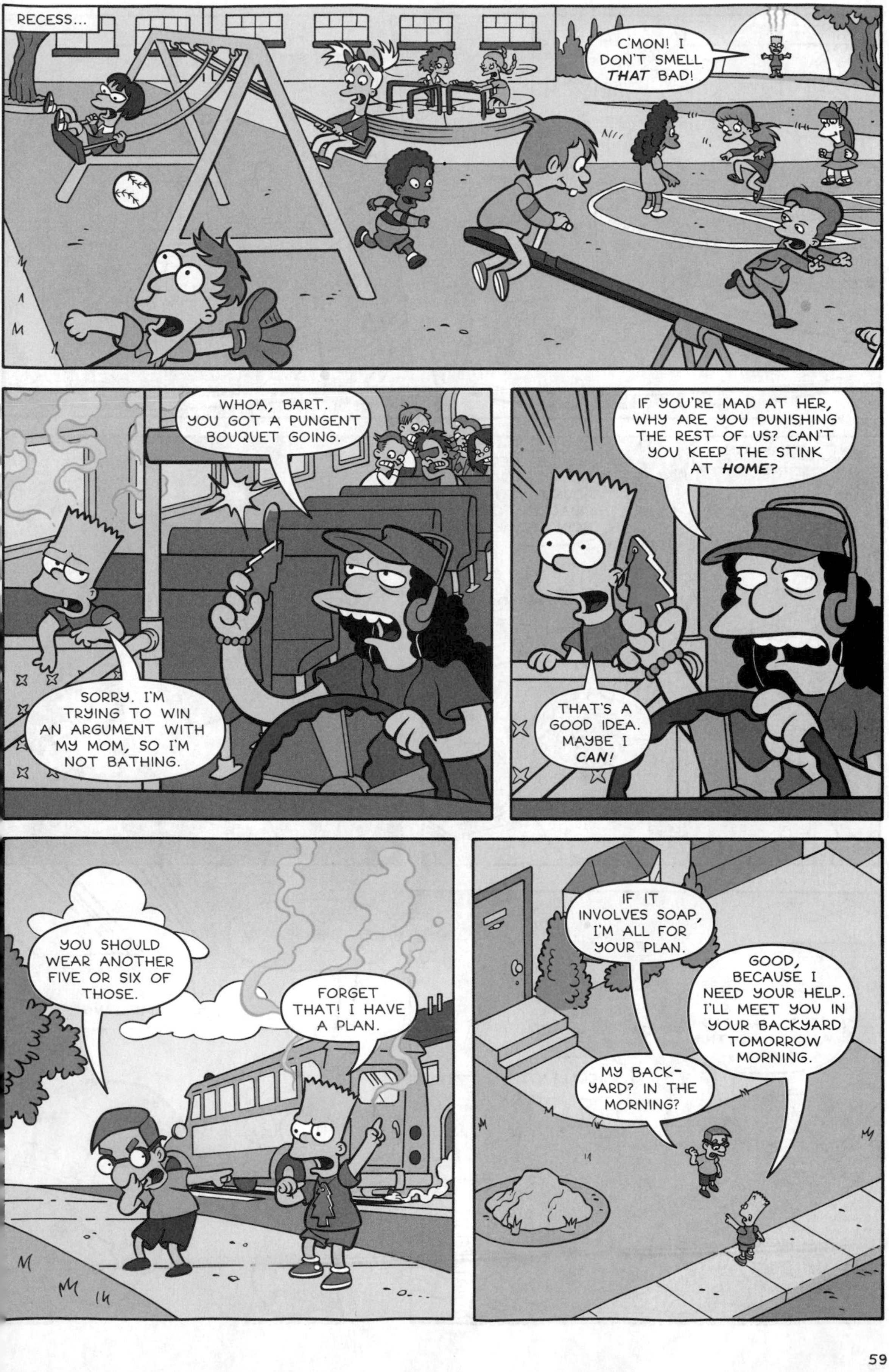
RECESS...
C'MON! I DON'T SMELL *THAT* BAD!
WHOA, BART. YOU GOT A PUNGENT BOUQUET GOING.
SORRY. I'M TRYING TO WIN AN ARGUMENT WITH MY MOM, SO I'M NOT BATHING.
IF YOU'RE MAD AT HER, WHY ARE YOU PUNISHING THE REST OF US? CAN'T YOU KEEP THE STINK AT *HOME*?
THAT'S A GOOD IDEA. MAYBE I *CAN*!
YOU SHOULD WEAR ANOTHER FIVE OR SIX OF THOSE.
FORGET THAT! I HAVE A PLAN.
IF IT INVOLVES SOAP, I'M ALL FOR YOUR PLAN.
GOOD, BECAUSE I NEED YOUR HELP. I'LL MEET YOU IN YOUR BACKYARD TOMORROW MORNING.
MY BACK-YARD? IN THE MORNING?

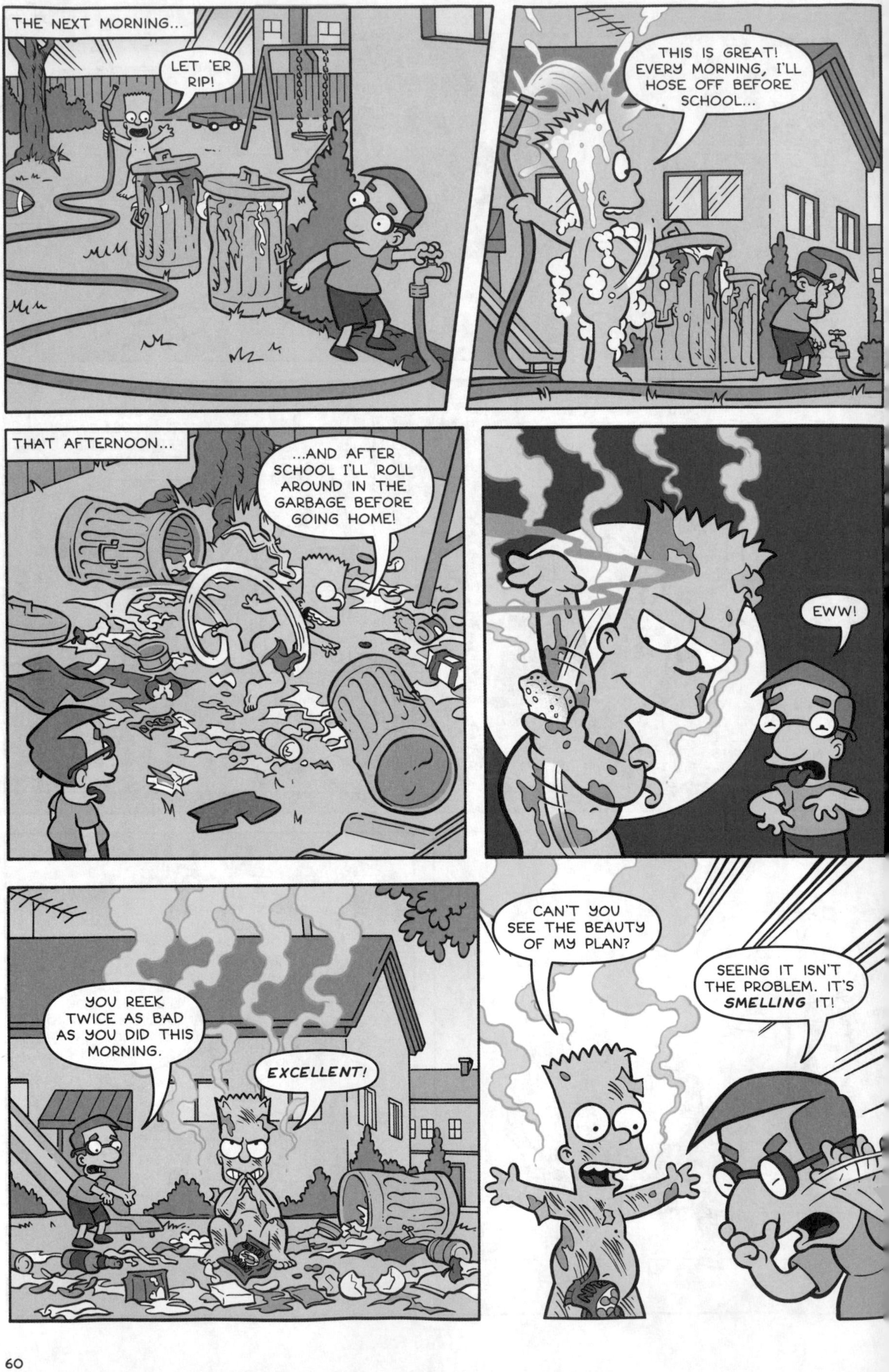
THE NEXT MORNING...
LET 'ER RIP!
THIS IS GREAT! EVERY MORNING, I'LL HOSE OFF BEFORE SCHOOL...
THAT AFTERNOON...
...AND AFTER SCHOOL I'LL ROLL AROUND IN THE GARBAGE BEFORE GOING HOME!
EWW!
YOU REEK TWICE AS BAD AS YOU DID THIS MORNING.
EXCELLENT!
CAN'T YOU SEE THE BEAUTY OF MY PLAN?
SEEING IT ISN'T THE PROBLEM. IT'S ***SMELLING*** IT!

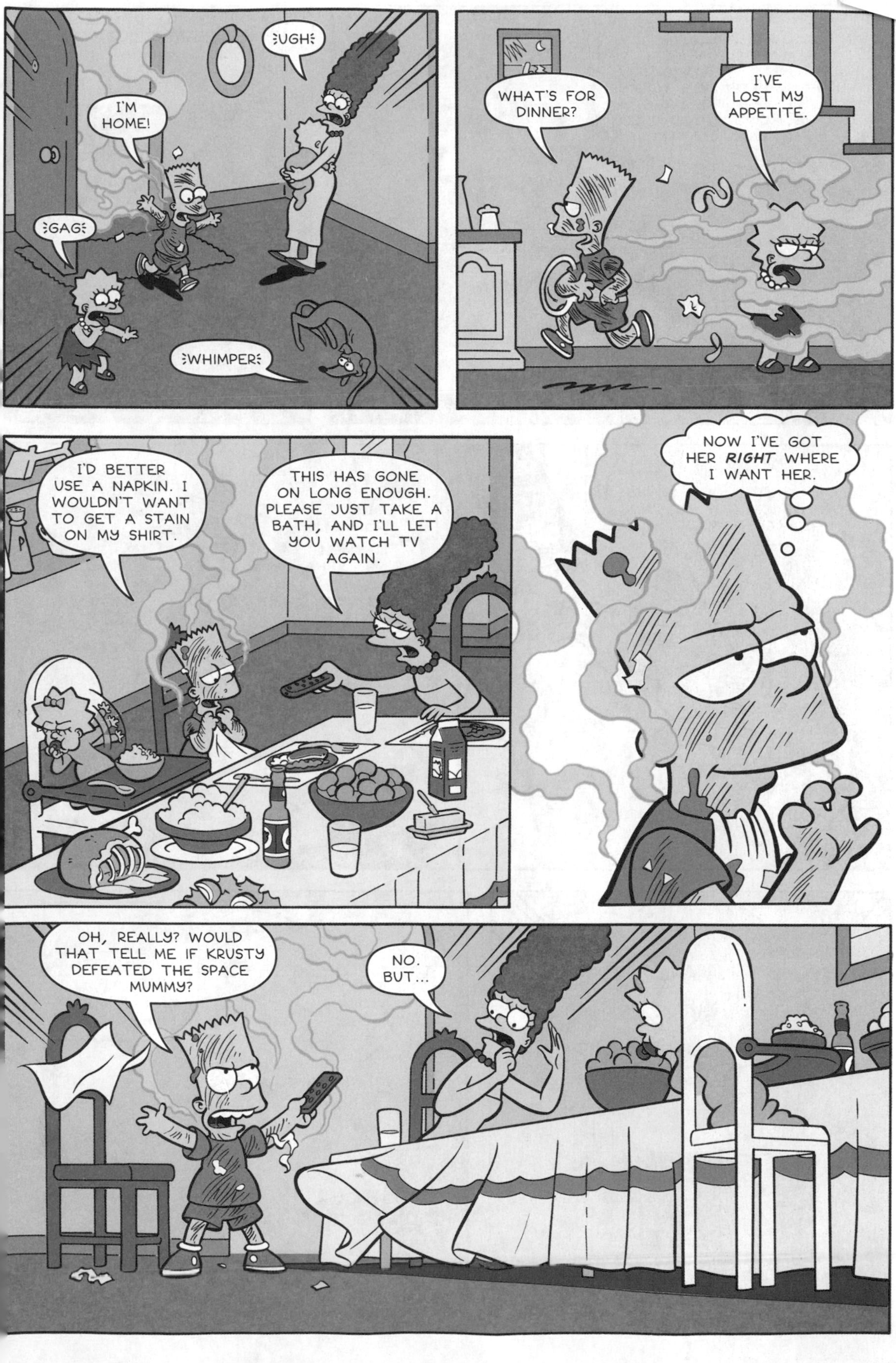

UGH
I'M HOME!
GAG
WHIMPER
WHAT'S FOR DINNER?
I'VE LOST MY APPETITE.
I'D BETTER USE A NAPKIN. I WOULDN'T WANT TO GET A STAIN ON MY SHIRT.
THIS HAS GONE ON LONG ENOUGH. PLEASE JUST TAKE A BATH, AND I'LL LET YOU WATCH TV AGAIN.
NOW I'VE GOT HER *RIGHT* WHERE I WANT HER.
OH, REALLY? WOULD THAT TELL ME IF KRUSTY DEFEATED THE SPACE MUMMY?
NO. BUT...

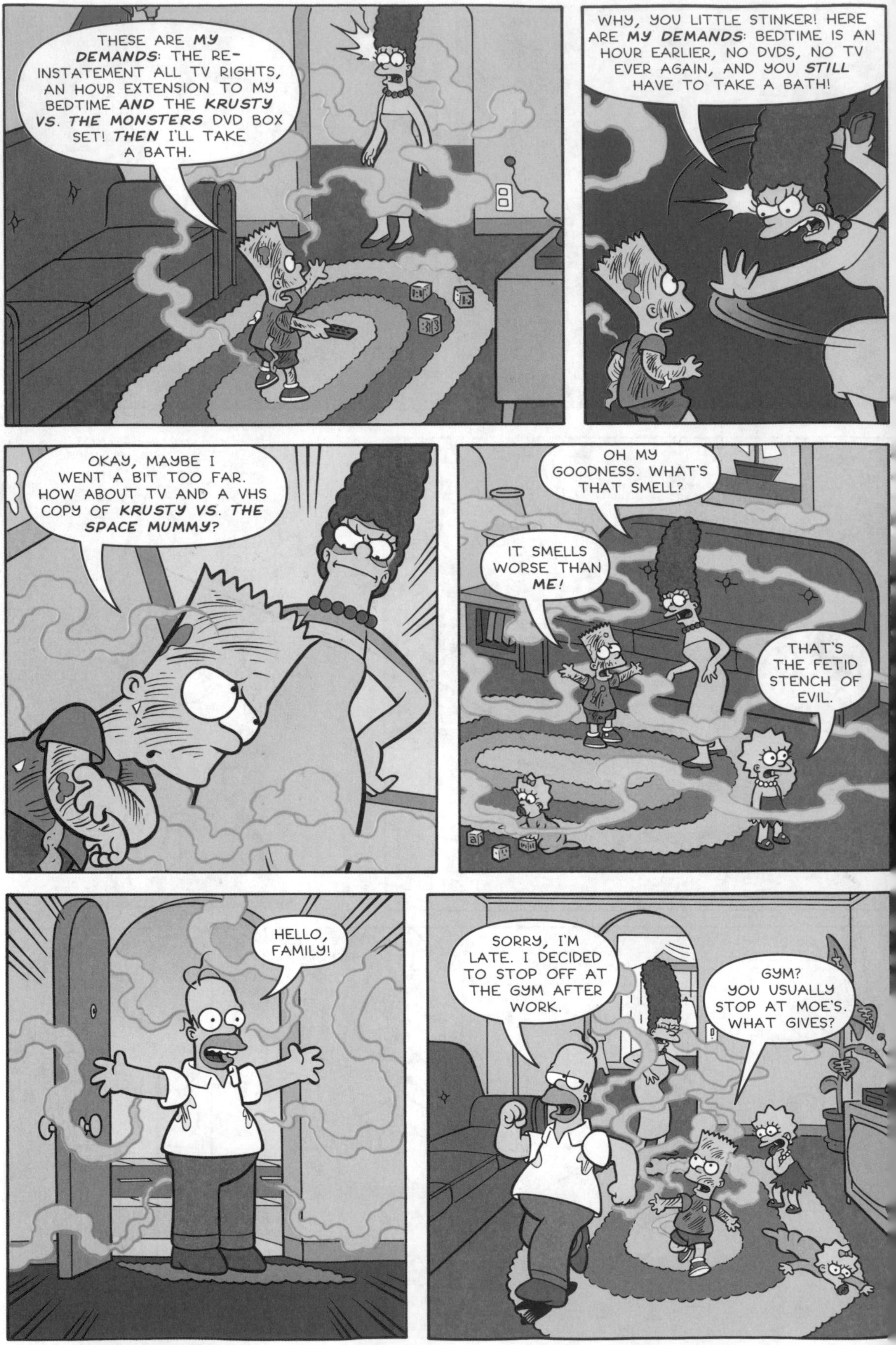
THESE ARE MY DEMANDS: THE RE-INSTATEMENT ALL TV RIGHTS, AN HOUR EXTENSION TO MY BEDTIME AND THE KRUSTY VS. THE MONSTERS DVD BOX SET! THEN I'LL TAKE A BATH.
WHY, YOU LITTLE STINKER! HERE ARE MY DEMANDS: BEDTIME IS AN HOUR EARLIER, NO DVDS, NO TV EVER AGAIN, AND YOU STILL HAVE TO TAKE A BATH!
OKAY, MAYBE I WENT A BIT TOO FAR. HOW ABOUT TV AND A VHS COPY OF KRUSTY VS. THE SPACE MUMMY?
OH MY GOODNESS. WHAT'S THAT SMELL?
IT SMELLS WORSE THAN ME!
THAT'S THE FETID STENCH OF EVIL.
HELLO, FAMILY!
SORRY, I'M LATE. I DECIDED TO STOP OFF AT THE GYM AFTER WORK.
GYM? YOU USUALLY STOP AT MOE'S. WHAT GIVES?

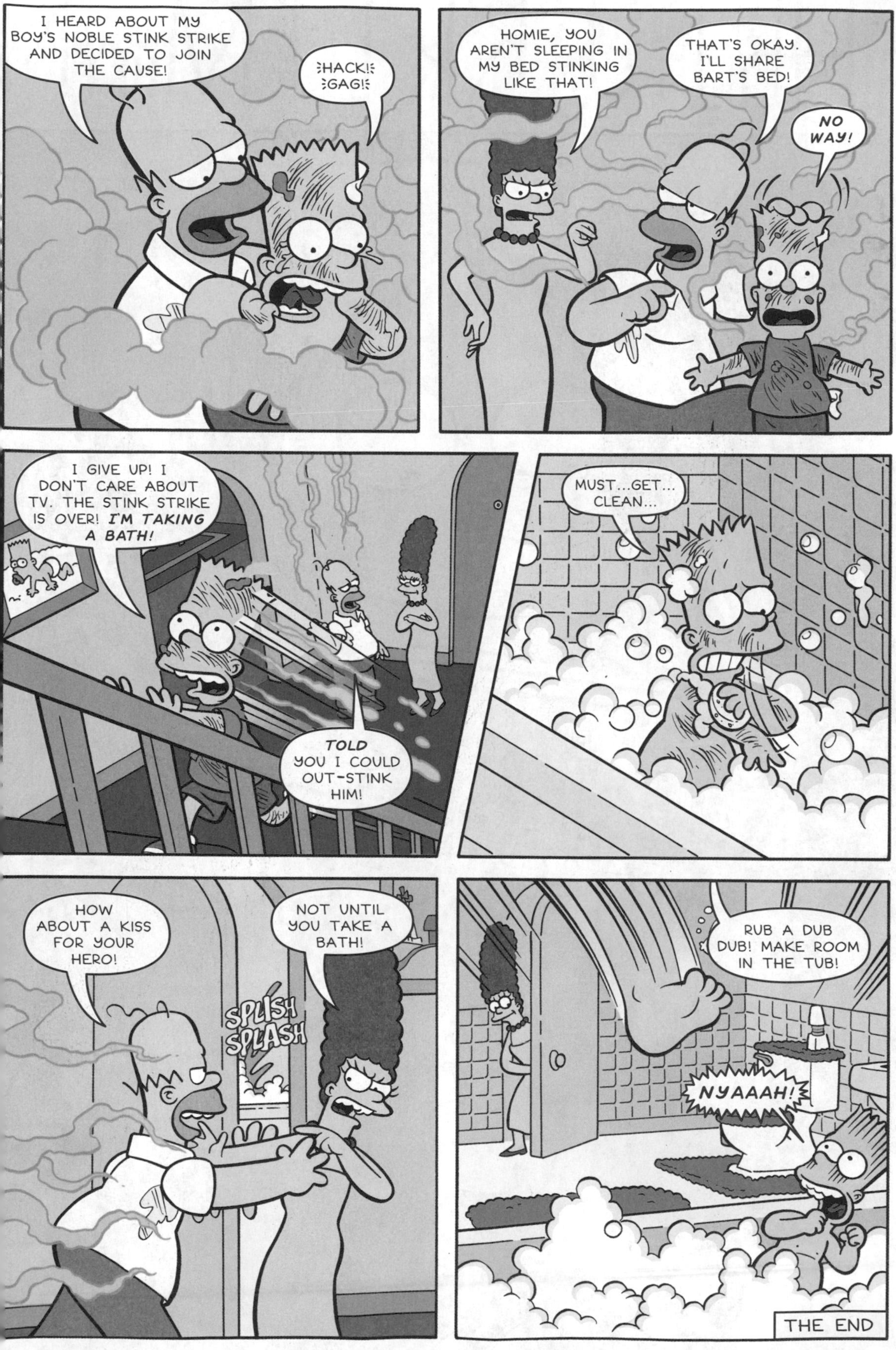
I HEARD ABOUT MY BOY'S NOBLE STINK STRIKE AND DECIDED TO JOIN THE CAUSE!
HACK! GAG!
HOMIE, YOU AREN'T SLEEPING IN MY BED STINKING LIKE THAT!
THAT'S OKAY. I'LL SHARE BART'S BED!
NO WAY!
I GIVE UP! I DON'T CARE ABOUT TV. THE STINK STRIKE IS OVER! I'M TAKING A BATH!
TOLD YOU I COULD OUT-STINK HIM!
MUST...GET... CLEAN...
HOW ABOUT A KISS FOR YOUR HERO!
NOT UNTIL YOU TAKE A BATH!
SPLISH SPLASH
RUB A DUB DUB! MAKE ROOM IN THE TUB!
NYAAAH!
THE END

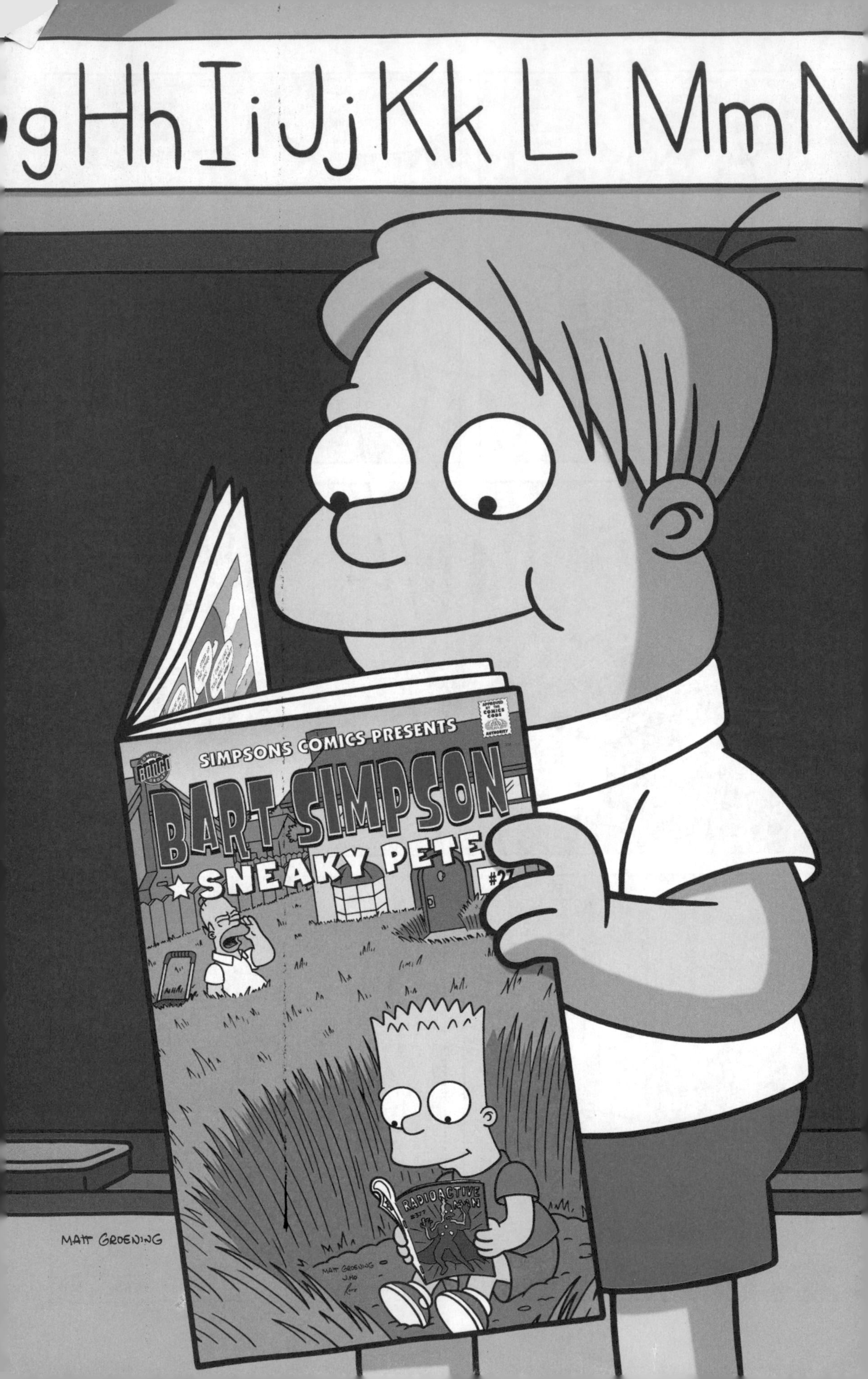
gHhIiJjKkLlMmN
SIMPSONS COMICS PRESENTS
BART SIMPSON
SNEAKY PETE
#27
RADIOACTIVE MAN
MATT GROENING

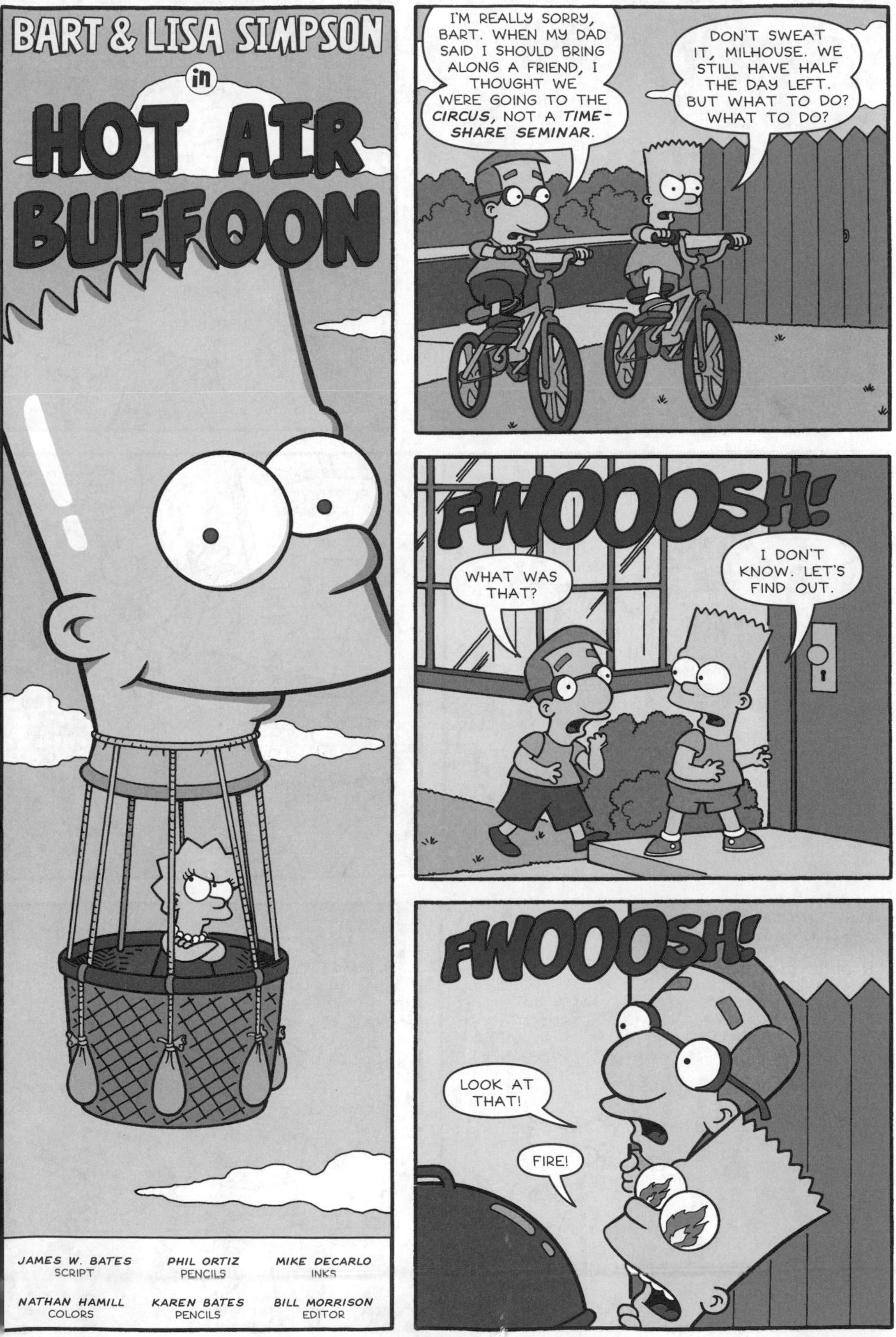
BART & LISA SIMPSON
in
HOT AIR BUFFOON
JAMES W. BATES SCRIPT
PHIL ORTIZ PENCILS
MIKE DECARLO INKS
NATHAN HAMILL COLORS
KAREN BATES PENCILS
BILL MORRISON EDITOR
I'M REALLY SORRY, BART. WHEN MY DAD SAID I SHOULD BRING ALONG A FRIEND, I THOUGHT WE WERE GOING TO THE CIRCUS, NOT A TIME-SHARE SEMINAR.
DON'T SWEAT IT, MILHOUSE. WE STILL HAVE HALF THE DAY LEFT. BUT WHAT TO DO? WHAT TO DO?
FWOOOSH!
WHAT WAS THAT?
I DON'T KNOW. LET'S FIND OUT.
FWOOOSH!
LOOK AT THAT!
FIRE!

FWOOOSH!

WHOA, MAMA!

COOL!

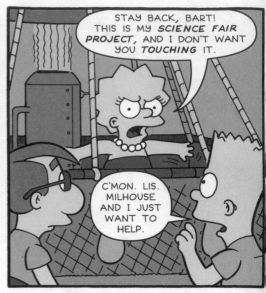

STAY BACK, BART! THIS IS MY *SCIENCE FAIR PROJECT*, AND I DON'T WANT YOU *TOUCHING* IT.

C'MON. LIS. MILHOUSE AND I JUST WANT TO HELP.

HEY! LET'S GO FOR A RIDE.

ABSOLUTELY NOT! I'M JUST TESTING THE FLAME APPARATUS AND THE BALLOON FABRIC TO MAKE SURE IT WILL FLY AT THE SCIENCE FAIR.

FLY? I'LL HELP YOU MAKE IT FLY ALL RIGHT.

ME, TOO!

WAIT, WAIT. YOU DON'T UNDERSTAND.

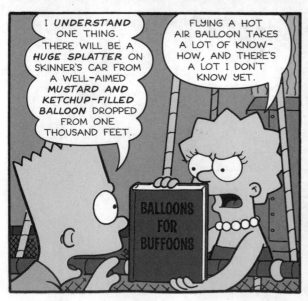

I *UNDERSTAND* ONE THING. THERE WILL BE A *HUGE SPLATTER* ON SKINNER'S CAR FROM A WELL-AIMED *MUSTARD AND KETCHUP-FILLED BALLOON* DROPPED FROM ONE THOUSAND FEET.

FLYING A HOT AIR BALLOON TAKES A LOT OF KNOW-HOW, AND THERE'S A LOT I DON'T KNOW YET.

BALLOONS FOR BUFFOONS

SORRY, BOYS. THERE WILL BE NO FLYING TODAY.

≥UMPH!≤

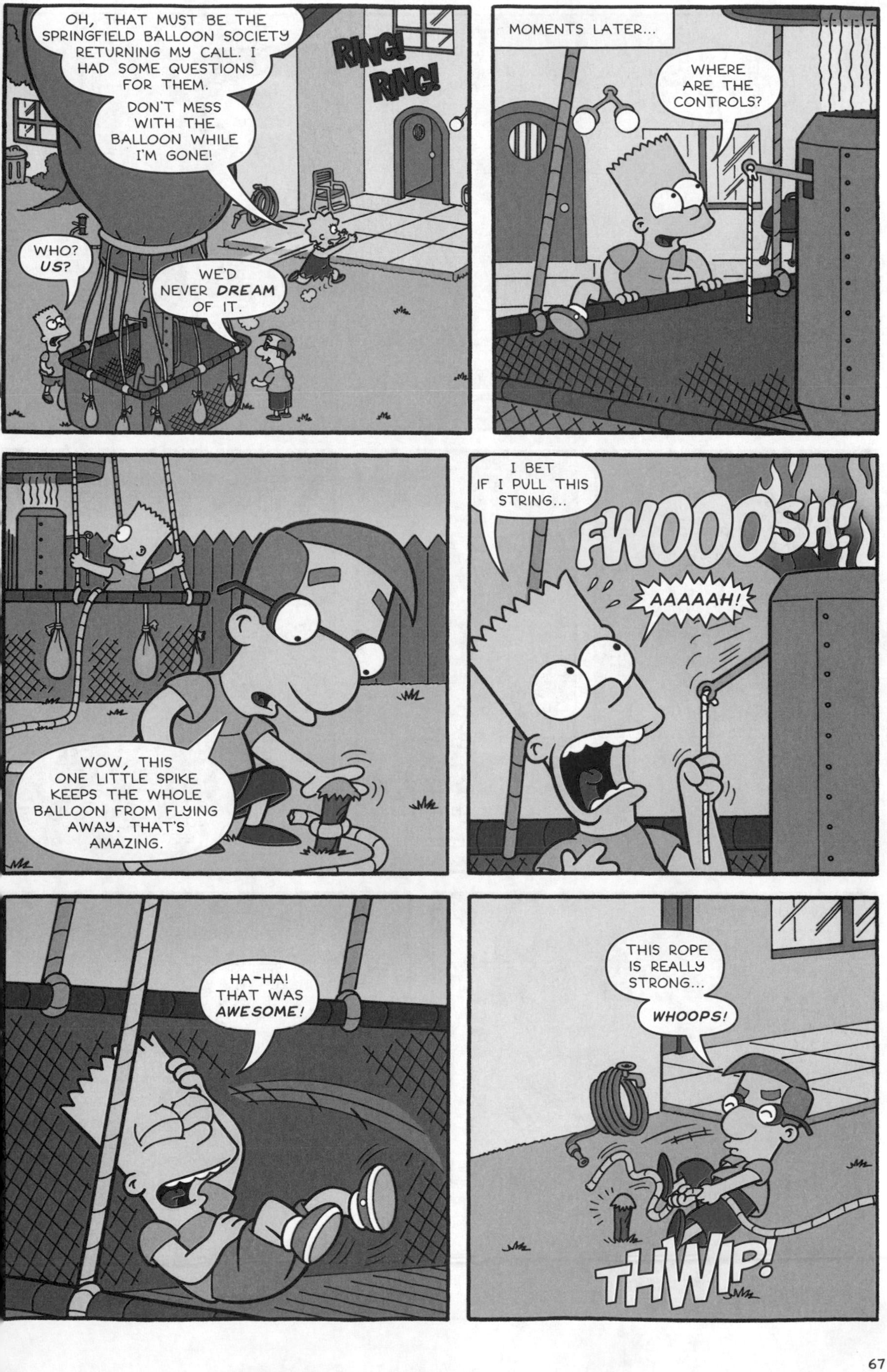

OH, THAT MUST BE THE SPRINGFIELD BALLOON SOCIETY RETURNING MY CALL. I HAD SOME QUESTIONS FOR THEM.
DON'T MESS WITH THE BALLOON WHILE I'M GONE!
RING! RING!
WHO? US?
WE'D NEVER DREAM OF IT.
MOMENTS LATER...
WHERE ARE THE CONTROLS?
WOW, THIS ONE LITTLE SPIKE KEEPS THE WHOLE BALLOON FROM FLYING AWAY. THAT'S AMAZING.
I BET IF I PULL THIS STRING...
FWOOOSH!
AAAAAH!
HA-HA! THAT WAS AWESOME!
THIS ROPE IS REALLY STRONG...
WHOOPS!
THWIP!

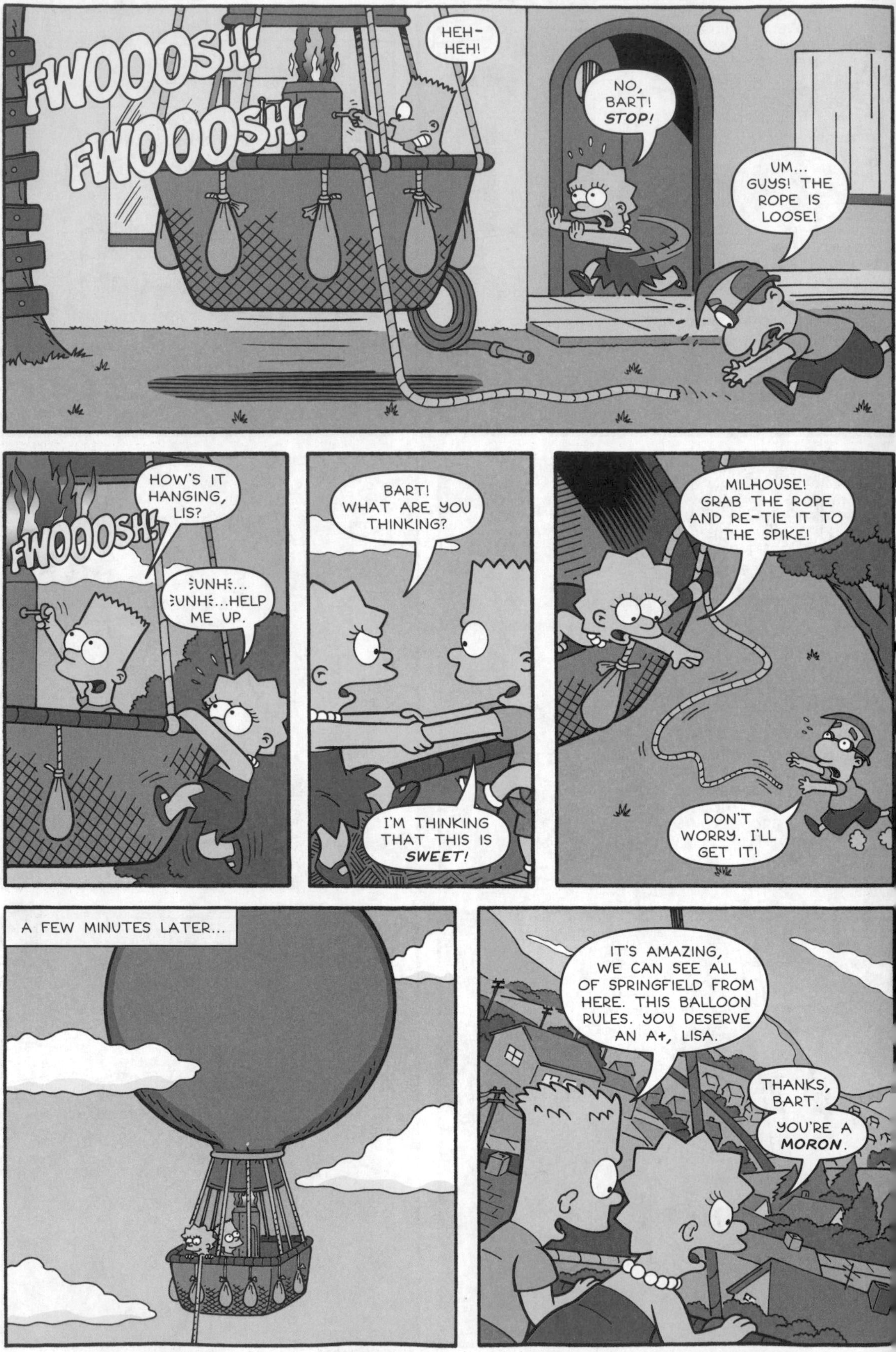
FWOOOSH!
FWOOOSH!
HEH-HEH!
NO, BART! STOP!
UM... GUYS! THE ROPE IS LOOSE!
FWOOOSH!
HOW'S IT HANGING, LIS?
UNH... UNH...HELP ME UP.
BART! WHAT ARE YOU THINKING?
I'M THINKING THAT THIS IS SWEET!
MILHOUSE! GRAB THE ROPE AND RE-TIE IT TO THE SPIKE!
DON'T WORRY. I'LL GET IT!
A FEW MINUTES LATER...
IT'S AMAZING, WE CAN SEE ALL OF SPRINGFIELD FROM HERE. THIS BALLOON RULES. YOU DESERVE AN A+, LISA.
THANKS, BART.
YOU'RE A MORON.

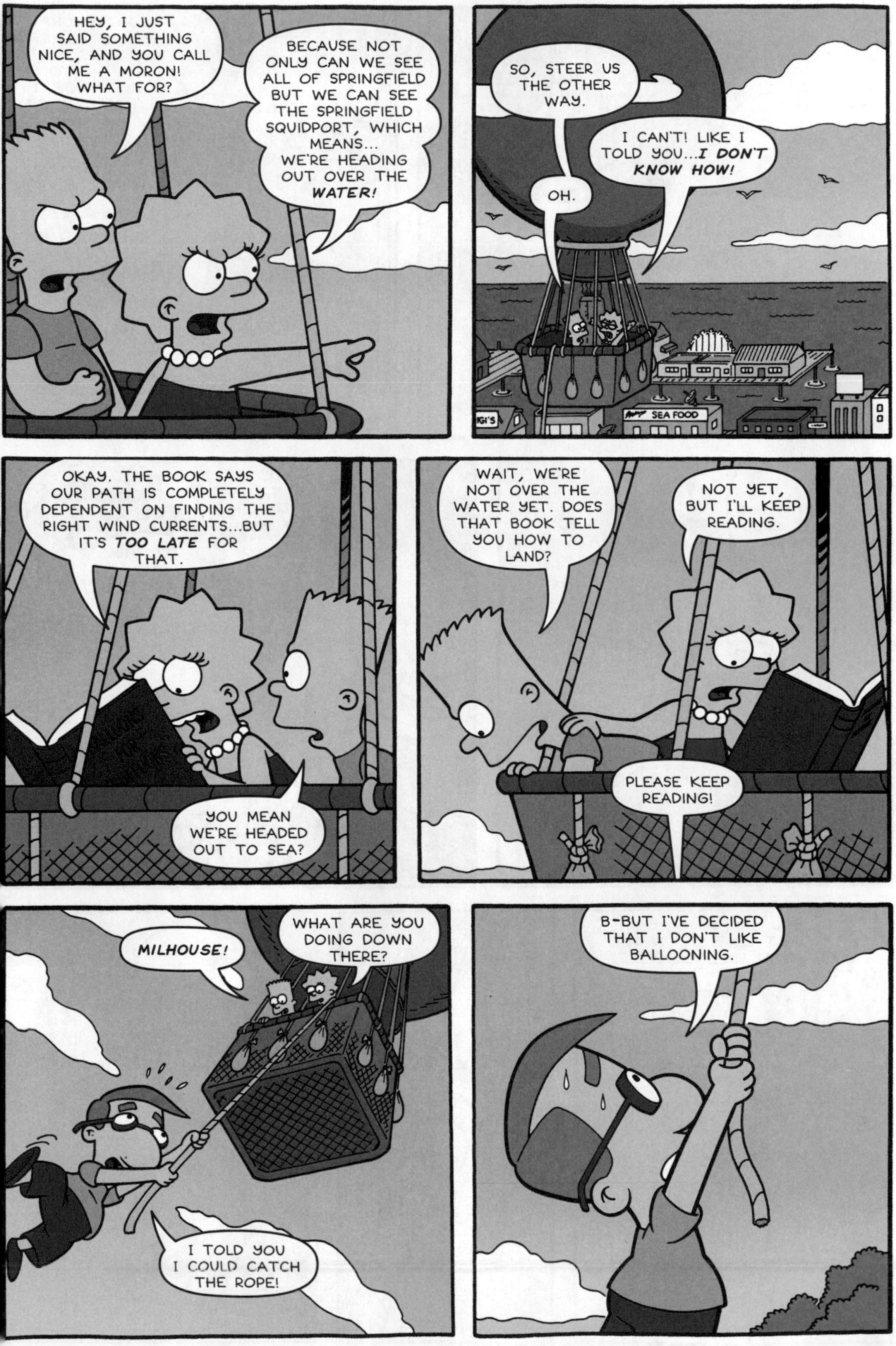
HEY, I JUST SAID SOMETHING NICE, AND YOU CALL ME A MORON! WHAT FOR?
BECAUSE NOT ONLY CAN WE SEE ALL OF SPRINGFIELD BUT WE CAN SEE THE SPRINGFIELD SQUIDPORT, WHICH MEANS... WE'RE HEADING OUT OVER THE WATER!
SO, STEER US THE OTHER WAY.
I CAN'T! LIKE I TOLD YOU...I DON'T KNOW HOW!
OH.
SEA FOOD
OKAY. THE BOOK SAYS OUR PATH IS COMPLETELY DEPENDENT ON FINDING THE RIGHT WIND CURRENTS...BUT IT'S TOO LATE FOR THAT.
YOU MEAN WE'RE HEADED OUT TO SEA?
WAIT, WE'RE NOT OVER THE WATER YET. DOES THAT BOOK TELL YOU HOW TO LAND?
NOT YET, BUT I'LL KEEP READING.
PLEASE KEEP READING!
MILHOUSE!
WHAT ARE YOU DOING DOWN THERE?
I TOLD YOU I COULD CATCH THE ROPE!
B-BUT I'VE DECIDED THAT I DON'T LIKE BALLOONING.

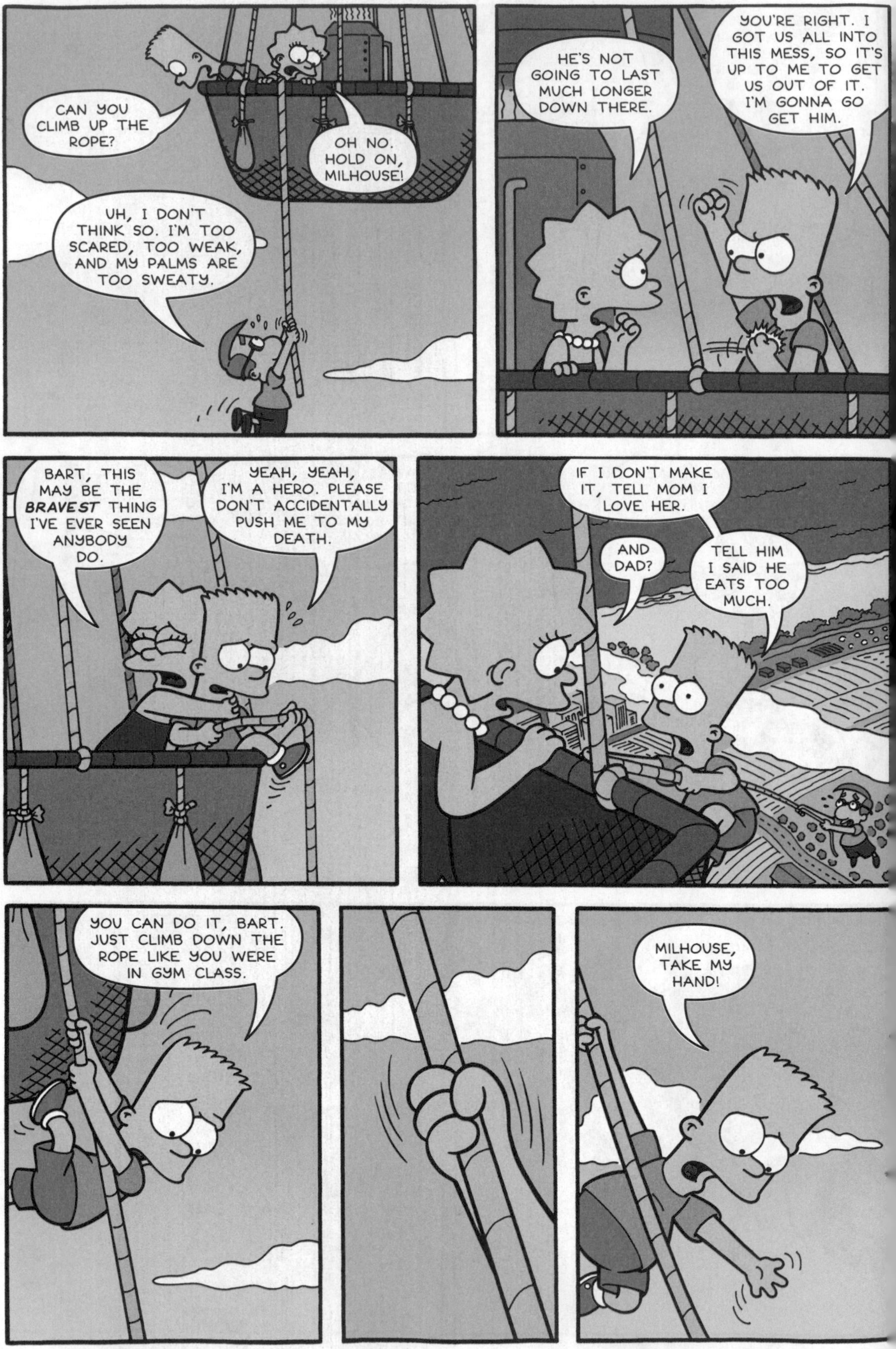

CAN YOU CLIMB UP THE ROPE?
OH NO. HOLD ON, MILHOUSE!
UH, I DON'T THINK SO. I'M TOO SCARED, TOO WEAK, AND MY PALMS ARE TOO SWEATY.
HE'S NOT GOING TO LAST MUCH LONGER DOWN THERE.
YOU'RE RIGHT. I GOT US ALL INTO THIS MESS, SO IT'S UP TO ME TO GET US OUT OF IT. I'M GONNA GO GET HIM.
BART, THIS MAY BE THE ***BRAVEST*** THING I'VE EVER SEEN ANYBODY DO.
YEAH, YEAH, I'M A HERO. PLEASE DON'T ACCIDENTALLY PUSH ME TO MY DEATH.
IF I DON'T MAKE IT, TELL MOM I LOVE HER.
AND DAD?
TELL HIM I SAID HE EATS TOO MUCH.
YOU CAN DO IT, BART. JUST CLIMB DOWN THE ROPE LIKE YOU WERE IN GYM CLASS.
MILHOUSE, TAKE MY HAND!

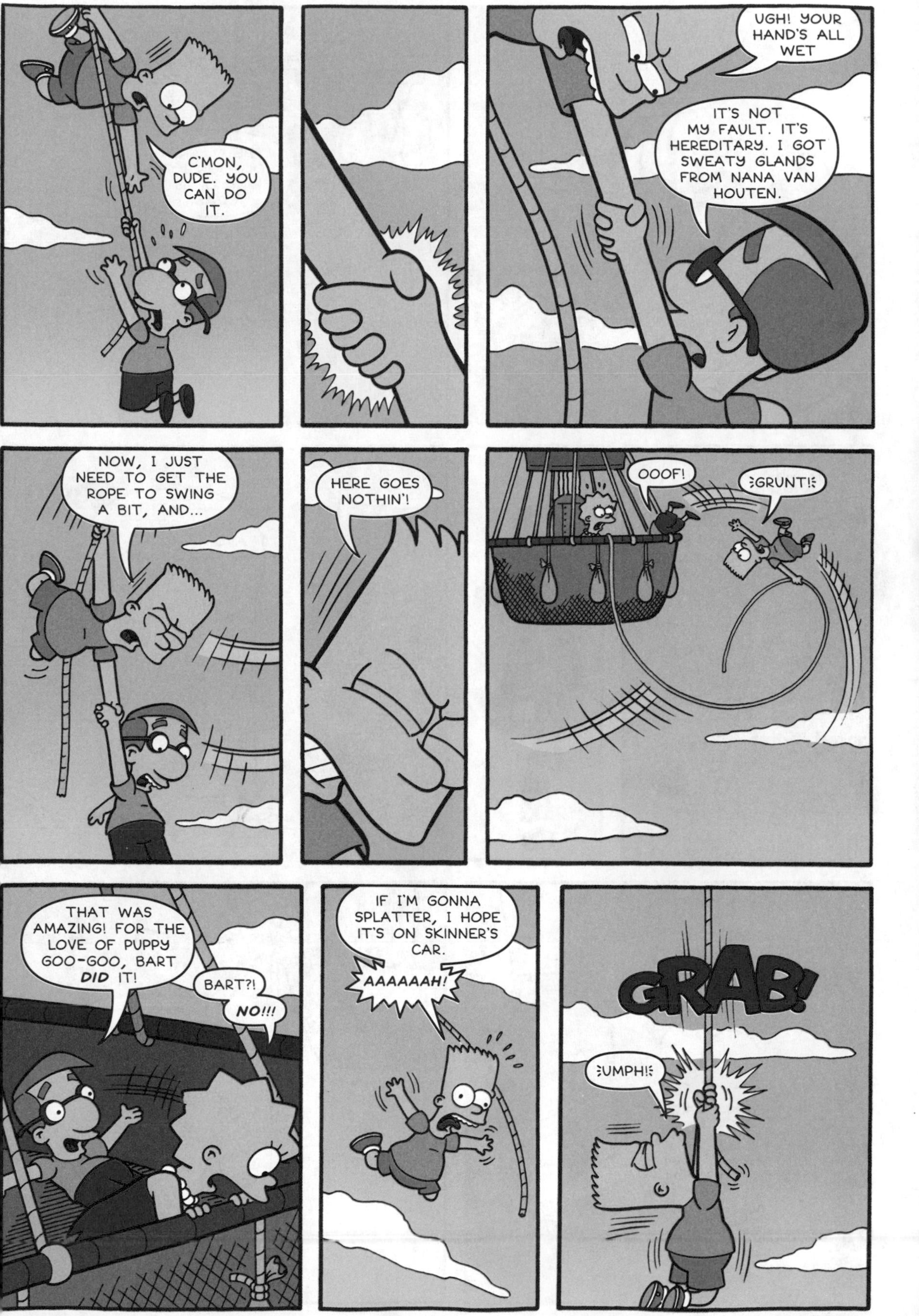
C'MON, DUDE. YOU CAN DO IT.
UGH! YOUR HAND'S ALL WET
IT'S NOT MY FAULT. IT'S HEREDITARY. I GOT SWEATY GLANDS FROM NANA VAN HOUTEN.
NOW, I JUST NEED TO GET THE ROPE TO SWING A BIT, AND...
HERE GOES NOTHIN'!
OOOF!
GRUNT!
THAT WAS AMAZING! FOR THE LOVE OF PUPPY GOO-GOO, BART DID IT!
BART?!
NO!!!
IF I'M GONNA SPLATTER, I HOPE IT'S ON SKINNER'S CAR.
AAAAAAH!
GRAB!
UMPH!

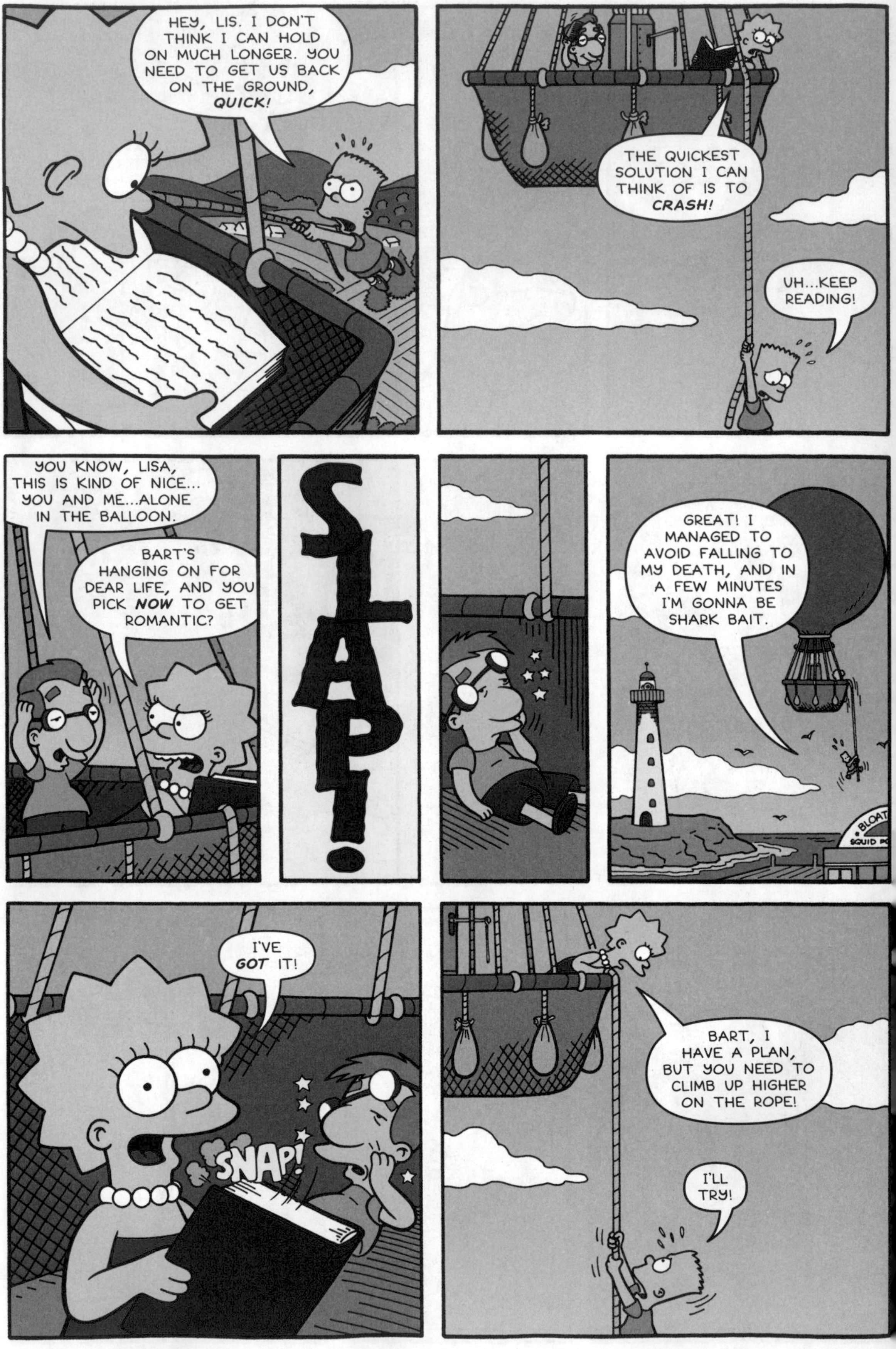
HEY, LIS. I DON'T THINK I CAN HOLD ON MUCH LONGER. YOU NEED TO GET US BACK ON THE GROUND, QUICK!
THE QUICKEST SOLUTION I CAN THINK OF IS TO CRASH!
UH...KEEP READING!
YOU KNOW, LISA, THIS IS KIND OF NICE... YOU AND ME...ALONE IN THE BALLOON.
BART'S HANGING ON FOR DEAR LIFE, AND YOU PICK NOW TO GET ROMANTIC?
SLAP!
GREAT! I MANAGED TO AVOID FALLING TO MY DEATH, AND IN A FEW MINUTES I'M GONNA BE SHARK BAIT.
I'VE GOT IT!
SNAP!
BART, I HAVE A PLAN, BUT YOU NEED TO CLIMB UP HIGHER ON THE ROPE!
I'LL TRY!

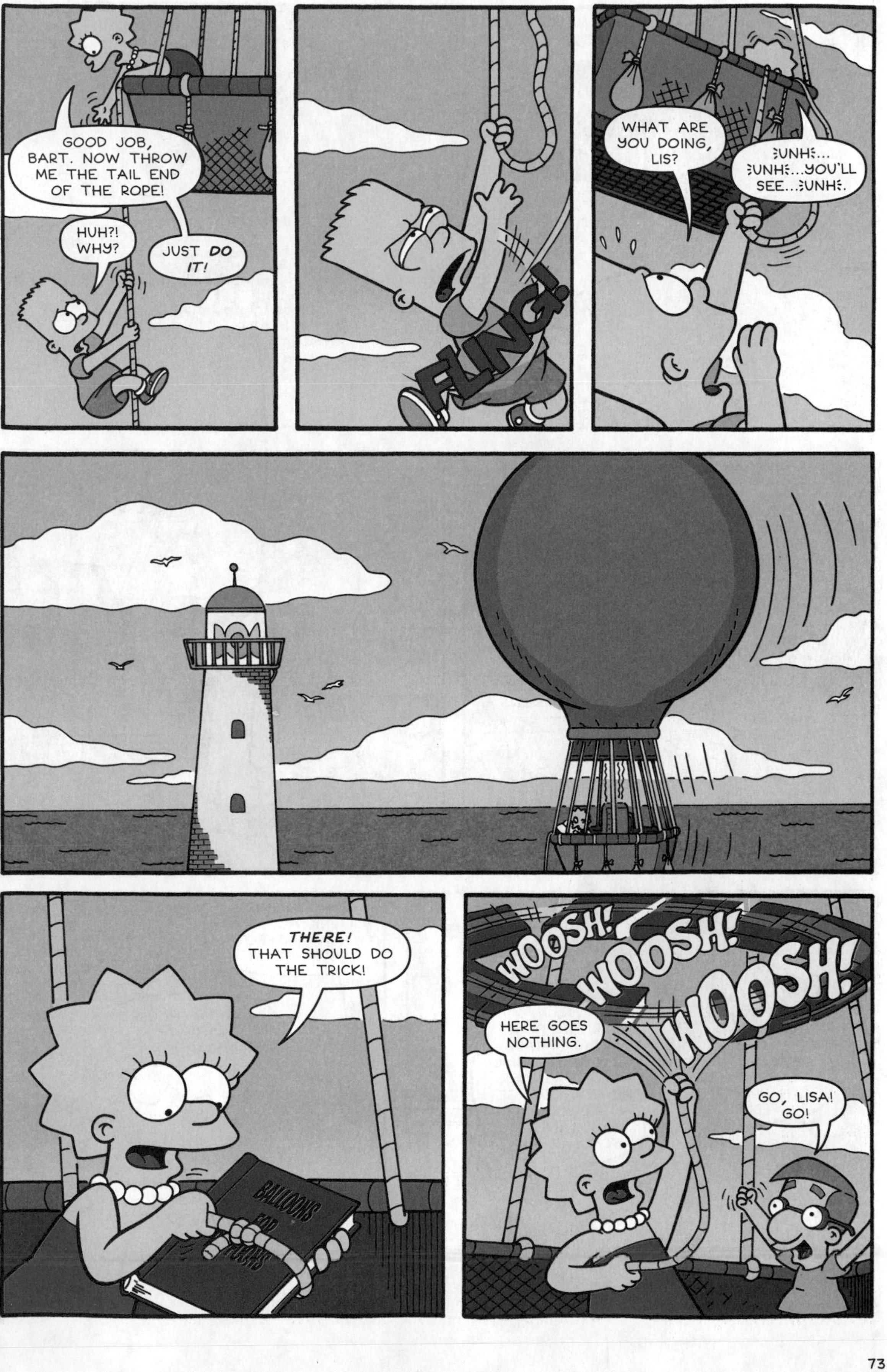

GOOD JOB, BART. NOW THROW ME THE TAIL END OF THE ROPE!
HUH?! WHY?
JUST DO IT!
FLING!
WHAT ARE YOU DOING, LIS?
UNH... UNH...YOU'LL SEE...UNH.
THERE! THAT SHOULD DO THE TRICK!
BALLOONS FOR FLIGHT
WOOSH! WOOSH! WOOSH!
HERE GOES NOTHING.
GO, LISA! GO!

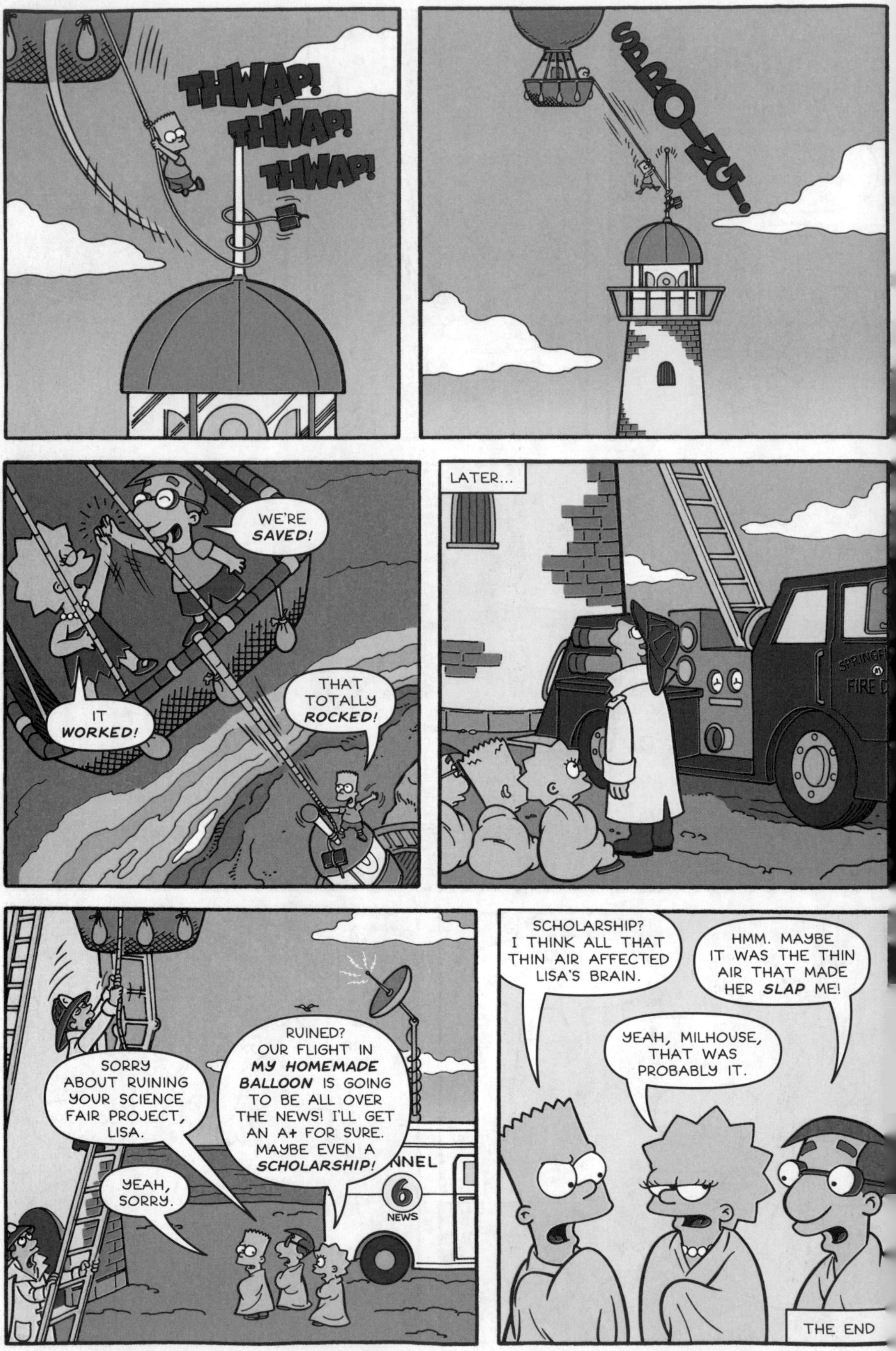
THWAP! THWAP! THWAP!
SPROING!
WE'RE *SAVED!*
IT *WORKED!*
THAT TOTALLY *ROCKED!*
LATER...
SORRY ABOUT RUINING YOUR SCIENCE FAIR PROJECT, LISA.
YEAH, SORRY.
RUINED? OUR FLIGHT IN ***MY HOMEMADE BALLOON*** IS GOING TO BE ALL OVER THE NEWS! I'LL GET AN A+ FOR SURE. MAYBE EVEN A ***SCHOLARSHIP!***
SCHOLARSHIP? I THINK ALL THAT THIN AIR AFFECTED LISA'S BRAIN.
HMM. MAYBE IT WAS THE THIN AIR THAT MADE HER ***SLAP*** ME!
YEAH, MILHOUSE, THAT WAS PROBABLY IT.
THE END

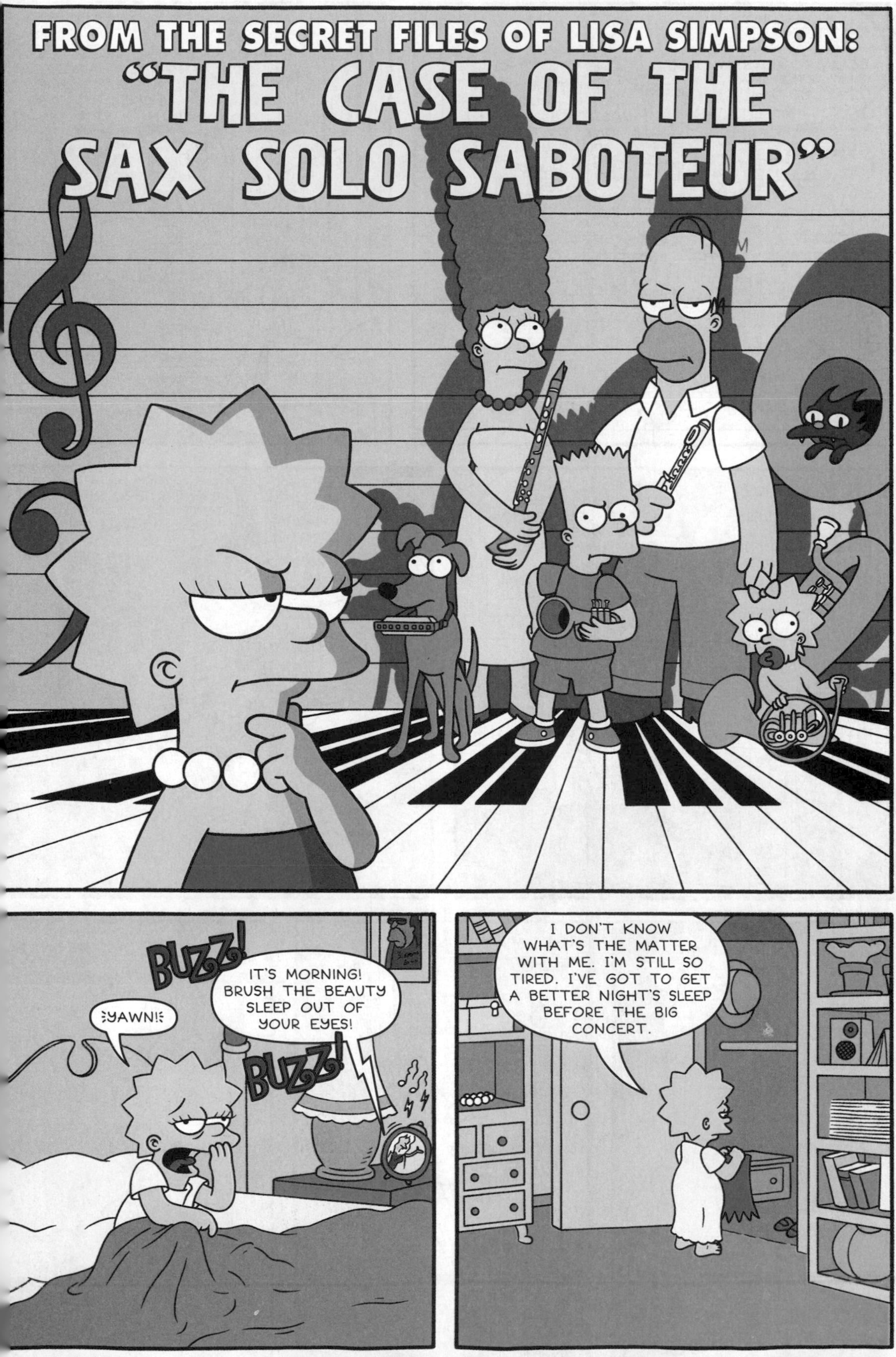
FROM THE SECRET FILES OF LISA SIMPSON:
"THE CASE OF THE SAX SOLO SABOTEUR"
BUZZ!
IT'S MORNING! BRUSH THE BEAUTY SLEEP OUT OF YOUR EYES!
YAWN!
BUZZ!
I DON'T KNOW WHAT'S THE MATTER WITH ME. I'M STILL SO TIRED. I'VE GOT TO GET A BETTER NIGHT'S SLEEP BEFORE THE BIG CONCERT.

JAMES W. BATES SCRIPT · MIKE WORLEY PENCILS · MIKE ROTE INKS · ART VILLANUEVA COLORS · KAREN BATES LETTERS · BILL MORRISON EDITOR

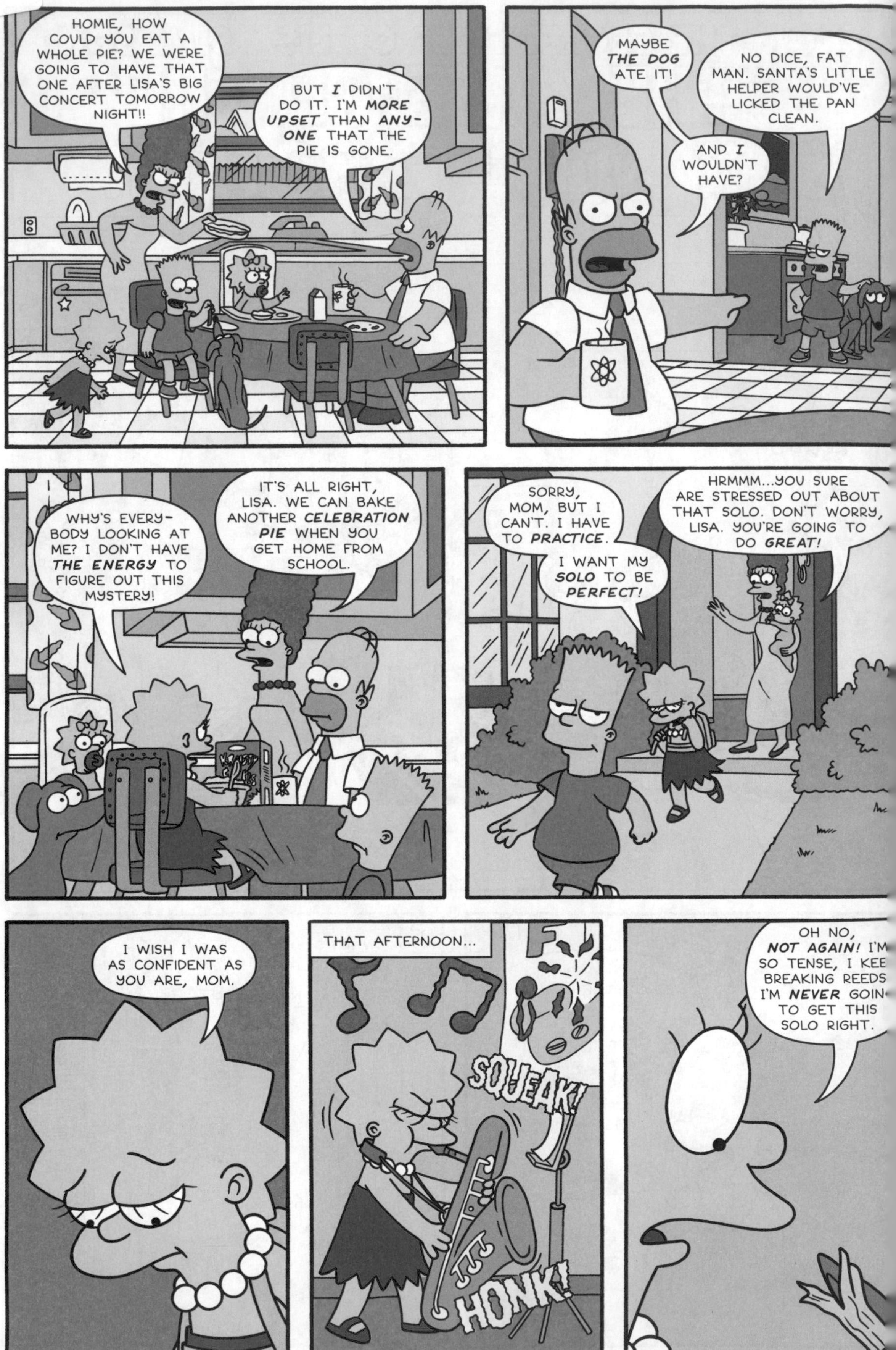
HOMIE, HOW COULD YOU EAT A WHOLE PIE? WE WERE GOING TO HAVE THAT ONE AFTER LISA'S BIG CONCERT TOMORROW NIGHT!!
BUT I DIDN'T DO IT. I'M MORE UPSET THAN ANYONE THAT THE PIE IS GONE.
MAYBE THE DOG ATE IT!
NO DICE, FAT MAN. SANTA'S LITTLE HELPER WOULD'VE LICKED THE PAN CLEAN.
AND I WOULDN'T HAVE?
WHY'S EVERYBODY LOOKING AT ME? I DON'T HAVE THE ENERGY TO FIGURE OUT THIS MYSTERY!
IT'S ALL RIGHT, LISA. WE CAN BAKE ANOTHER CELEBRATION PIE WHEN YOU GET HOME FROM SCHOOL.
SORRY, MOM, BUT I CAN'T. I HAVE TO PRACTICE.
I WANT MY SOLO TO BE PERFECT!
HRMMM...YOU SURE ARE STRESSED OUT ABOUT THAT SOLO. DON'T WORRY, LISA. YOU'RE GOING TO DO GREAT!
I WISH I WAS AS CONFIDENT AS YOU ARE, MOM.
THAT AFTERNOON...
SQUEAK!
HONK!
OH NO, NOT AGAIN! I'M SO TENSE, I KEE BREAKING REEDS I'M NEVER GOIN TO GET THIS SOLO RIGHT.

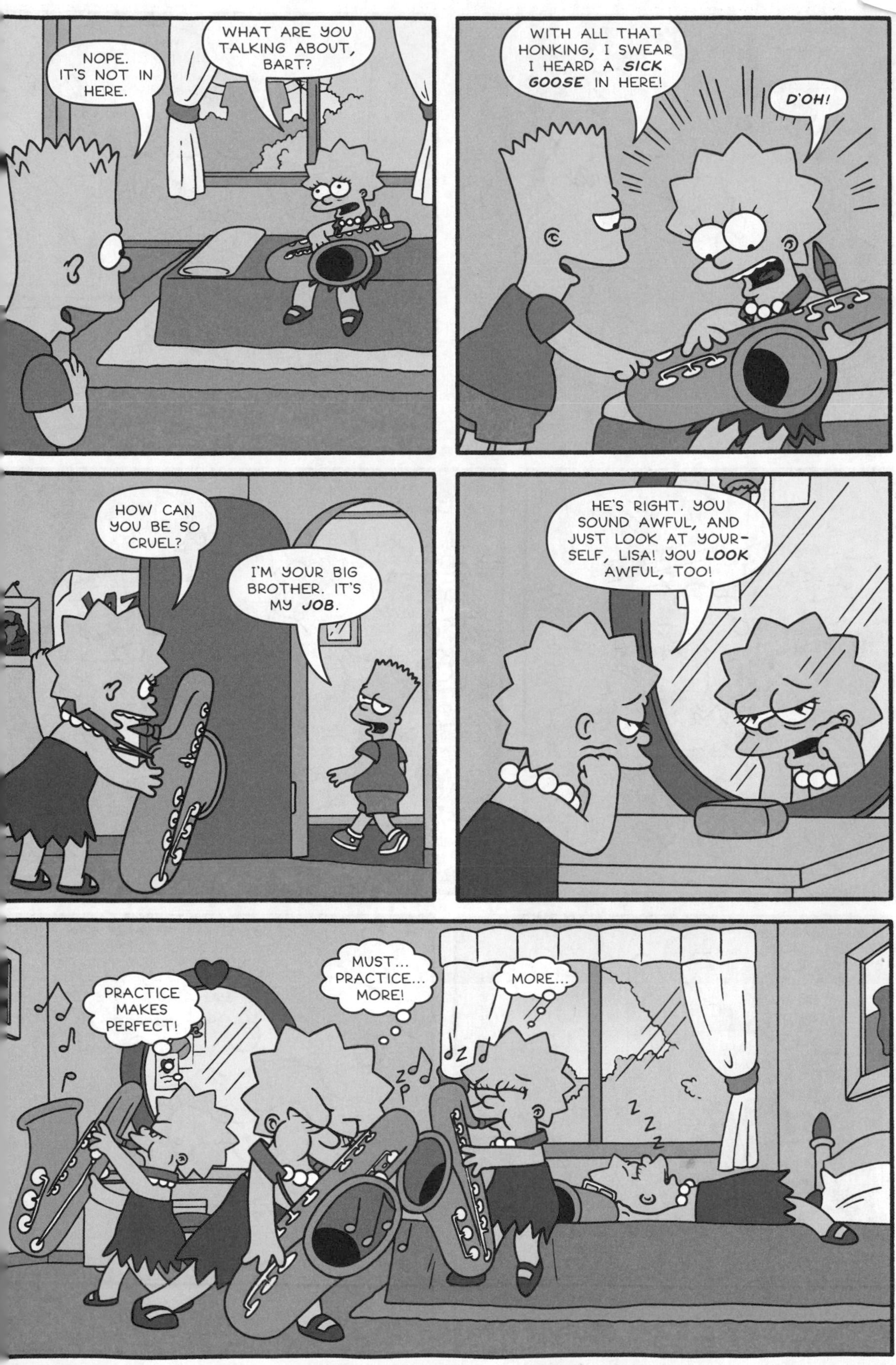
NOPE. IT'S NOT IN HERE.
WHAT ARE YOU TALKING ABOUT, BART?
WITH ALL THAT HONKING, I SWEAR I HEARD A SICK GOOSE IN HERE!
D'OH!
HOW CAN YOU BE SO CRUEL?
I'M YOUR BIG BROTHER. IT'S MY JOB.
HE'S RIGHT. YOU SOUND AWFUL, AND JUST LOOK AT YOURSELF, LISA! YOU LOOK AWFUL, TOO!
PRACTICE MAKES PERFECT!
MUST... PRACTICE... MORE!
MORE...
Z Z Z

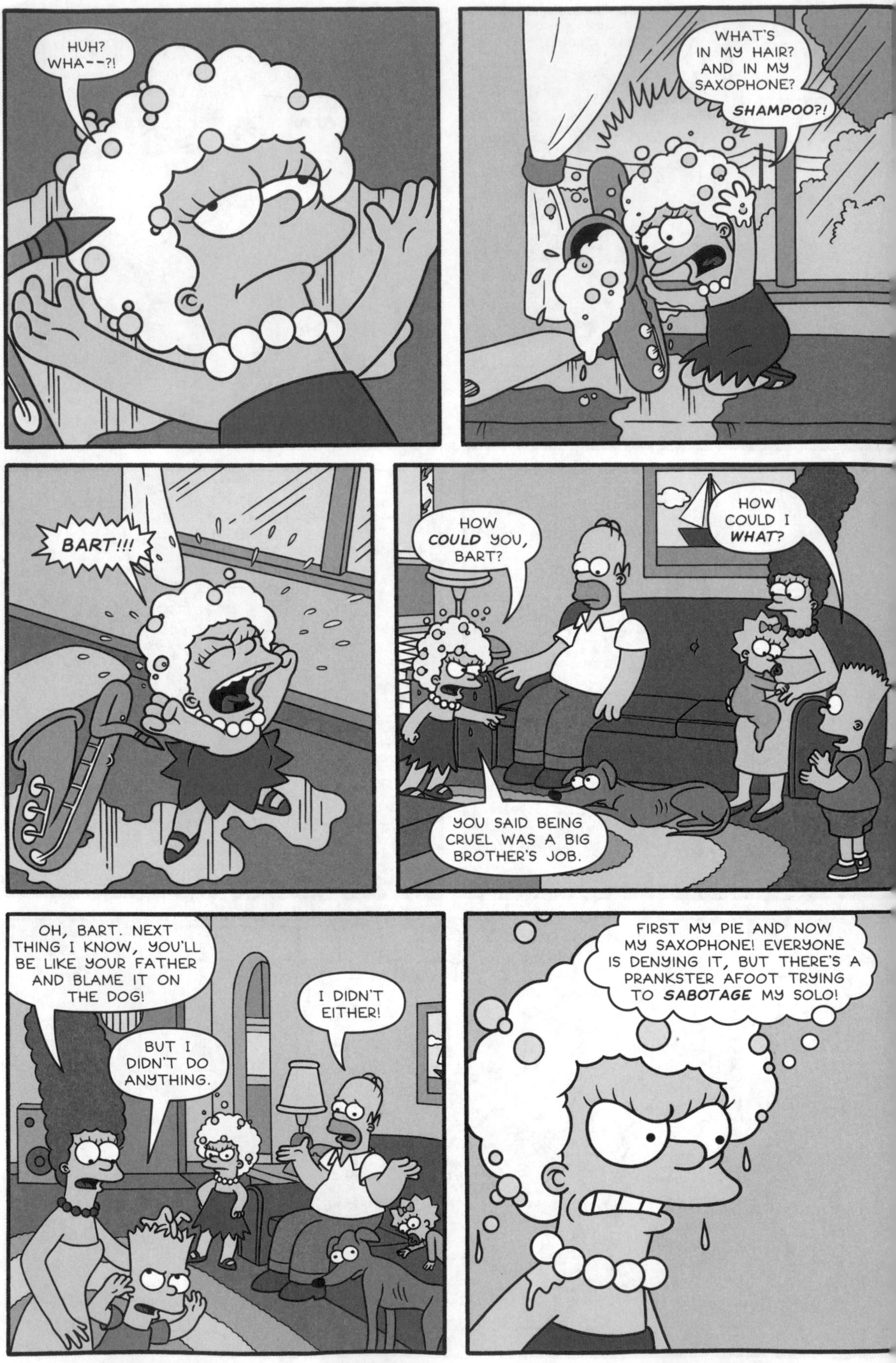
HUH? WHA--?!
WHAT'S IN MY HAIR? AND IN MY SAXOPHONE? SHAMPOO?!
BART!!!
HOW COULD YOU, BART?
HOW COULD I WHAT?
YOU SAID BEING CRUEL WAS A BIG BROTHER'S JOB.
OH, BART. NEXT THING I KNOW, YOU'LL BE LIKE YOUR FATHER AND BLAME IT ON THE DOG!
BUT I DIDN'T DO ANYTHING.
I DIDN'T EITHER!
FIRST MY PIE AND NOW MY SAXOPHONE! EVERYONE IS DENYING IT, BUT THERE'S A PRANKSTER AFOOT TRYING TO SABOTAGE MY SOLO!

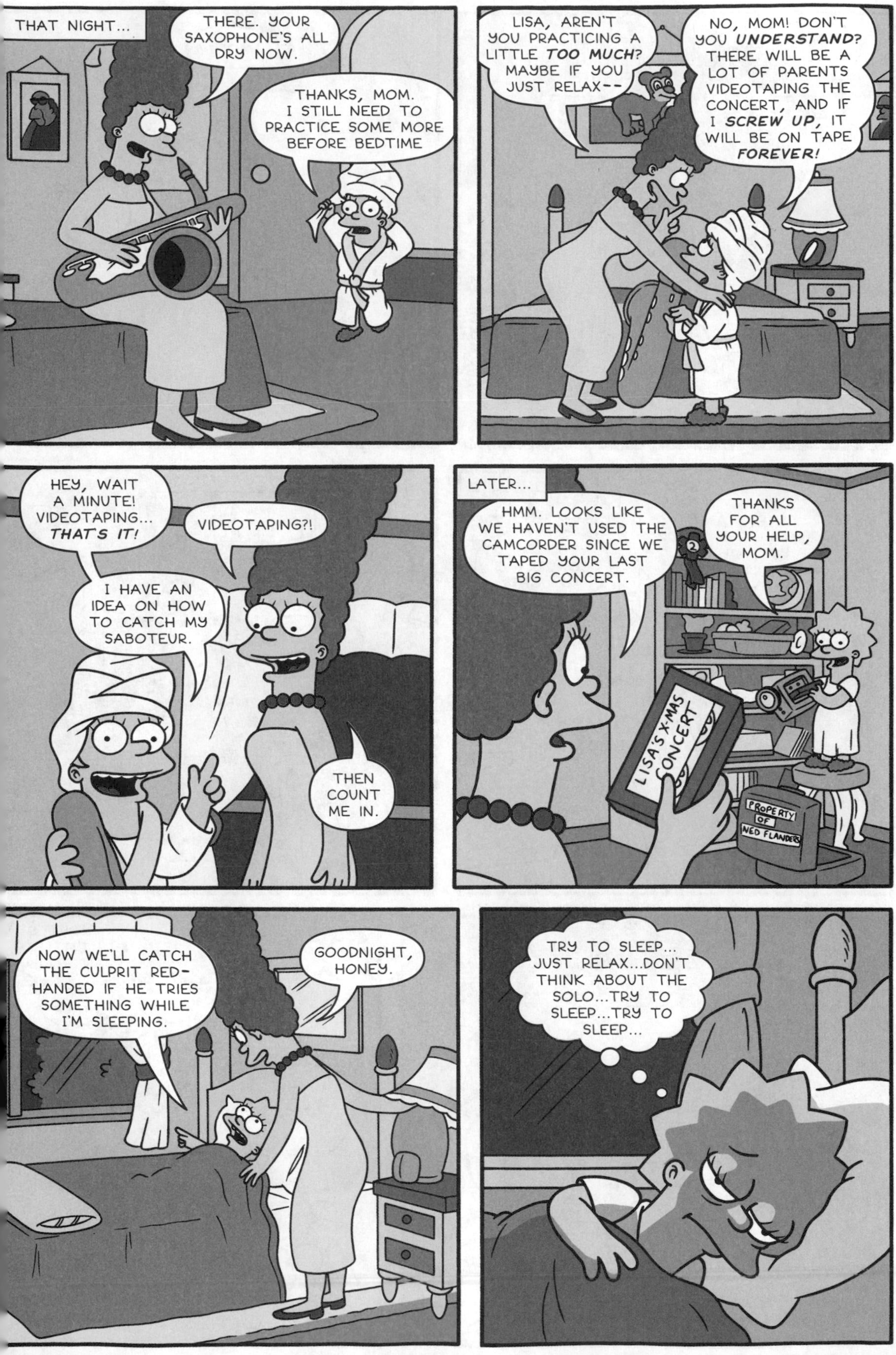
THAT NIGHT...
THERE. YOUR SAXOPHONE'S ALL DRY NOW.
THANKS, MOM. I STILL NEED TO PRACTICE SOME MORE BEFORE BEDTIME
LISA, AREN'T YOU PRACTICING A LITTLE TOO MUCH? MAYBE IF YOU JUST RELAX--
NO, MOM! DON'T YOU UNDERSTAND? THERE WILL BE A LOT OF PARENTS VIDEOTAPING THE CONCERT, AND IF I SCREW UP, IT WILL BE ON TAPE FOREVER!
HEY, WAIT A MINUTE! VIDEOTAPING... THAT'S IT!
VIDEOTAPING?!
I HAVE AN IDEA ON HOW TO CATCH MY SABOTEUR.
THEN COUNT ME IN.
LATER...
HMM. LOOKS LIKE WE HAVEN'T USED THE CAMCORDER SINCE WE TAPED YOUR LAST BIG CONCERT.
THANKS FOR ALL YOUR HELP, MOM.
LISA'S X-MAS CONCERT
PROPERTY OF NED FLANDERS
NOW WE'LL CATCH THE CULPRIT RED-HANDED IF HE TRIES SOMETHING WHILE I'M SLEEPING.
GOODNIGHT, HONEY.
TRY TO SLEEP... JUST RELAX...DON'T THINK ABOUT THE SOLO...TRY TO SLEEP...TRY TO SLEEP...

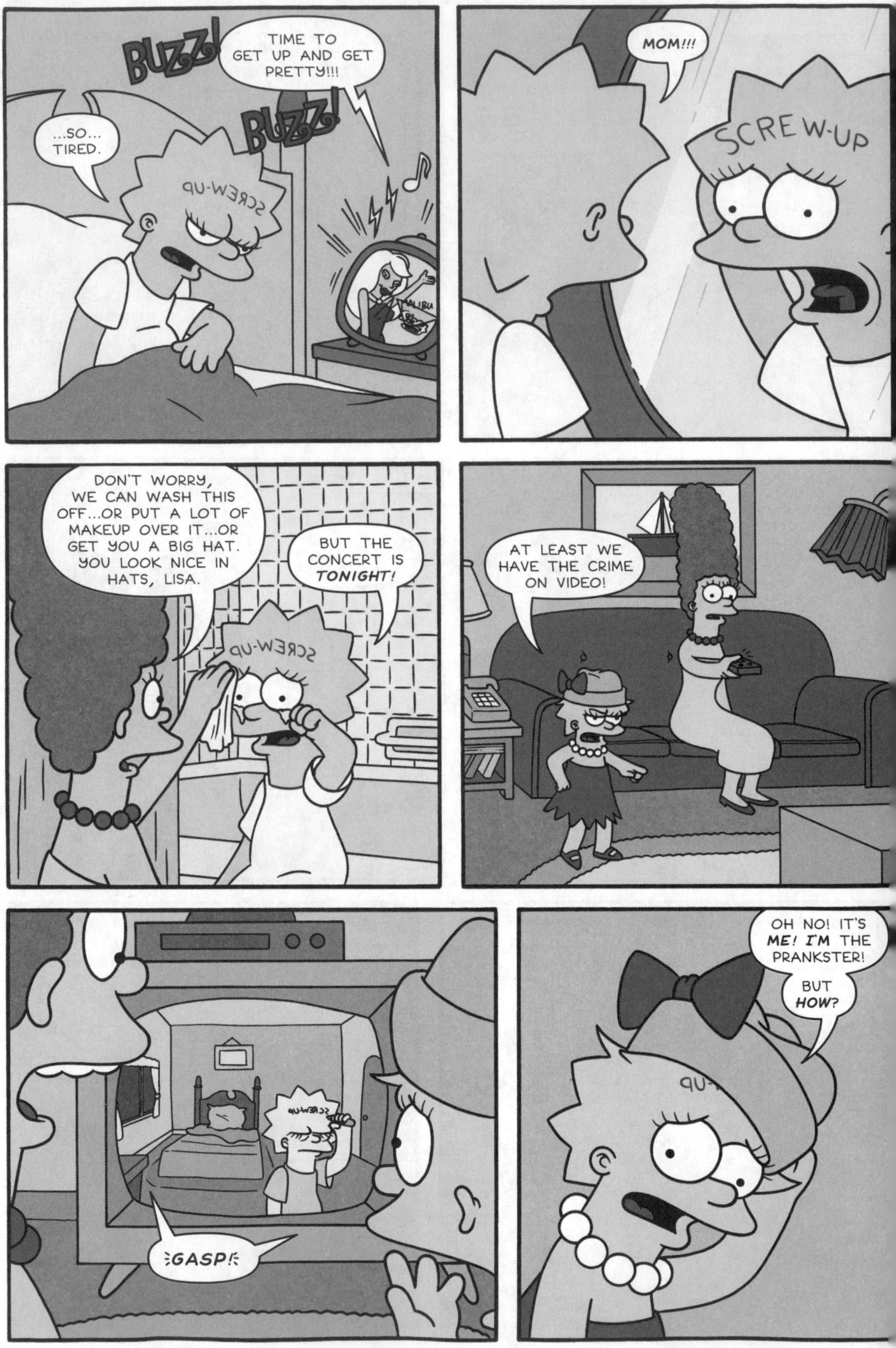
BUZZ!
TIME TO GET UP AND GET PRETTY!!!
BUZZ!
...SO... TIRED.
MALIBU
MOM!!!
SCREW-UP
DON'T WORRY, WE CAN WASH THIS OFF...OR PUT A LOT OF MAKEUP OVER IT...OR GET YOU A BIG HAT. YOU LOOK NICE IN HATS, LISA.
BUT THE CONCERT IS **TONIGHT**!
AT LEAST WE HAVE THE CRIME ON VIDEO!
GASP!
OH NO! IT'S **ME! I'M** THE PRANKSTER!
BUT **HOW**?

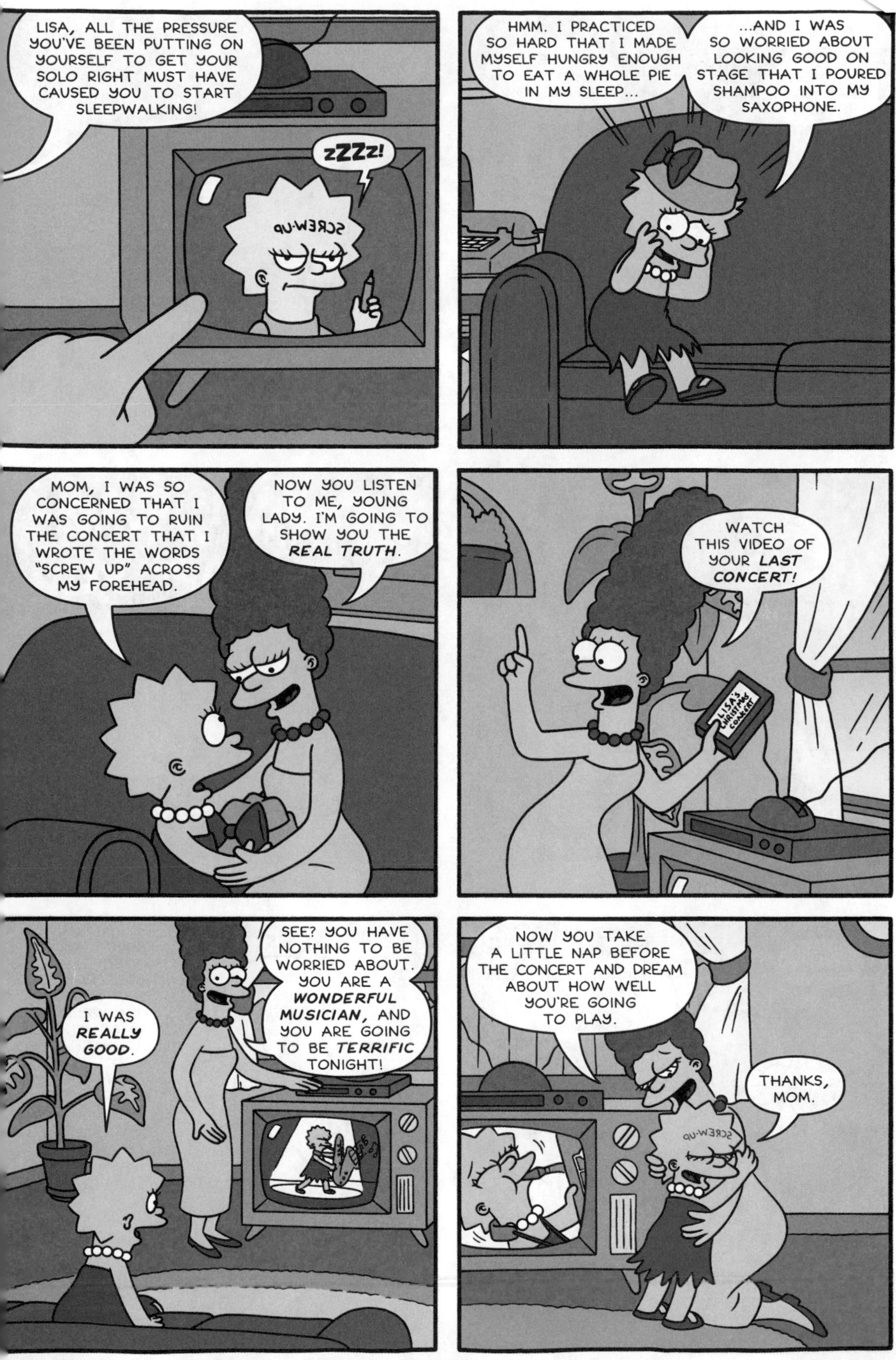
LISA, ALL THE PRESSURE YOU'VE BEEN PUTTING ON YOURSELF TO GET YOUR SOLO RIGHT MUST HAVE CAUSED YOU TO START SLEEPWALKING!
zZZz!
HMM. I PRACTICED SO HARD THAT I MADE MYSELF HUNGRY ENOUGH TO EAT A WHOLE PIE IN MY SLEEP...
...AND I WAS SO WORRIED ABOUT LOOKING GOOD ON STAGE THAT I POURED SHAMPOO INTO MY SAXOPHONE.
MOM, I WAS SO CONCERNED THAT I WAS GOING TO RUIN THE CONCERT THAT I WROTE THE WORDS "SCREW UP" ACROSS MY FOREHEAD.
NOW YOU LISTEN TO ME, YOUNG LADY. I'M GOING TO SHOW YOU THE REAL TRUTH.
WATCH THIS VIDEO OF YOUR LAST CONCERT!
LISA'S CHRISTMAS CONCERT
I WAS REALLY GOOD.
SEE? YOU HAVE NOTHING TO BE WORRIED ABOUT. YOU ARE A WONDERFUL MUSICIAN, AND YOU ARE GOING TO BE TERRIFIC TONIGHT!
NOW YOU TAKE A LITTLE NAP BEFORE THE CONCERT AND DREAM ABOUT HOW WELL YOU'RE GOING TO PLAY.
THANKS, MOM.

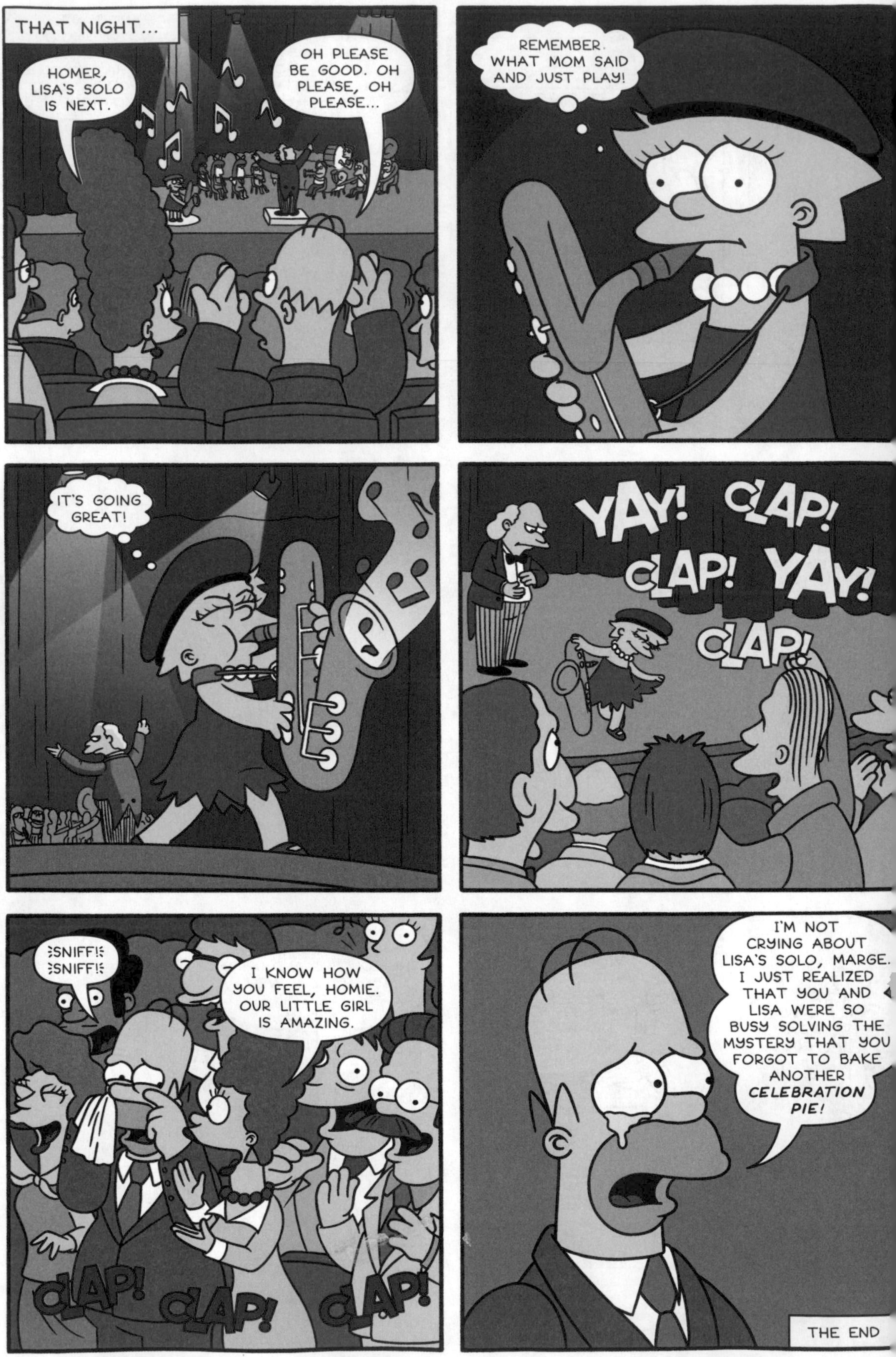
THAT NIGHT...
HOMER, LISA'S SOLO IS NEXT.
OH PLEASE BE GOOD. OH PLEASE, OH PLEASE...
REMEMBER. WHAT MOM SAID AND JUST PLAY!
IT'S GOING GREAT!
YAY! CLAP! CLAP! YAY! CLAP!
SNIFF! SNIFF!
I KNOW HOW YOU FEEL, HOMIE. OUR LITTLE GIRL IS AMAZING.
CLAP! CLAP! CLAP!
I'M NOT CRYING ABOUT LISA'S SOLO, MARGE. I JUST REALIZED THAT YOU AND LISA WERE SO BUSY SOLVING THE MYSTERY THAT YOU FORGOT TO BAKE ANOTHER *CELEBRATION PIE!*
THE END

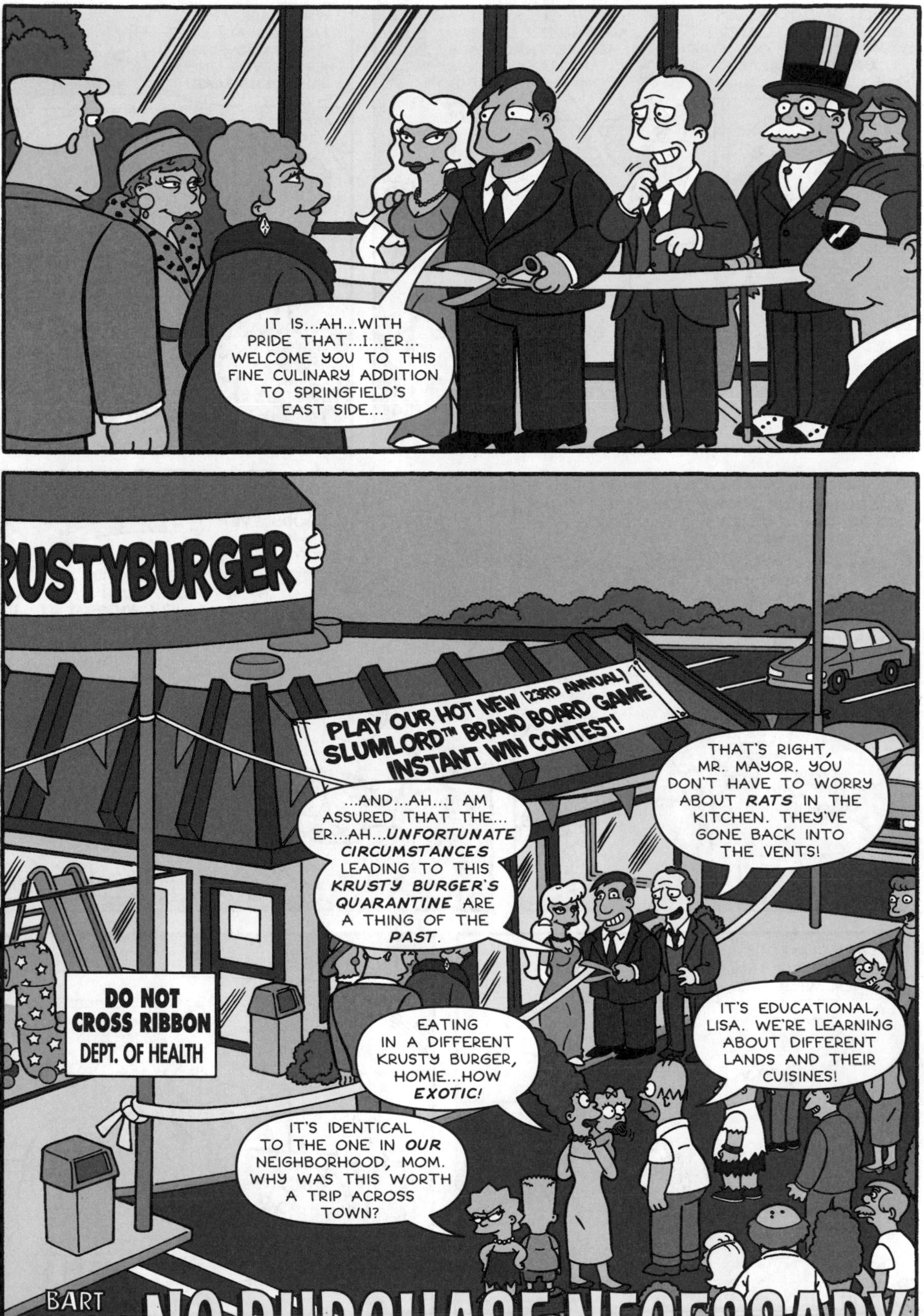
IT IS...AH...WITH PRIDE THAT...I...ER... WELCOME YOU TO THIS FINE CULINARY ADDITION TO SPRINGFIELD'S EAST SIDE...
KRUSTYBURGER
PLAY OUR HOT NEW (23RD ANNUAL) SLUMLORD™ BRAND BOARD GAME INSTANT WIN CONTEST!
...AND...AH...I AM ASSURED THAT THE... ER...AH...UNFORTUNATE CIRCUMSTANCES LEADING TO THIS KRUSTY BURGER'S QUARANTINE ARE A THING OF THE PAST.
THAT'S RIGHT, MR. MAYOR. YOU DON'T HAVE TO WORRY ABOUT RATS IN THE KITCHEN. THEY'VE GONE BACK INTO THE VENTS!
DO NOT CROSS RIBBON DEPT. OF HEALTH
EATING IN A DIFFERENT KRUSTY BURGER, HOMIE...HOW EXOTIC!
IT'S EDUCATIONAL, LISA. WE'RE LEARNING ABOUT DIFFERENT LANDS AND THEIR CUISINES!
IT'S IDENTICAL TO THE ONE IN OUR NEIGHBORHOOD, MOM. WHY WAS THIS WORTH A TRIP ACROSS TOWN?
BART SIMPSON IN
NO PURCHASE NECESSARY

JOHN JACKSON MILLER SCRIPT · **PHIL ORTIZ** PENCILS · **MIKE DECARLO** INKS · **NATHAN HAMILL** COLORS · **KAREN BATES** LETTERS · **BILL MORRISON** EDITOR

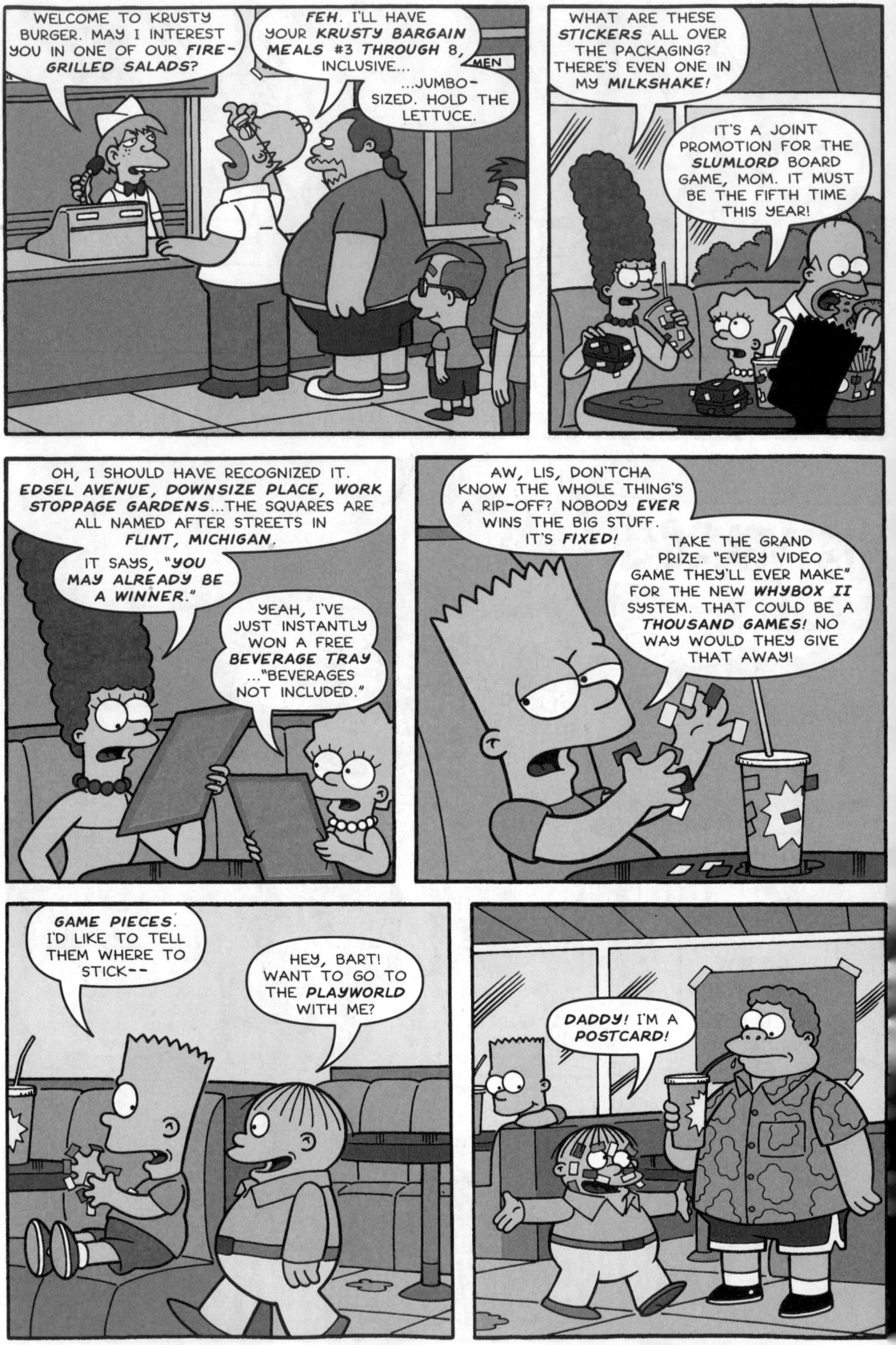
WELCOME TO KRUSTY BURGER. MAY I INTEREST YOU IN ONE OF OUR FIRE-GRILLED SALADS?
FEH. I'LL HAVE YOUR KRUSTY BARGAIN MEALS #3 THROUGH 8, INCLUSIVE...
MEN
...JUMBO-SIZED. HOLD THE LETTUCE.
WHAT ARE THESE STICKERS ALL OVER THE PACKAGING? THERE'S EVEN ONE IN MY MILKSHAKE!
IT'S A JOINT PROMOTION FOR THE SLUMLORD BOARD GAME, MOM. IT MUST BE THE FIFTH TIME THIS YEAR!
OH, I SHOULD HAVE RECOGNIZED IT. EDSEL AVENUE, DOWNSIZE PLACE, WORK STOPPAGE GARDENS...THE SQUARES ARE ALL NAMED AFTER STREETS IN FLINT, MICHIGAN.
IT SAYS, "YOU MAY ALREADY BE A WINNER."
YEAH, I'VE JUST INSTANTLY WON A FREE BEVERAGE TRAY ..."BEVERAGES NOT INCLUDED."
AW, LIS, DON'TCHA KNOW THE WHOLE THING'S A RIP-OFF? NOBODY EVER WINS THE BIG STUFF. IT'S FIXED!
TAKE THE GRAND PRIZE. "EVERY VIDEO GAME THEY'LL EVER MAKE" FOR THE NEW WHYBOX II SYSTEM. THAT COULD BE A THOUSAND GAMES! NO WAY WOULD THEY GIVE THAT AWAY!
GAME PIECES. I'D LIKE TO TELL THEM WHERE TO STICK--
HEY, BART! WANT TO GO TO THE PLAYWORLD WITH ME?
DADDY! I'M A POSTCARD!

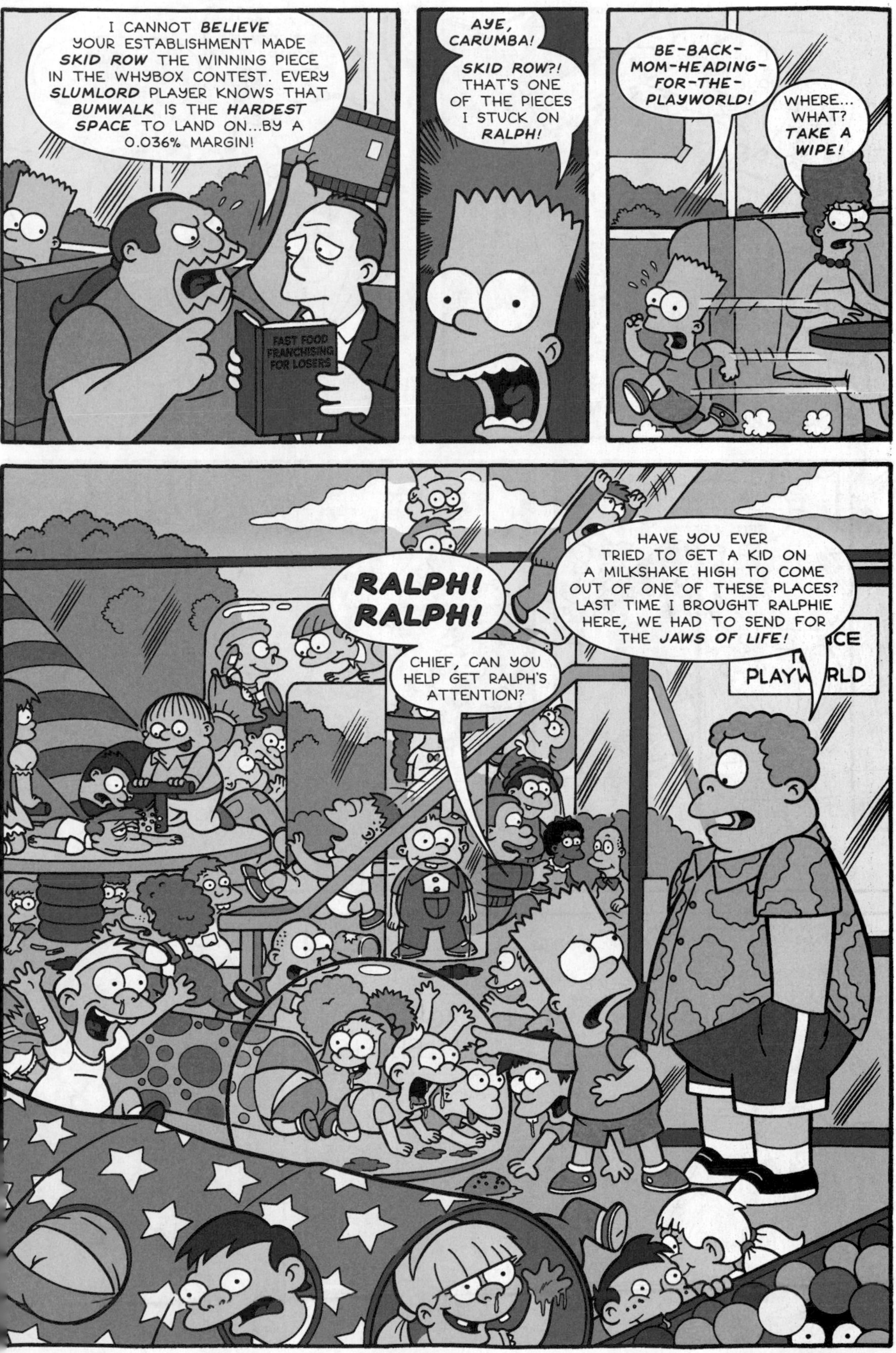
I CANNOT BELIEVE YOUR ESTABLISHMENT MADE SKID ROW THE WINNING PIECE IN THE WHYBOX CONTEST. EVERY SLUMLORD PLAYER KNOWS THAT BUMWALK IS THE HARDEST SPACE TO LAND ON...BY A 0.036% MARGIN!
FAST FOOD FRANCHISING FOR LOSERS
AYE, CARUMBA!
SKID ROW?! THAT'S ONE OF THE PIECES I STUCK ON RALPH!
BE-BACK-MOM-HEADING-FOR-THE-PLAYWORLD!
WHERE... WHAT? TAKE A WIPE!
RALPH! RALPH!
CHIEF, CAN YOU HELP GET RALPH'S ATTENTION?
HAVE YOU EVER TRIED TO GET A KID ON A MILKSHAKE HIGH TO COME OUT OF ONE OF THESE PLACES? LAST TIME I BROUGHT RALPHIE HERE, WE HAD TO SEND FOR THE JAWS OF LIFE!
PLAYWRLD

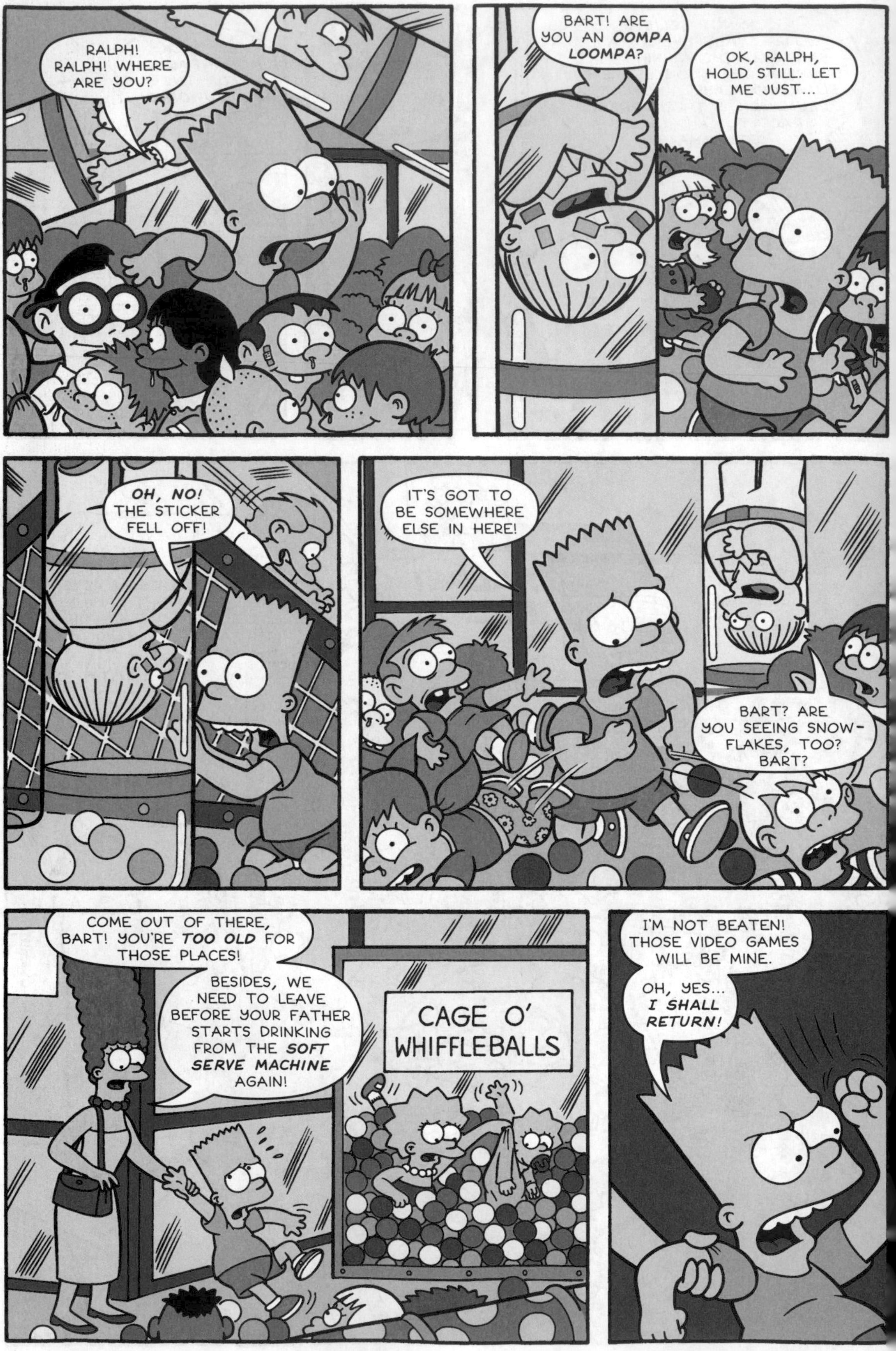
RALPH! RALPH! WHERE ARE YOU?
BART! ARE YOU AN OOMPA LOOMPA?
OK, RALPH, HOLD STILL. LET ME JUST...
OH, NO! THE STICKER FELL OFF!
IT'S GOT TO BE SOMEWHERE ELSE IN HERE!
BART? ARE YOU SEEING SNOW-FLAKES, TOO? BART?
COME OUT OF THERE, BART! YOU'RE TOO OLD FOR THOSE PLACES!
BESIDES, WE NEED TO LEAVE BEFORE YOUR FATHER STARTS DRINKING FROM THE SOFT SERVE MACHINE AGAIN!
CAGE O' WHIFFLEBALLS
I'M NOT BEATEN! THOSE VIDEO GAMES WILL BE MINE.
OH, YES... I SHALL RETURN!

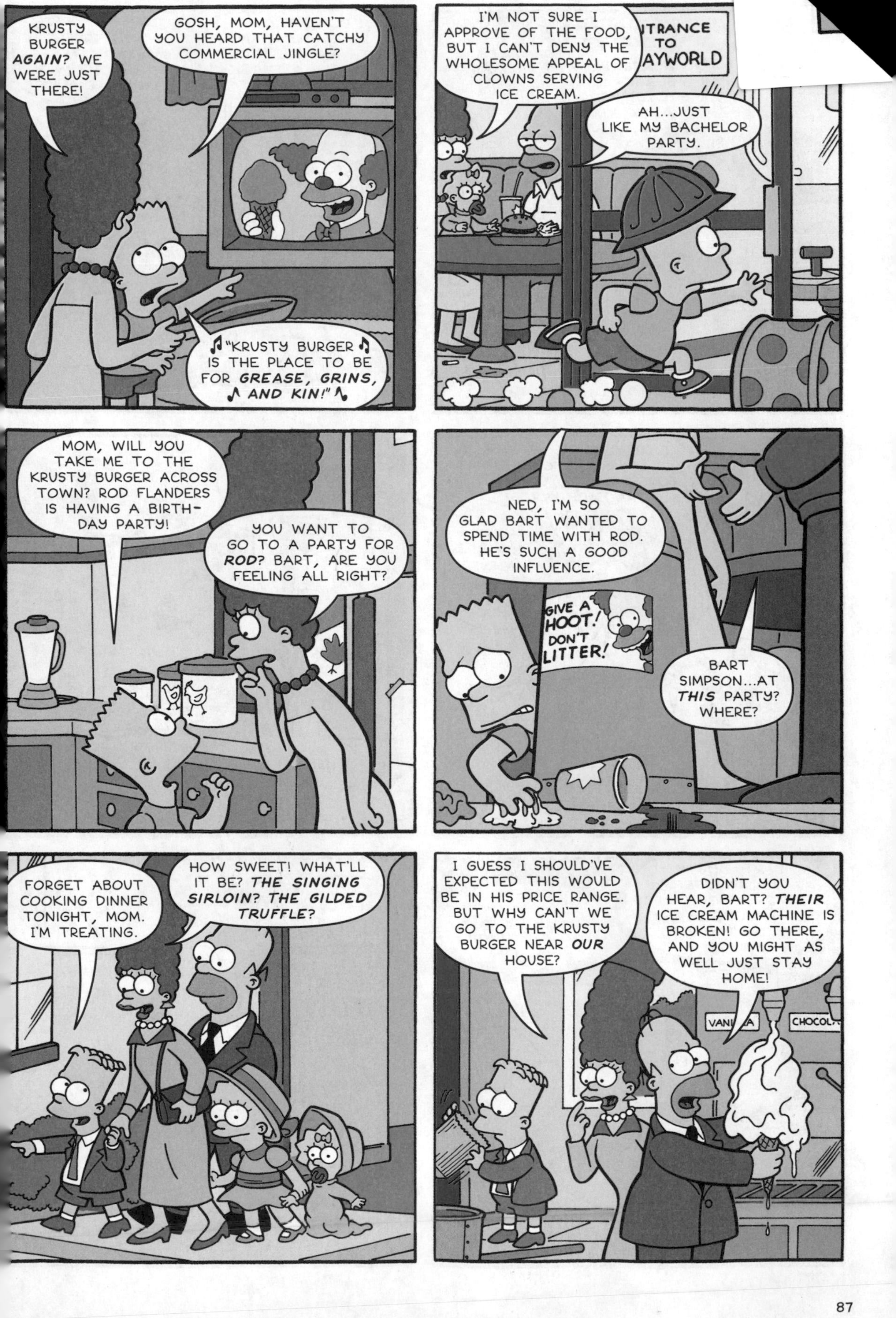
KRUSTY BURGER AGAIN? WE WERE JUST THERE!
GOSH, MOM, HAVEN'T YOU HEARD THAT CATCHY COMMERCIAL JINGLE?
♫ "KRUSTY BURGER ♫ IS THE PLACE TO BE FOR GREASE, GRINS, ♪ AND KIN!" ♪
I'M NOT SURE I APPROVE OF THE FOOD, BUT I CAN'T DENY THE WHOLESOME APPEAL OF CLOWNS SERVING ICE CREAM.
AH...JUST LIKE MY BACHELOR PARTY.
MOM, WILL YOU TAKE ME TO THE KRUSTY BURGER ACROSS TOWN? ROD FLANDERS IS HAVING A BIRTH-DAY PARTY!
YOU WANT TO GO TO A PARTY FOR ROD? BART, ARE YOU FEELING ALL RIGHT?
NED, I'M SO GLAD BART WANTED TO SPEND TIME WITH ROD. HE'S SUCH A GOOD INFLUENCE.
GIVE A HOOT! DON'T LITTER!
BART SIMPSON...AT THIS PARTY? WHERE?
FORGET ABOUT COOKING DINNER TONIGHT, MOM. I'M TREATING.
HOW SWEET! WHAT'LL IT BE? THE SINGING SIRLOIN? THE GILDED TRUFFLE?
I GUESS I SHOULD'VE EXPECTED THIS WOULD BE IN HIS PRICE RANGE. BUT WHY CAN'T WE GO TO THE KRUSTY BURGER NEAR OUR HOUSE?
DIDN'T YOU HEAR, BART? THEIR ICE CREAM MACHINE IS BROKEN! GO THERE, AND YOU MIGHT AS WELL JUST STAY HOME!

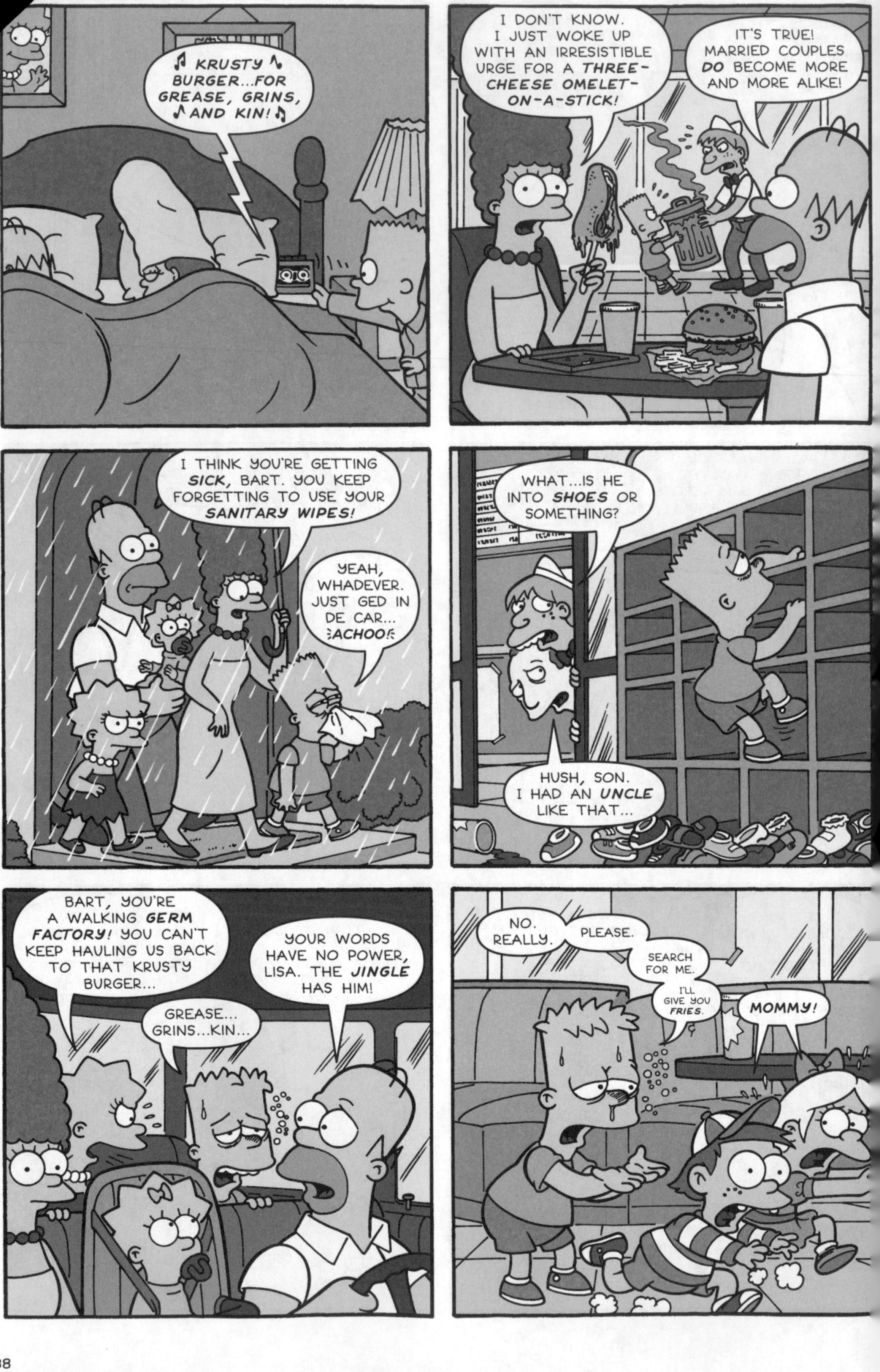
♪ KRUSTY ♪ BURGER...FOR GREASE, GRINS, ♪ AND KIN! ♪
I DON'T KNOW. I JUST WOKE UP WITH AN IRRESISTIBLE URGE FOR A THREE-CHEESE OMELET-ON-A-STICK!
IT'S TRUE! MARRIED COUPLES DO BECOME MORE AND MORE ALIKE!
I THINK YOU'RE GETTING SICK, BART. YOU KEEP FORGETTING TO USE YOUR SANITARY WIPES!
YEAH, WHADEVER. JUST GED IN DE CAR... ACHOO!
WHAT...IS HE INTO SHOES OR SOMETHING?
HUSH, SON. I HAD AN UNCLE LIKE THAT...
BART, YOU'RE A WALKING GERM FACTORY! YOU CAN'T KEEP HAULING US BACK TO THAT KRUSTY BURGER...
GREASE... GRINS...KIN...
YOUR WORDS HAVE NO POWER, LISA. THE JINGLE HAS HIM!
NO. REALLY.
PLEASE.
SEARCH FOR ME.
I'LL GIVE YOU FRIES.
MOMMY!

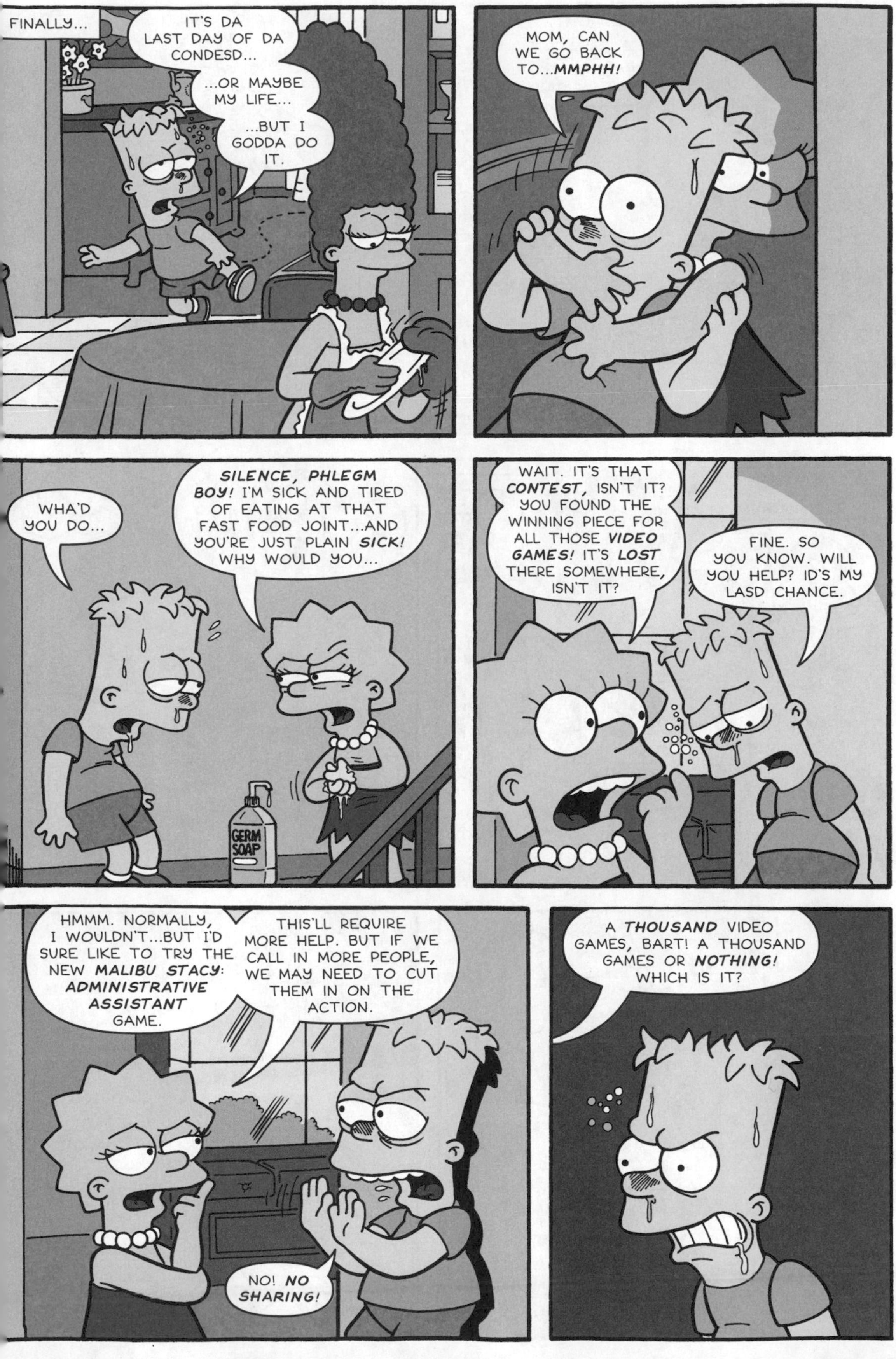

FINALLY...
IT'S DA LAST DAY OF DA CONDESD...
...OR MAYBE MY LIFE...
...BUT I GODDA DO IT.
MOM, CAN WE GO BACK TO...MMPHH!
WHA'D YOU DO...
SILENCE, PHLEGM BOY! I'M SICK AND TIRED OF EATING AT THAT FAST FOOD JOINT...AND YOU'RE JUST PLAIN SICK! WHY WOULD YOU...
GERM SOAP
WAIT. IT'S THAT CONTEST, ISN'T IT? YOU FOUND THE WINNING PIECE FOR ALL THOSE VIDEO GAMES! IT'S LOST THERE SOMEWHERE, ISN'T IT?
FINE. SO YOU KNOW. WILL YOU HELP? ID'S MY LASD CHANCE.
HMMM. NORMALLY, I WOULDN'T...BUT I'D SURE LIKE TO TRY THE NEW MALIBU STACY: ADMINISTRATIVE ASSISTANT GAME.
THIS'LL REQUIRE MORE HELP. BUT IF WE CALL IN MORE PEOPLE, WE MAY NEED TO CUT THEM IN ON THE ACTION.
NO! NO SHARING!
A THOUSAND VIDEO GAMES, BART! A THOUSAND GAMES OR NOTHING! WHICH IS IT?

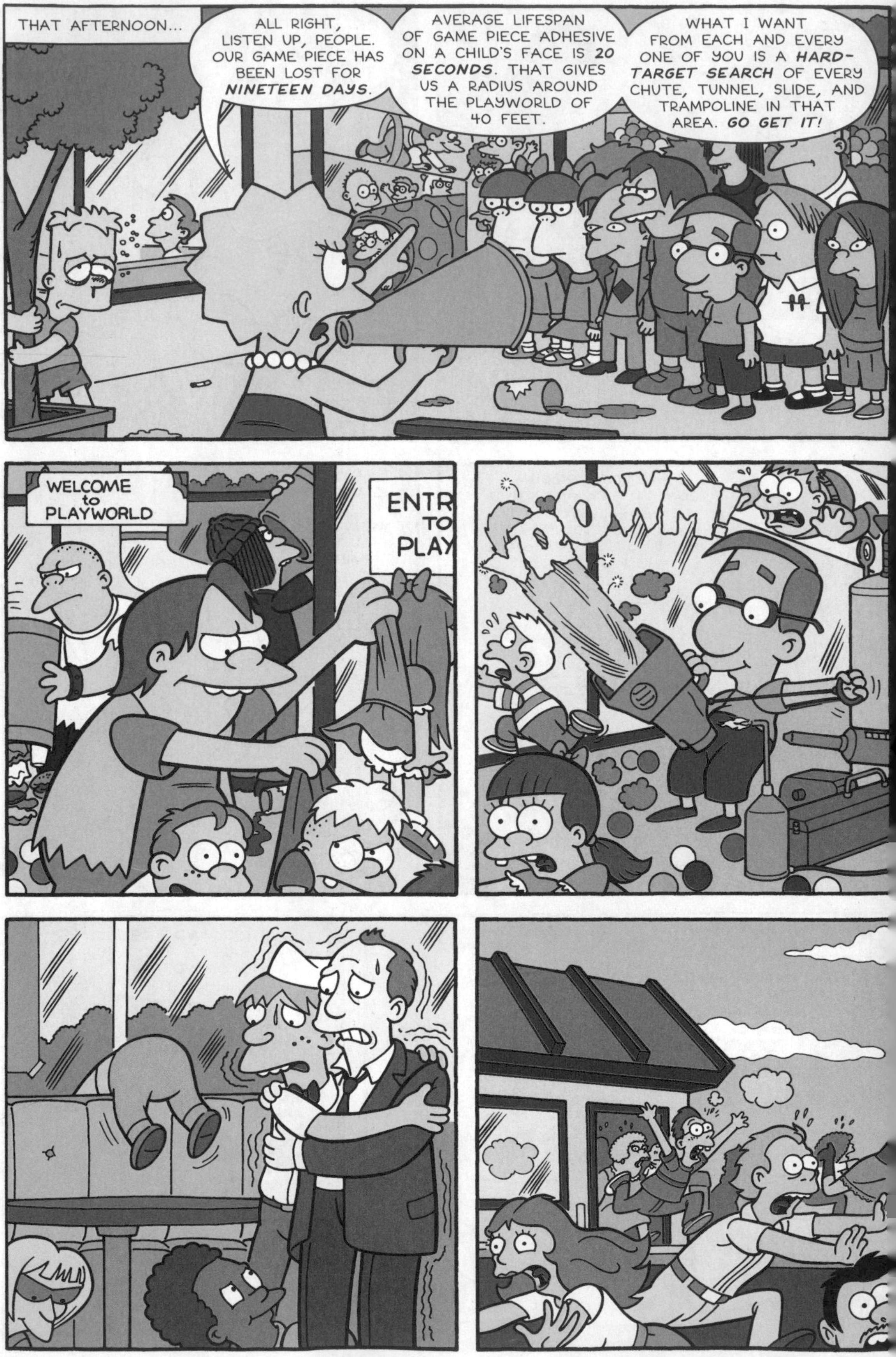
THAT AFTERNOON...
ALL RIGHT, LISTEN UP, PEOPLE. OUR GAME PIECE HAS BEEN LOST FOR NINETEEN DAYS.
AVERAGE LIFESPAN OF GAME PIECE ADHESIVE ON A CHILD'S FACE IS 20 SECONDS. THAT GIVES US A RADIUS AROUND THE PLAYWORLD OF 40 FEET.
WHAT I WANT FROM EACH AND EVERY ONE OF YOU IS A HARD-TARGET SEARCH OF EVERY CHUTE, TUNNEL, SLIDE, AND TRAMPOLINE IN THAT AREA. GO GET IT!
WELCOME to PLAYWORLD
ENTR TO PLAY
POWW!

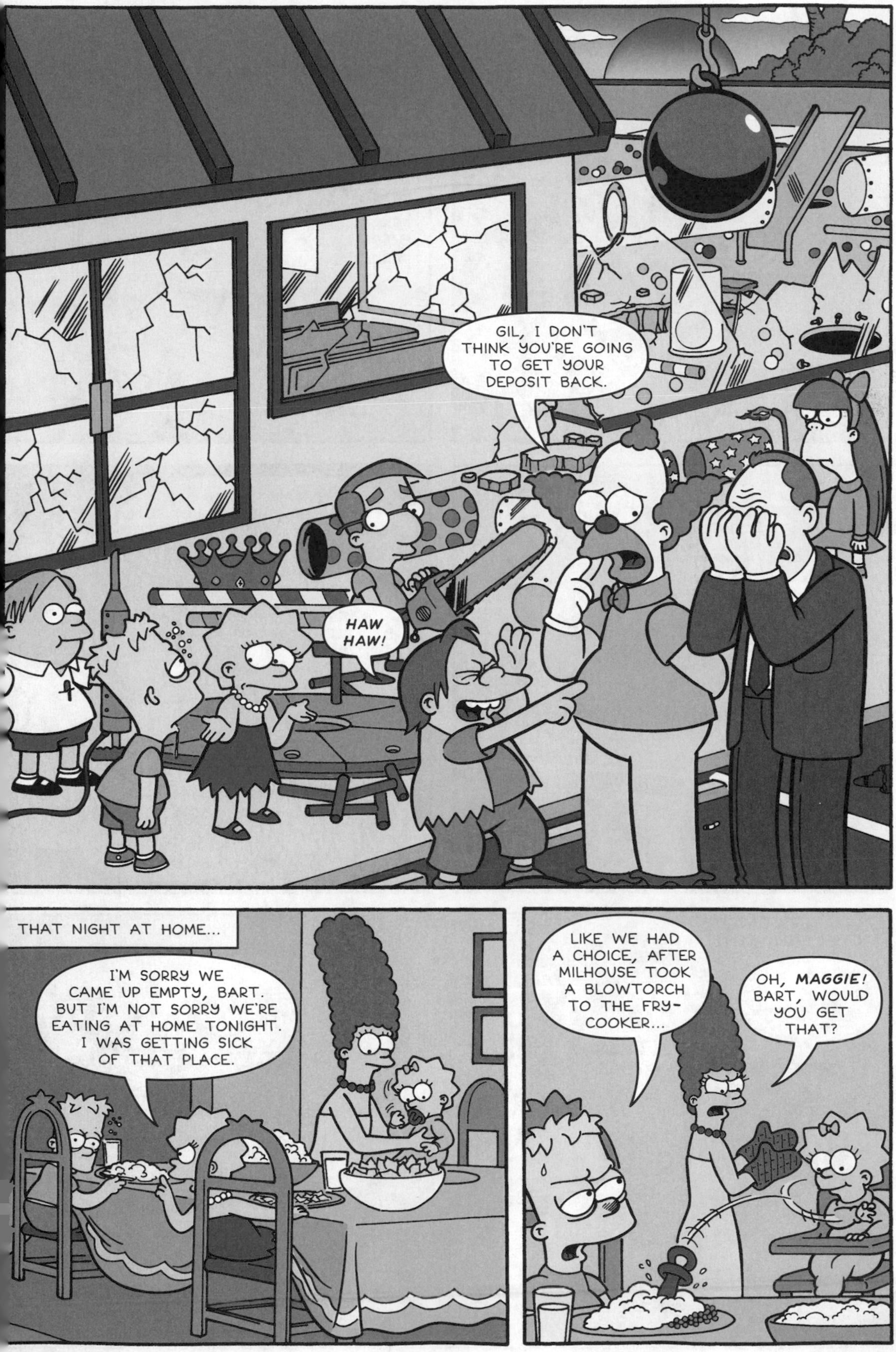
GIL, I DON'T THINK YOU'RE GOING TO GET YOUR DEPOSIT BACK.
HAW HAW!
THAT NIGHT AT HOME...
I'M SORRY WE CAME UP EMPTY, BART. BUT I'M NOT SORRY WE'RE EATING AT HOME TONIGHT. I WAS GETTING SICK OF THAT PLACE.
LIKE WE HAD A CHOICE, AFTER MILHOUSE TOOK A BLOWTORCH TO THE FRY-COOKER...
OH, MAGGIE! BART, WOULD YOU GET THAT?

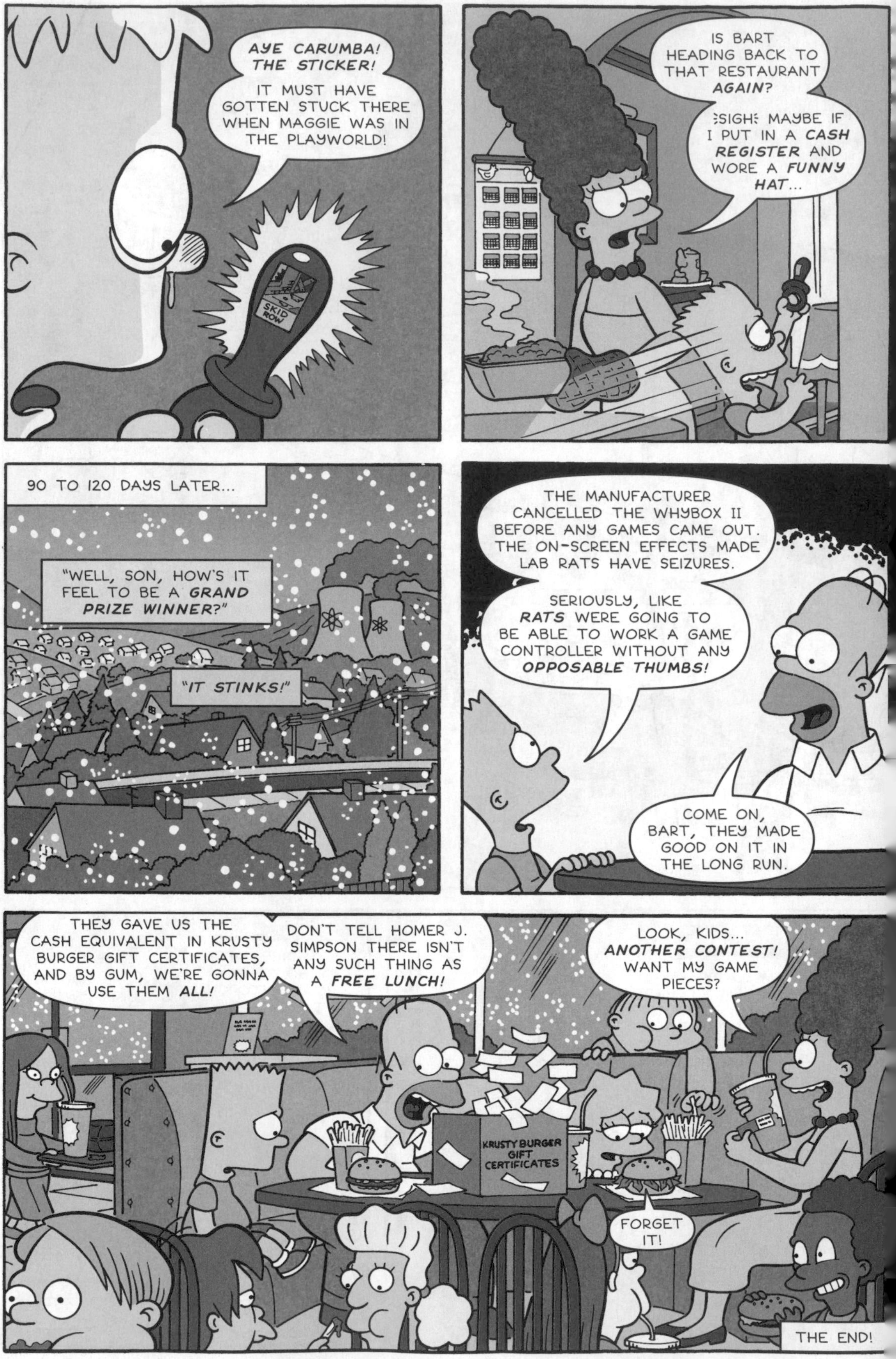
AYE CARUMBA! THE STICKER!
IT MUST HAVE GOTTEN STUCK THERE WHEN MAGGIE WAS IN THE PLAYWORLD!
SKID ROW
IS BART HEADING BACK TO THAT RESTAURANT AGAIN?
:SIGH: MAYBE IF I PUT IN A CASH REGISTER AND WORE A FUNNY HAT...
90 TO 120 DAYS LATER...
"WELL, SON, HOW'S IT FEEL TO BE A GRAND PRIZE WINNER?"
"IT STINKS!"
THE MANUFACTURER CANCELLED THE WHYBOX II BEFORE ANY GAMES CAME OUT. THE ON-SCREEN EFFECTS MADE LAB RATS HAVE SEIZURES.
SERIOUSLY, LIKE RATS WERE GOING TO BE ABLE TO WORK A GAME CONTROLLER WITHOUT ANY OPPOSABLE THUMBS!
COME ON, BART, THEY MADE GOOD ON IT IN THE LONG RUN.
THEY GAVE US THE CASH EQUIVALENT IN KRUSTY BURGER GIFT CERTIFICATES, AND BY GUM, WE'RE GONNA USE THEM ALL!
DON'T TELL HOMER J. SIMPSON THERE ISN'T ANY SUCH THING AS A FREE LUNCH!
LOOK, KIDS... ANOTHER CONTEST! WANT MY GAME PIECES?
KRUSTY BURGER GIFT CERTIFICATES
FORGET IT!
THE END!

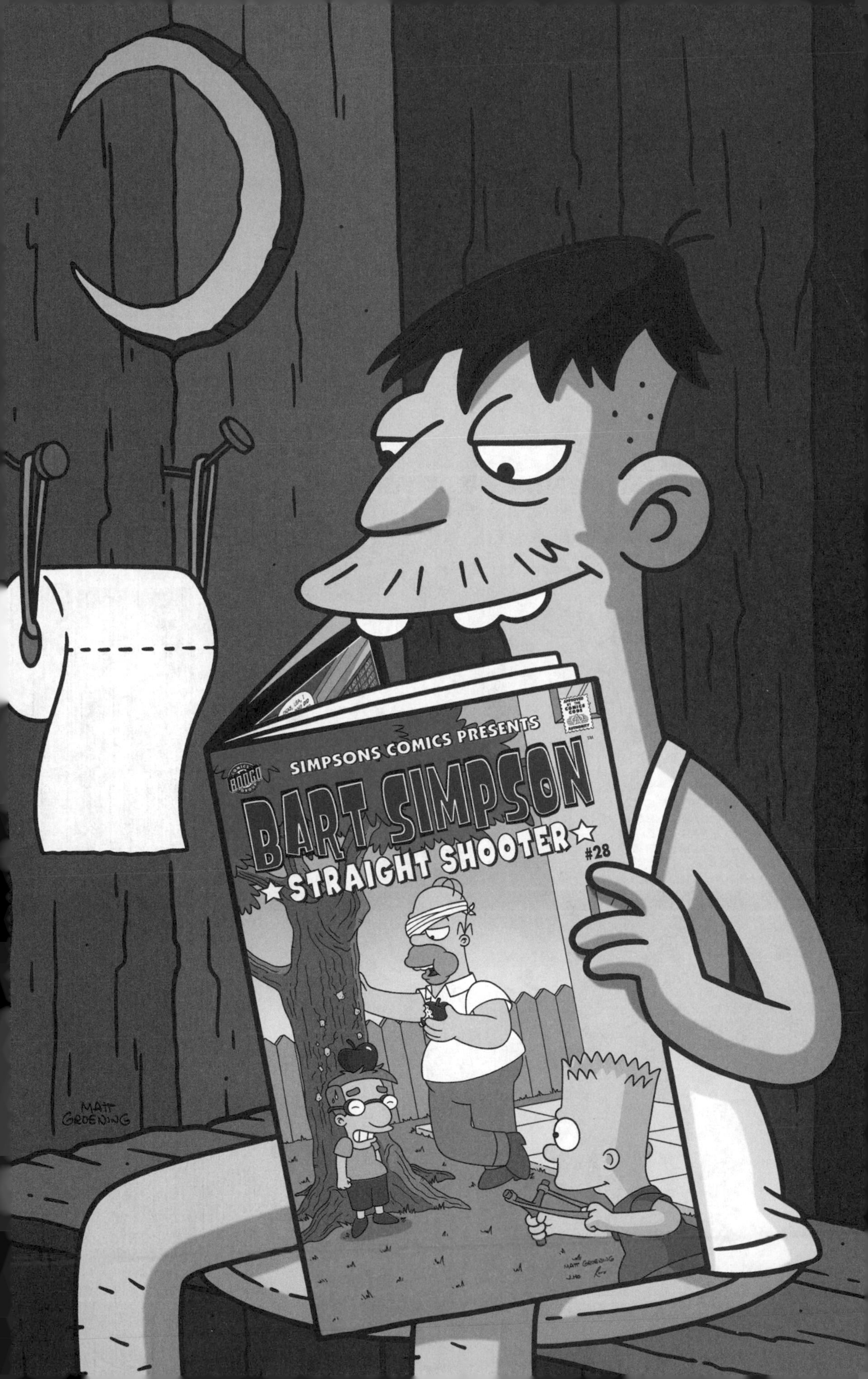
SIMPSONS COMICS PRESENTS
BART SIMPSON
STRAIGHT SHOOTER
#28
MATT GROENING

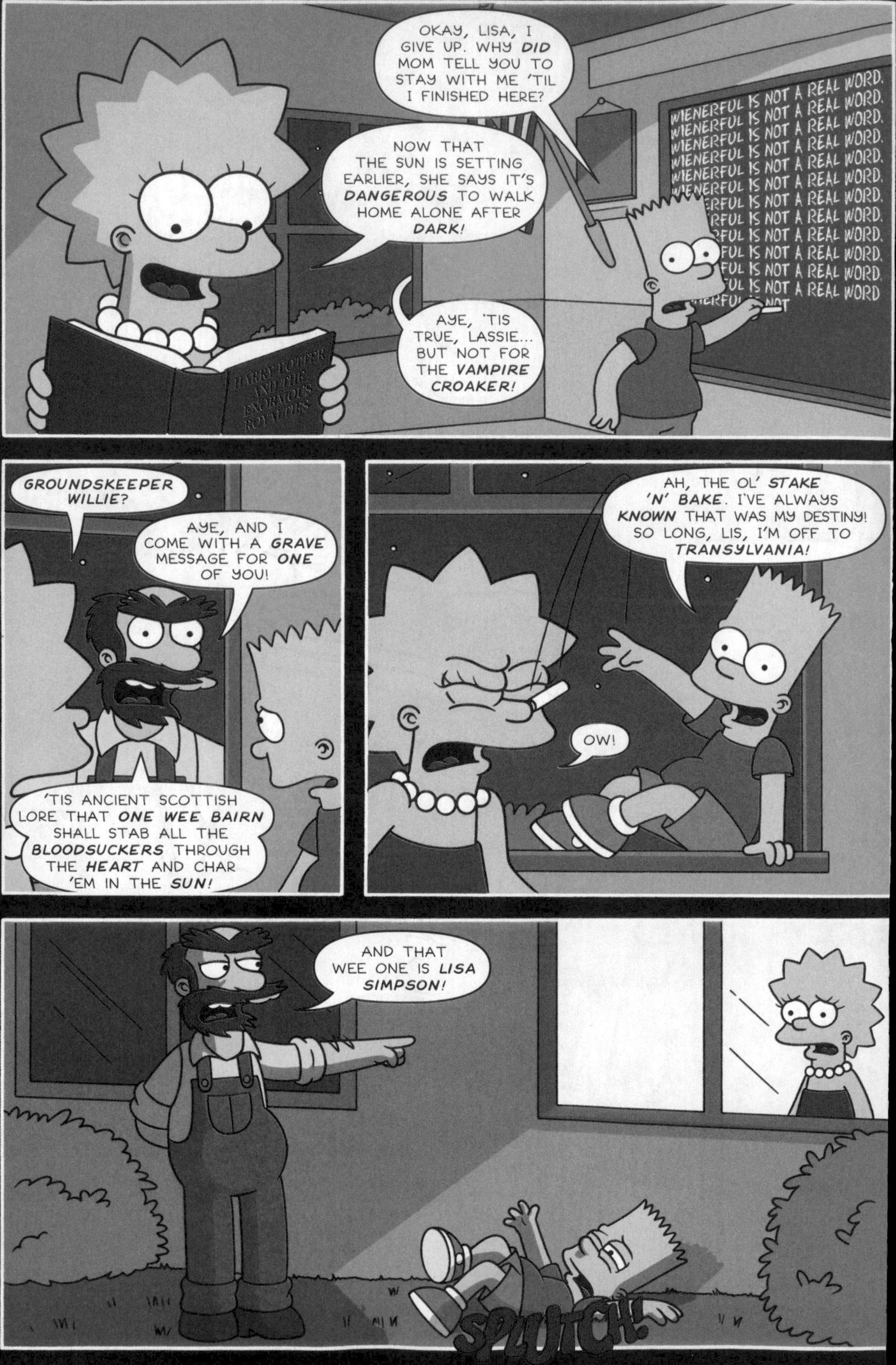

OKAY, LISA, I GIVE UP. WHY *DID* MOM TELL YOU TO STAY WITH ME 'TIL I FINISHED HERE?
WIENERFUL IS NOT A REAL WORD.
WIENERFUL IS NOT A REAL WORD.
WIENERFUL IS NOT A REAL WORD.
WIENERFUL IS NOT A REAL WORD.
WIENERFUL IS NOT A REAL WORD.
WIENERFUL IS NOT A REAL WORD.
WIENERFUL IS NOT A REAL WORD.
NOW THAT THE SUN IS SETTING EARLIER, SHE SAYS IT'S *DANGEROUS* TO WALK HOME ALONE AFTER *DARK!*
AYE, 'TIS TRUE, LASSIE... BUT NOT FOR THE *VAMPIRE CROAKER!*
HARRY LOTPER AND THE ENORMOUS ROYALTIES
GROUNDSKEEPER WILLIE?
AYE, AND I COME WITH A *GRAVE* MESSAGE FOR *ONE* OF YOU!
'TIS ANCIENT SCOTTISH LORE THAT *ONE WEE BAIRN* SHALL STAB ALL THE *BLOODSUCKERS* THROUGH THE *HEART* AND CHAR 'EM IN THE *SUN!*
AH, THE OL' *STAKE 'N' BAKE*. I'VE ALWAYS *KNOWN* THAT WAS MY DESTINY! SO LONG, LIS, I'M OFF TO *TRANSYLVANIA!*
OW!
AND THAT WEE ONE IS *LISA SIMPSON!*
SPLUTCH!

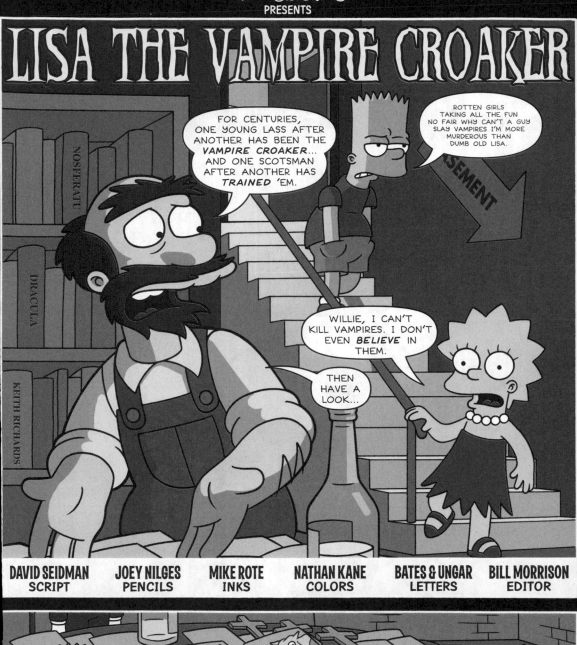

MATT GROENING
PRESENTS

LISA THE VAMPIRE CROAKER

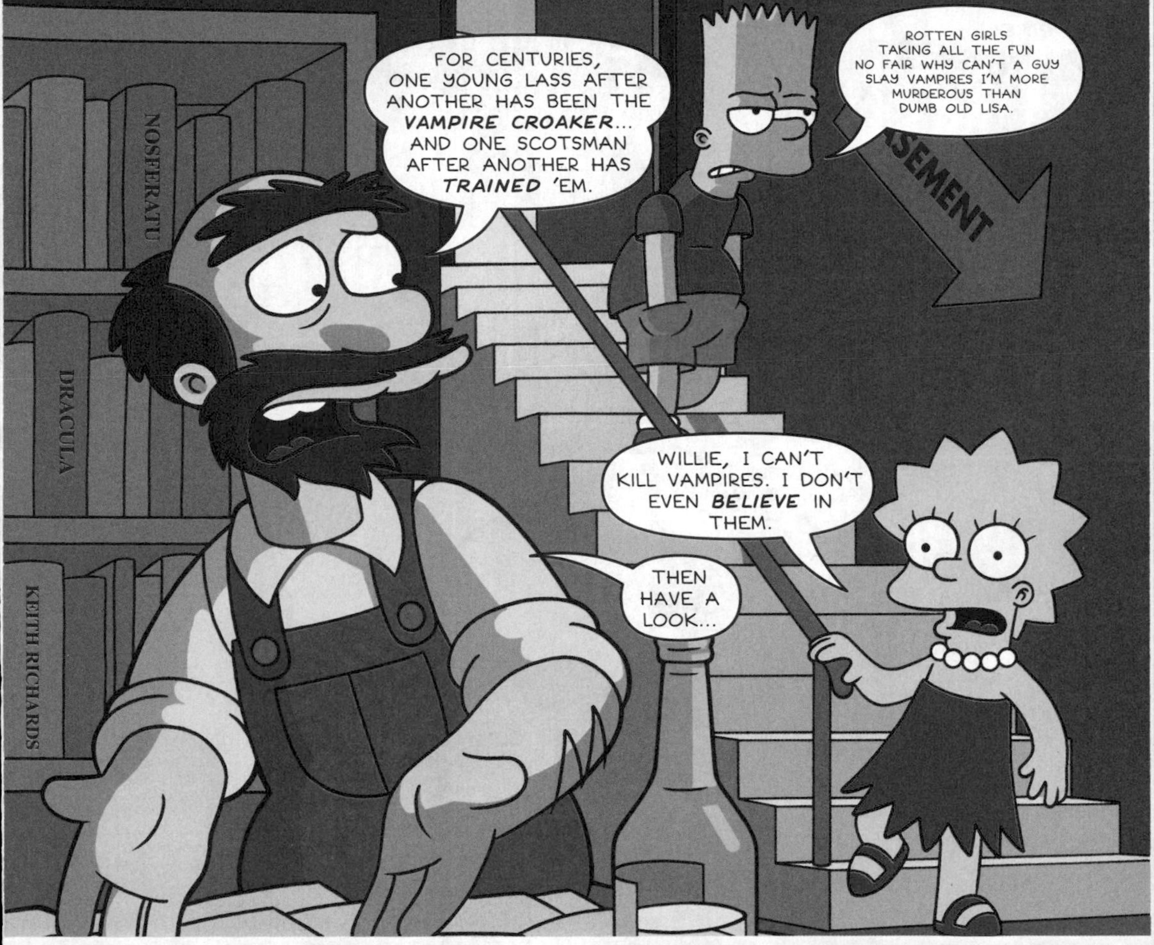
FOR CENTURIES, ONE YOUNG LASS AFTER ANOTHER HAS BEEN THE *VAMPIRE CROAKER*... AND ONE SCOTSMAN AFTER ANOTHER HAS *TRAINED* 'EM.
ROTTEN GIRLS TAKING ALL THE FUN NO FAIR WHY CAN'T A GUY SLAY VAMPIRES I'M MORE MURDEROUS THAN DUMB OLD LISA.
WILLIE, I CAN'T KILL VAMPIRES. I DON'T EVEN *BELIEVE* IN THEM.
THEN HAVE A LOOK...
NOSFERATU
DRACULA
KEITH RICHARDS

DAVID SEIDMAN	JOEY NILGES	MIKE ROTE	NATHAN KANE	BATES & UNGAR	BILL MORRISON
SCRIPT	PENCILS	INKS	COLORS	LETTERS	EDITOR

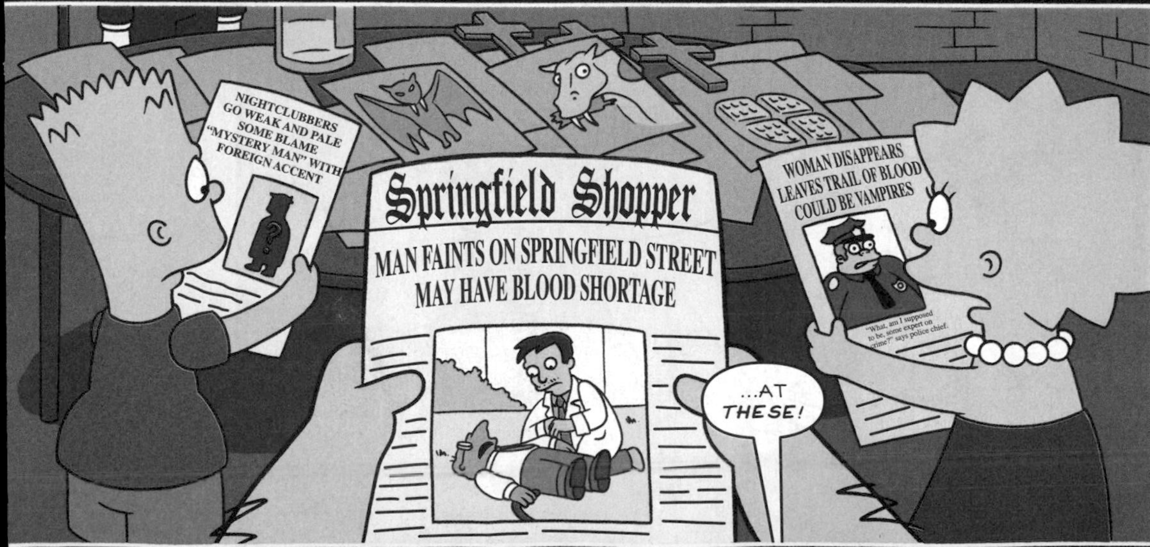
NIGHTCLUBBERS GO WEAK AND PALE SOME BLAME "MYSTERY MAN" WITH FOREIGN ACCENT
Springfield Shopper
MAN FAINTS ON SPRINGFIELD STREET MAY HAVE BLOOD SHORTAGE
WOMAN DISAPPEARS LEAVES TRAIL OF BLOOD COULD BE VAMPIRES
"What, am I supposed to be, some expert on crime?" says police chief.
...AT *THESE!*

OKAY, **SOME** WEIRD STUFF'S GOING ON, BUT THERE'S NO PROOF THAT **VAMPIRES**--

HEAR **THAT**, WILLIE? GIRLS ARE TOO **NAMBY-PAMBY** TO STALK THE UNDEAD!

A TOME OF MYSTERY - JO LOSS "CAN'T UNDER-LAND IT" SAYS WITNESS

FIRE UP THE **LESSONS**, WILLIE. I'VE GOT SOMETHING TO **PROVE** FOR ALL OF **GIRLKIND**!

HOOT MON!

SOON...

NOW, LASSIE, THE EASIEST WAY TA KILL A VAMPIRE IS TA **EXPOSE** HIM--

KNOW YOUR

ENEMY

I GOT IT, WILLIE! SEE?

NOT SO GOOD →

--TA **SUNLIGHT**!

OOPS.

PLUS, YE NEED TO GET ACQUAINTED WITH THE TOOLS TO **KILL** THE FIENDS.

YOU MEAN...

...LIKE THIS...

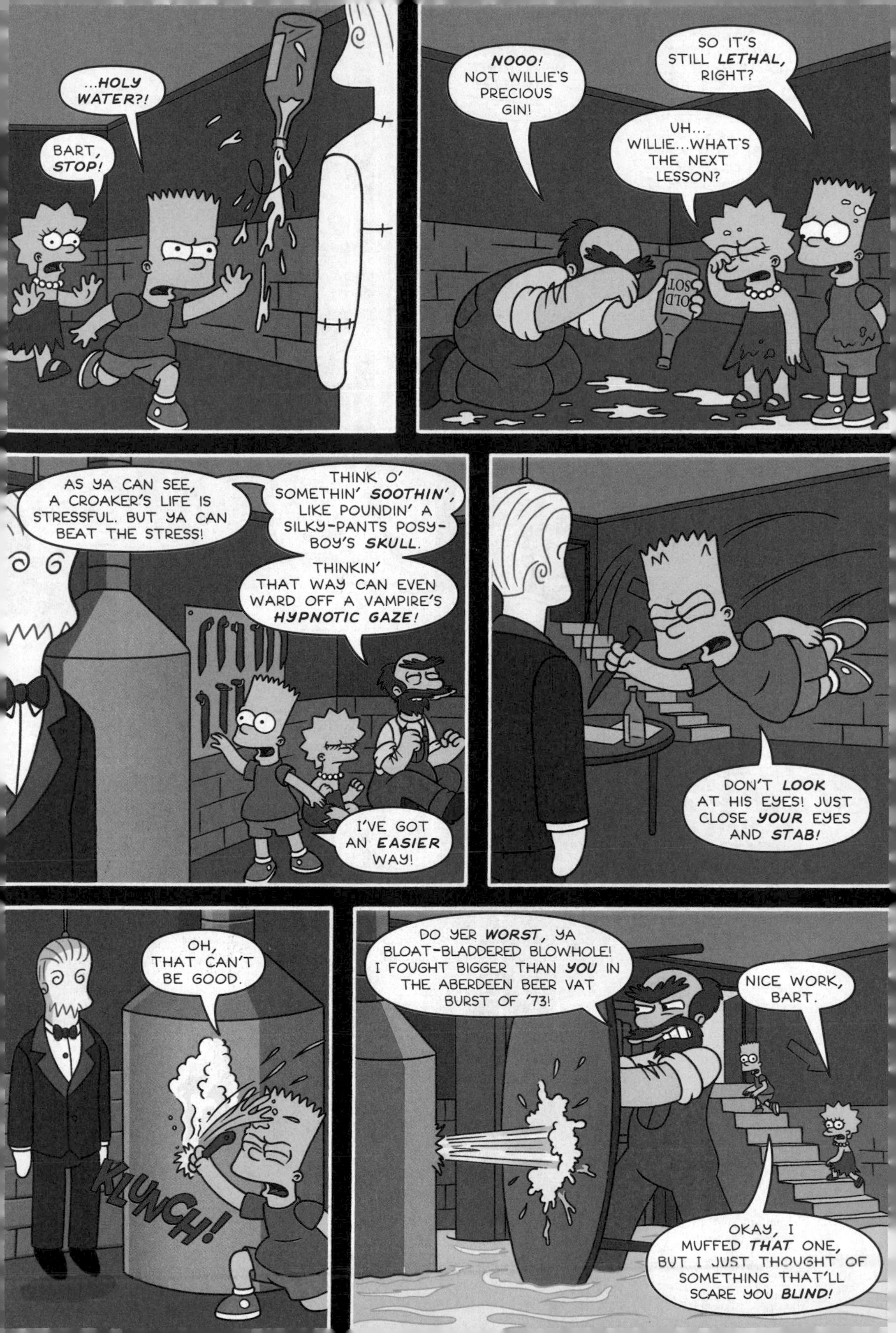

BART, STOP!
...HOLY WATER?!
NOOO! NOT WILLIE'S PRECIOUS GIN!
SO IT'S STILL LETHAL, RIGHT?
UH... WILLIE...WHAT'S THE NEXT LESSON?
OLD SOT
AS YA CAN SEE, A CROAKER'S LIFE IS STRESSFUL. BUT YA CAN BEAT THE STRESS!
THINK O' SOMETHIN' SOOTHIN', LIKE POUNDIN' A SILKY-PANTS POSY-BOY'S SKULL.
THINKIN' THAT WAY CAN EVEN WARD OFF A VAMPIRE'S HYPNOTIC GAZE!
I'VE GOT AN EASIER WAY!
DON'T LOOK AT HIS EYES! JUST CLOSE YOUR EYES AND STAB!
OH, THAT CAN'T BE GOOD.
KLUNCH!
DO YER WORST, YA BLOAT-BLADDERED BLOWHOLE! I FOUGHT BIGGER THAN YOU IN THE ABERDEEN BEER VAT BURST OF '73!
NICE WORK, BART.
OKAY, I MUFFED THAT ONE, BUT I JUST THOUGHT OF SOMETHING THAT'LL SCARE YOU BLIND!

I DIDN'T SEE WHY WILLIE PICKED *YOU* OVER *ME* UNTIL IT HIT ME: HE WANTED A *LAME-O* TO LEAD THE VAMPIRE HUNT 'CAUSE HE'S A BLOODSUCKER *HIMSELF!*

SCARY, RIGHT? BETCHA WANNA *QUIT* NOW!

HARDLY. GOT ANY *PROOF?*

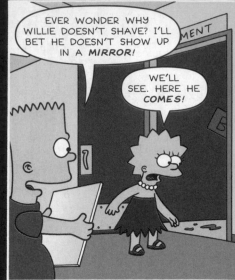

EVER WONDER WHY WILLIE DOESN'T SHAVE? I'LL BET HE DOESN'T SHOW UP IN A *MIRROR!*

WE'LL SEE. HERE HE *COMES!*

NAY! NAY!

AH-HAH!

ME *SPLIT ENDS!* I GEL 'EM AND GEL 'EM, BUT NOTHIN' HOLDS 'EM *TOGETHER!*

AW, MAN!

I'VE HAD ENOUGH. LET'S GO, LIS.

SEE YOU TOMORROW, WILLIE!

THAT NIGHT...

STUPID SCHOOL *BUDGET CUTS!* THIS TEXTBOOK IS USELESS!

PSST! LASSIE!

World War I: We won.

WE'VE GOT TO *GO!* THERE'S VAMPIRES AFOOT!

BUT I HAVEN'T FINISHED MY--

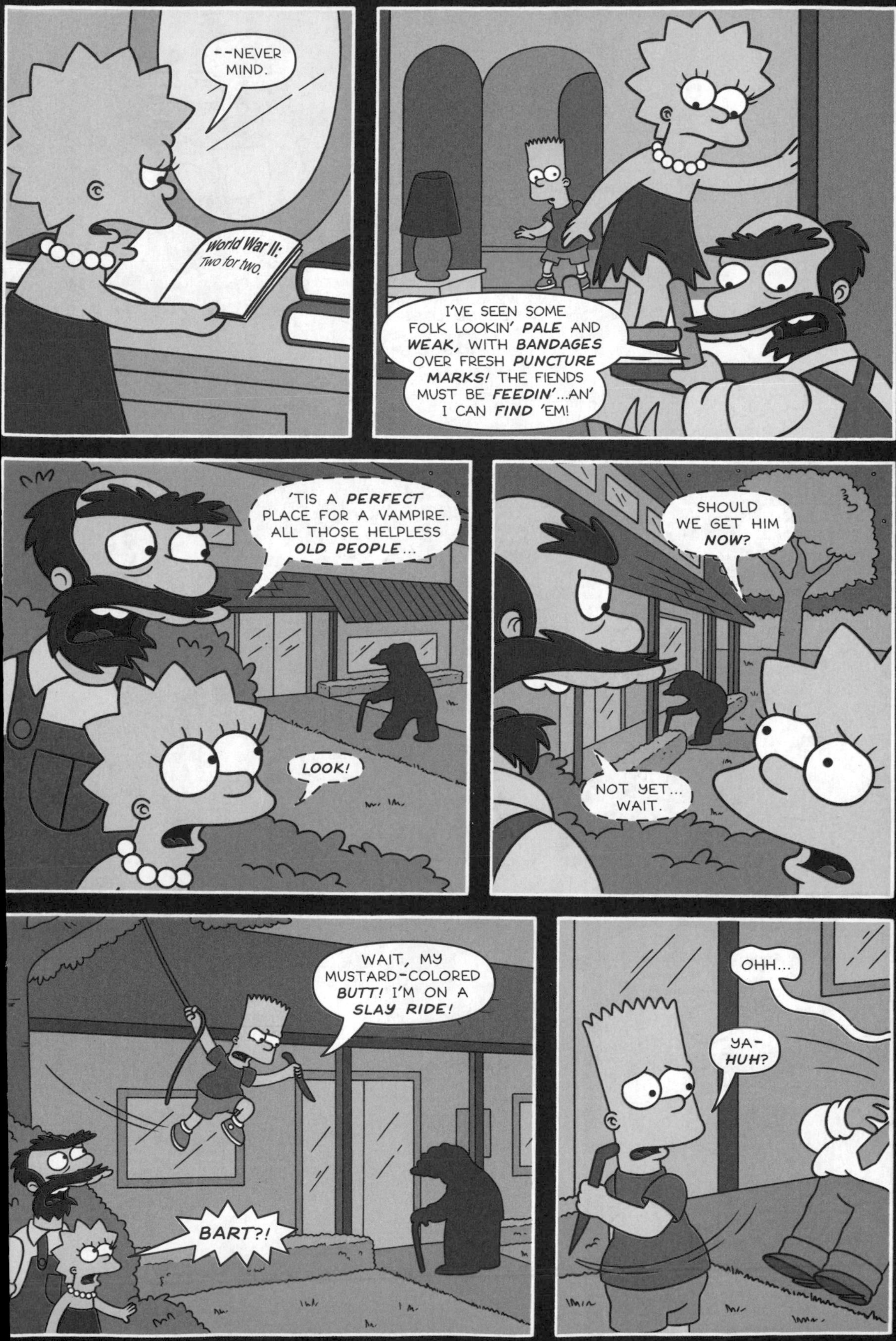
--NEVER MIND.
World War II: Two for two.
I'VE SEEN SOME FOLK LOOKIN' PALE AND WEAK, WITH BANDAGES OVER FRESH PUNCTURE MARKS! THE FIENDS MUST BE FEEDIN'...AN' I CAN FIND 'EM!
'TIS A PERFECT PLACE FOR A VAMPIRE. ALL THOSE HELPLESS OLD PEOPLE...
LOOK!
SHOULD WE GET HIM NOW?
NOT YET... WAIT.
WAIT, MY MUSTARD-COLORED BUTT! I'M ON A SLAY RIDE!
BART?!
OHH...
YA-HUH?

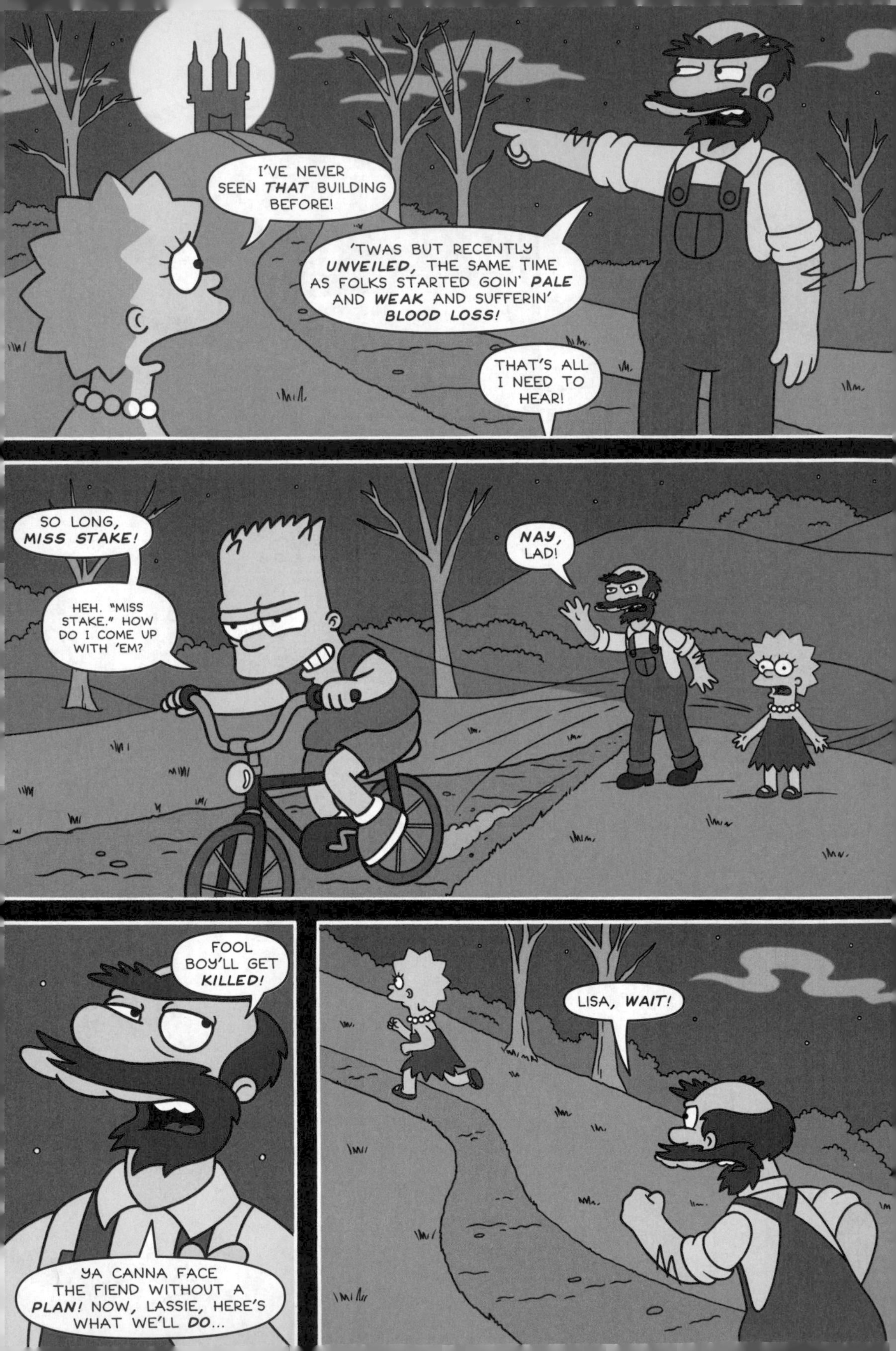
I'VE NEVER SEEN THAT BUILDING BEFORE!
'TWAS BUT RECENTLY UNVEILED, THE SAME TIME AS FOLKS STARTED GOIN' PALE AND WEAK AND SUFFERIN' BLOOD LOSS!
THAT'S ALL I NEED TO HEAR!
SO LONG, MISS STAKE!
HEH. "MISS STAKE." HOW DO I COME UP WITH 'EM?
NAY, LAD!
FOOL BOY'LL GET KILLED!
YA CANNA FACE THE FIEND WITHOUT A PLAN! NOW, LASSIE, HERE'S WHAT WE'LL DO...
LISA, WAIT!

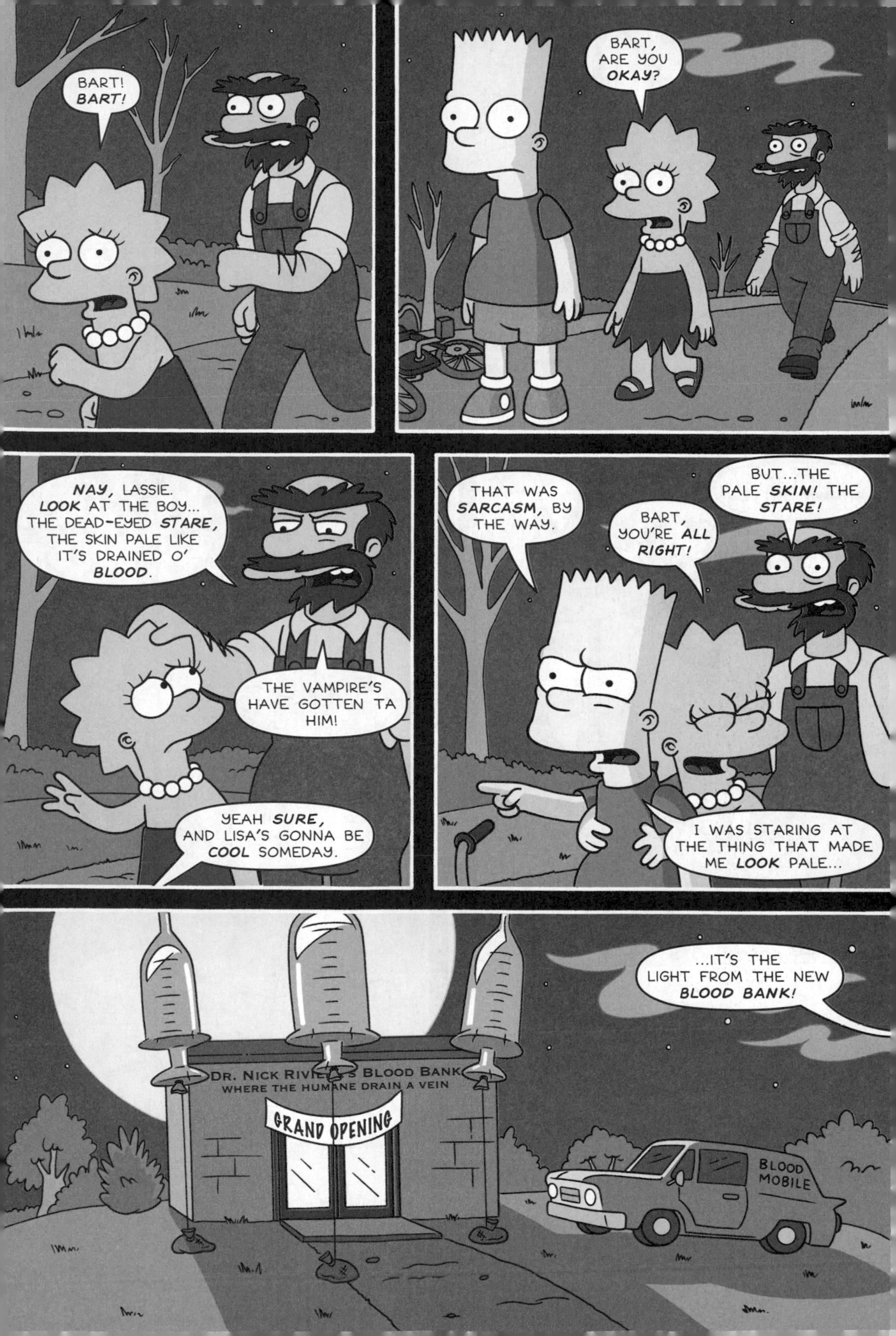
BART! BART!
BART, ARE YOU OKAY?
NAY, LASSIE. LOOK AT THE BOY... THE DEAD-EYED STARE, THE SKIN PALE LIKE IT'S DRAINED O' BLOOD.
THE VAMPIRE'S HAVE GOTTEN TA HIM!
YEAH SURE, AND LISA'S GONNA BE COOL SOMEDAY.
THAT WAS SARCASM, BY THE WAY.
BART, YOU'RE ALL RIGHT!
BUT...THE PALE SKIN! THE STARE!
I WAS STARING AT THE THING THAT MADE ME LOOK PALE...
DR. NICK RIVIE S BLOOD BANK
WHERE THE HUMANE DRAIN A VEIN
GRAND OPENING
BLOOD MOBILE
...IT'S THE LIGHT FROM THE NEW BLOOD BANK!

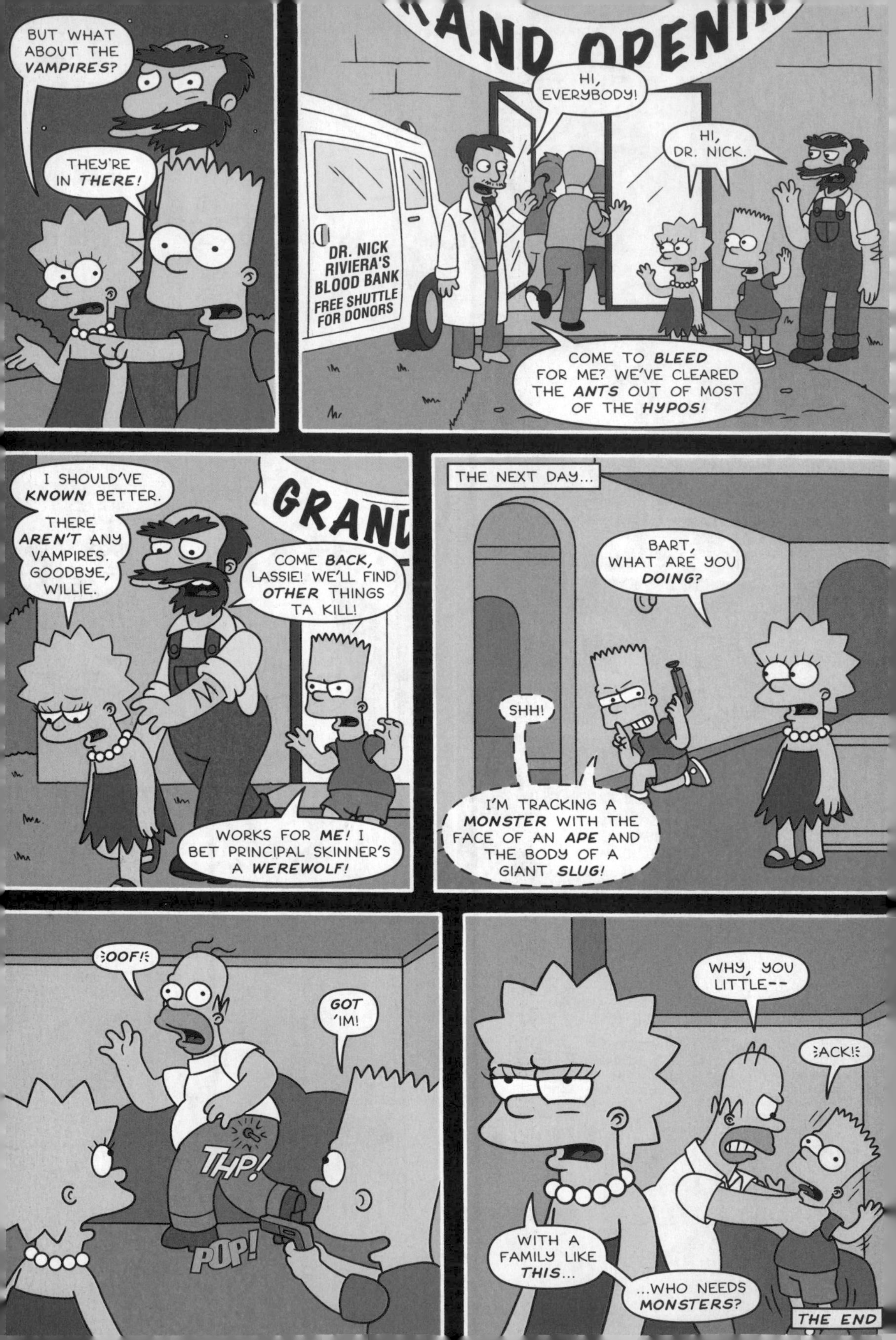
BUT WHAT ABOUT THE VAMPIRES?
THEY'RE IN THERE!
...AND OPENIN...
DR. NICK RIVIERA'S BLOOD BANK FREE SHUTTLE FOR DONORS
HI, EVERYBODY!
HI, DR. NICK.
COME TO BLEED FOR ME? WE'VE CLEARED THE ANTS OUT OF MOST OF THE HYPOS!
I SHOULD'VE KNOWN BETTER.
THERE AREN'T ANY VAMPIRES. GOODBYE, WILLIE.
GRAND
COME BACK, LASSIE! WE'LL FIND OTHER THINGS TA KILL!
WORKS FOR ME! I BET PRINCIPAL SKINNER'S A WEREWOLF!
THE NEXT DAY...
BART, WHAT ARE YOU DOING?
SHH!
I'M TRACKING A MONSTER WITH THE FACE OF AN APE AND THE BODY OF A GIANT SLUG!
OOF!
GOT 'IM!
THP!
POP!
WHY, YOU LITTLE--
ACK!
WITH A FAMILY LIKE THIS...
...WHO NEEDS MONSTERS?
THE END

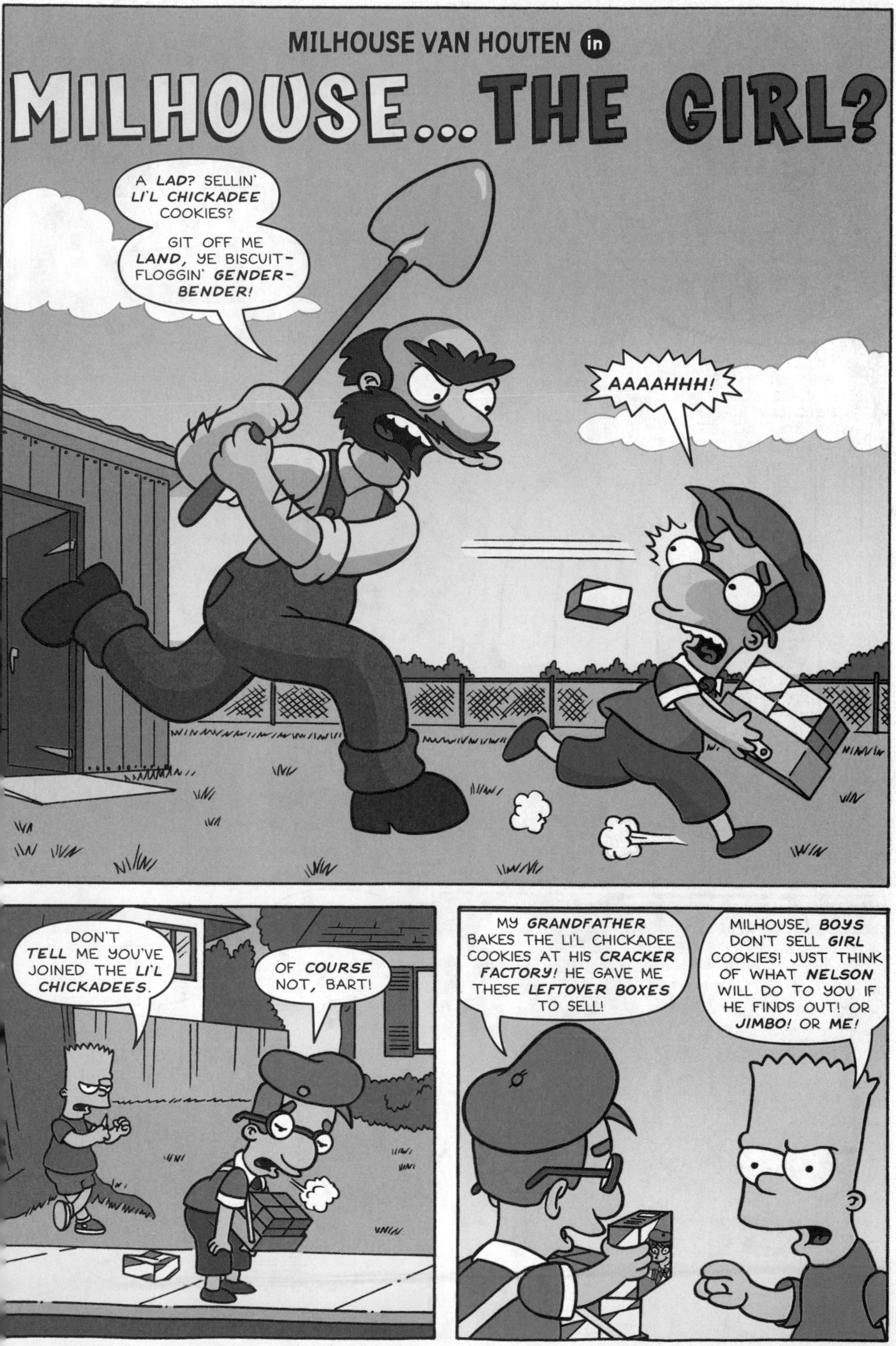
MILHOUSE VAN HOUTEN in
MILHOUSE...THE GIRL?
A LAD? SELLIN' LI'L CHICKADEE COOKIES?
GIT OFF ME LAND, YE BISCUIT-FLOGGIN' GENDER-BENDER!
AAAAHHH!
DON'T TELL ME YOU'VE JOINED THE LI'L CHICKADEES.
OF COURSE NOT, BART!
MY GRANDFATHER BAKES THE LI'L CHICKADEE COOKIES AT HIS CRACKER FACTORY! HE GAVE ME THESE LEFTOVER BOXES TO SELL!
MILHOUSE, BOYS DON'T SELL GIRL COOKIES! JUST THINK OF WHAT NELSON WILL DO TO YOU IF HE FINDS OUT! OR JIMBO! OR ME!

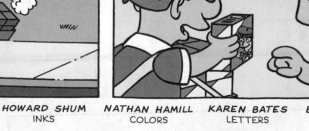

TOM PEYER SCRIPT | MIKE WORLEY PENCILS | HOWARD SHUM INKS | NATHAN HAMILL COLORS | KAREN BATES LETTERS | BILL MORRISON EDITOR

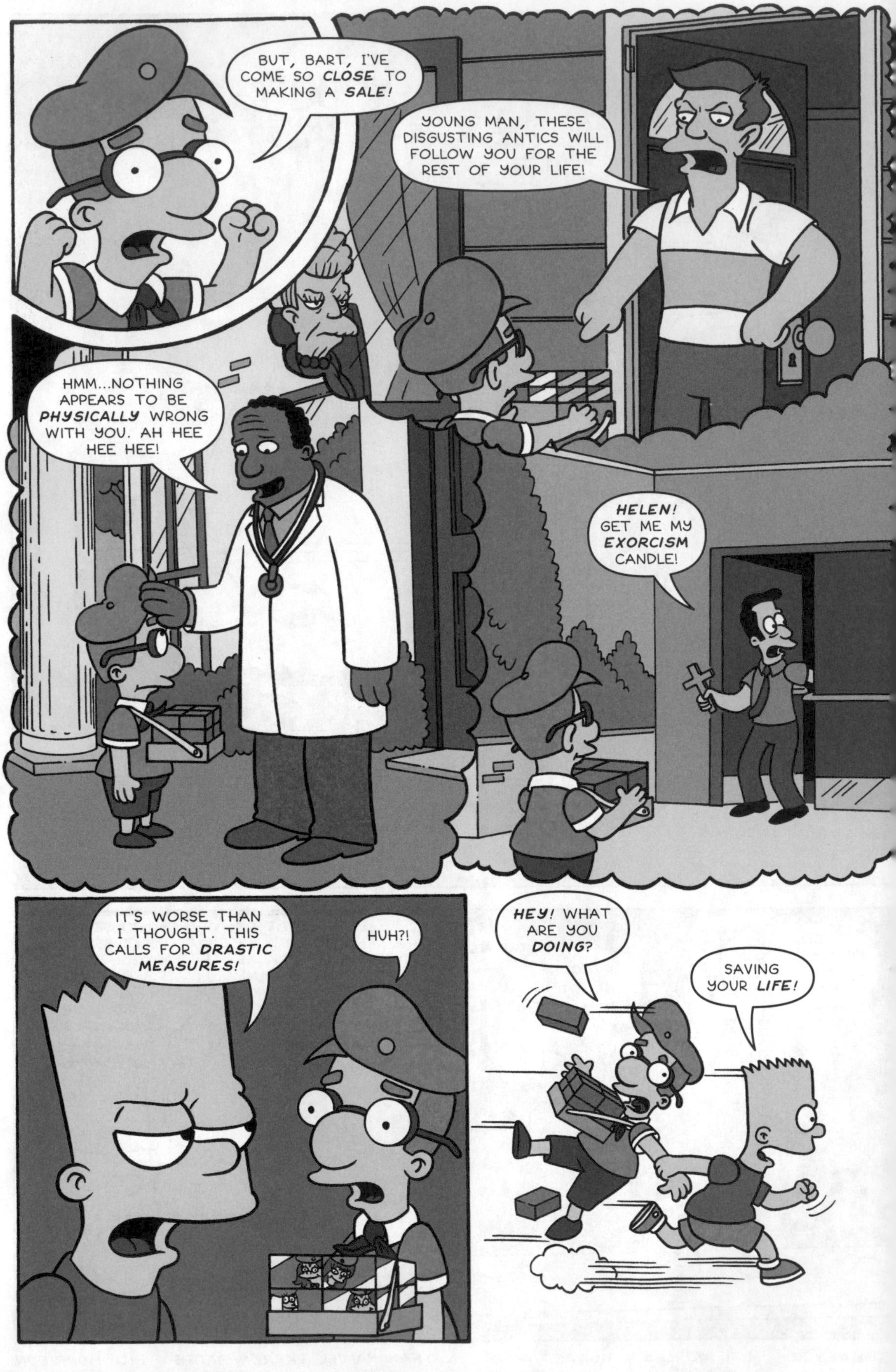
BUT, BART, I'VE COME SO **CLOSE** TO MAKING A **SALE**!
YOUNG MAN, THESE DISGUSTING ANTICS WILL FOLLOW YOU FOR THE REST OF YOUR LIFE!
HMM...NOTHING APPEARS TO BE **PHYSICALLY** WRONG WITH YOU. AH HEE HEE HEE!
HELEN! GET ME MY **EXORCISM** CANDLE!
IT'S WORSE THAN I THOUGHT. THIS CALLS FOR **DRASTIC MEASURES**!
HUH?!
HEY! WHAT ARE YOU **DOING**?
SAVING YOUR **LIFE**!

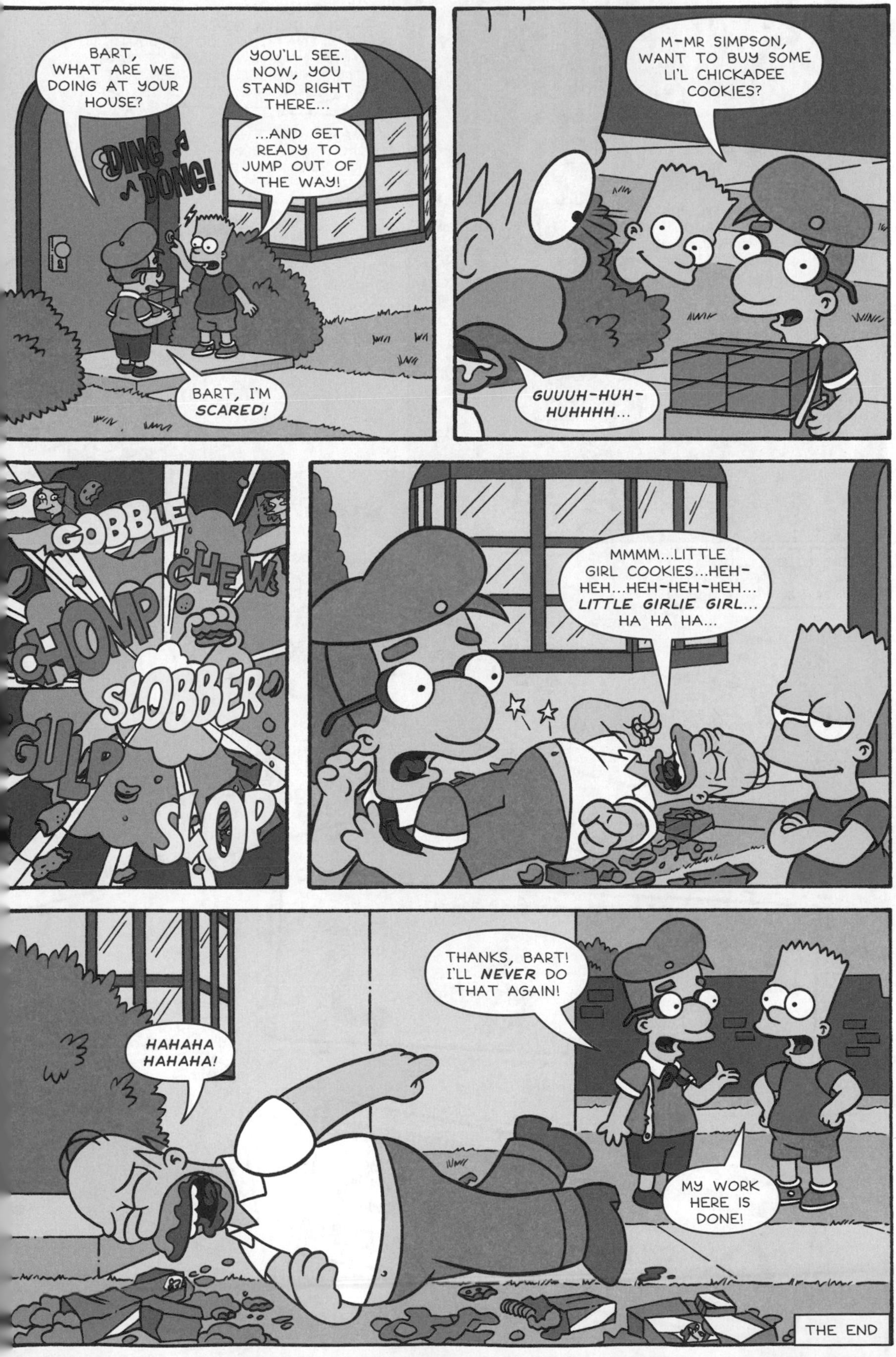
BART, WHAT ARE WE DOING AT YOUR HOUSE?
YOU'LL SEE. NOW, YOU STAND RIGHT THERE...
...AND GET READY TO JUMP OUT OF THE WAY!
DING DONG!
BART, I'M SCARED!
M-MR SIMPSON, WANT TO BUY SOME LI'L CHICKADEE COOKIES?
GUUUH-HUH-HUHHHH...
GOBBLE
CHEW
CHOMP
SLOBBER
GULP
SLOP
MMMM...LITTLE GIRL COOKIES...HEH-HEH...HEH-HEH-HEH... LITTLE GIRLIE GIRL... HA HA HA...
THANKS, BART! I'LL NEVER DO THAT AGAIN!
HAHAHA HAHAHA!
MY WORK HERE IS DONE!
THE END

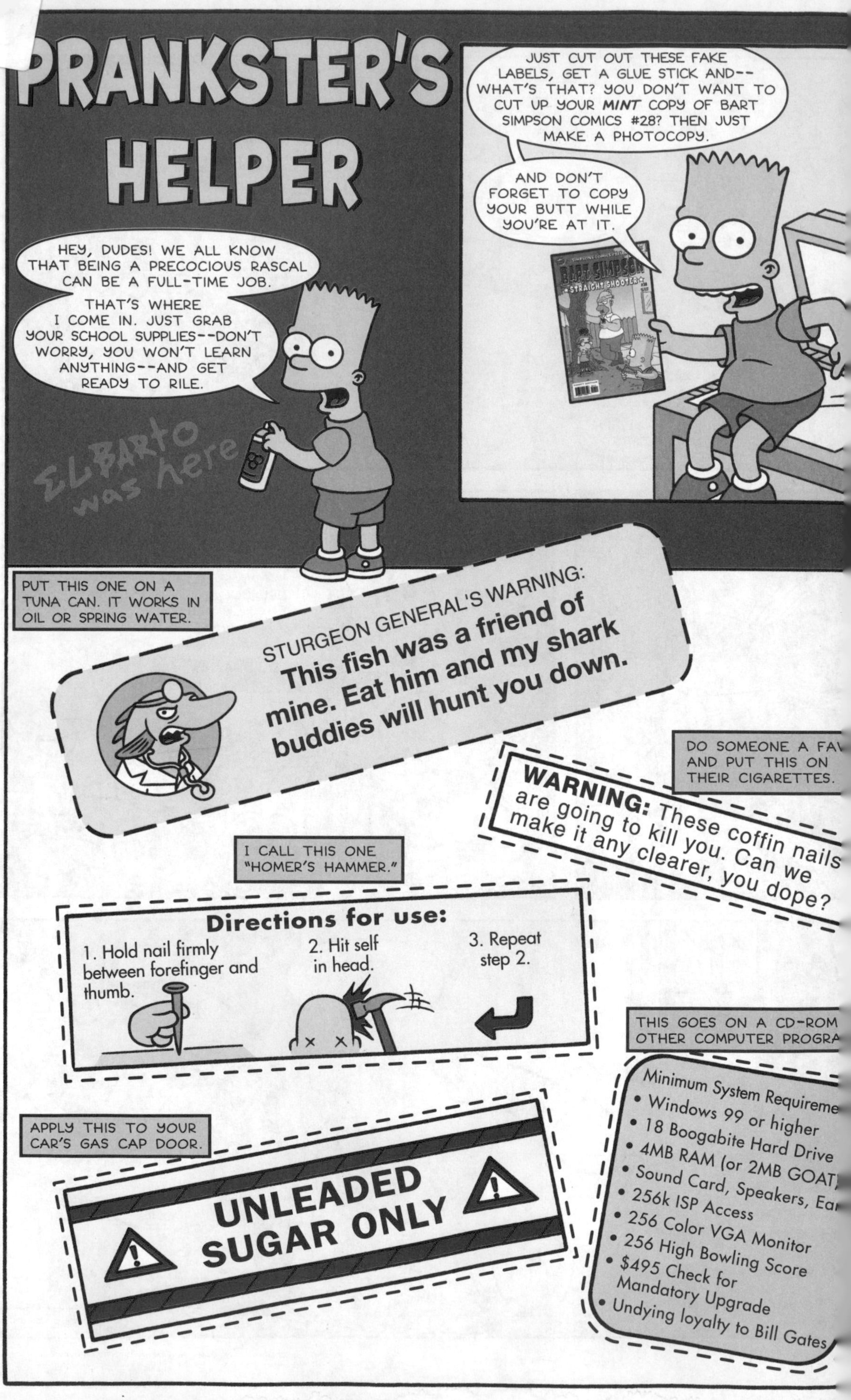
PRANKSTER'S HELPER
HEY, DUDES! WE ALL KNOW THAT BEING A PRECOCIOUS RASCAL CAN BE A FULL-TIME JOB.
THAT'S WHERE I COME IN. JUST GRAB YOUR SCHOOL SUPPLIES--DON'T WORRY, YOU WON'T LEARN ANYTHING--AND GET READY TO RILE.
EL BARTO was here
JUST CUT OUT THESE FAKE LABELS, GET A GLUE STICK AND--WHAT'S THAT? YOU DON'T WANT TO CUT UP YOUR *MINT* COPY OF BART SIMPSON COMICS #28? THEN JUST MAKE A PHOTOCOPY.
AND DON'T FORGET TO COPY YOUR BUTT WHILE YOU'RE AT IT.
BART SIMPSON
STRAIGHT SHOOTER
PUT THIS ONE ON A TUNA CAN. IT WORKS IN OIL OR SPRING WATER.
STURGEON GENERAL'S WARNING:
This fish was a friend of mine. Eat him and my shark buddies will hunt you down.
DO SOMEONE A FA
AND PUT THIS ON THEIR CIGARETTES.
WARNING: These coffin nails are going to kill you. Can we make it any clearer, you dope?
I CALL THIS ONE "HOMER'S HAMMER."
Directions for use:
1. Hold nail firmly between forefinger and thumb.
2. Hit self in head.
3. Repeat step 2.
THIS GOES ON A CD-ROM
OTHER COMPUTER PROGRA
Minimum System Requireme
• Windows 99 or higher
• 18 Boogabite Hard Drive
• 4MB RAM (or 2MB GOAT
• Sound Card, Speakers, Ea
• 256k ISP Access
• 256 Color VGA Monitor
• 256 High Bowling Score
• $495 Check for Mandatory Upgrade
• Undying loyalty to Bill Gates
APPLY THIS TO YOUR CAR'S GAS CAP DOOR.
UNLEADED SUGAR ONLY

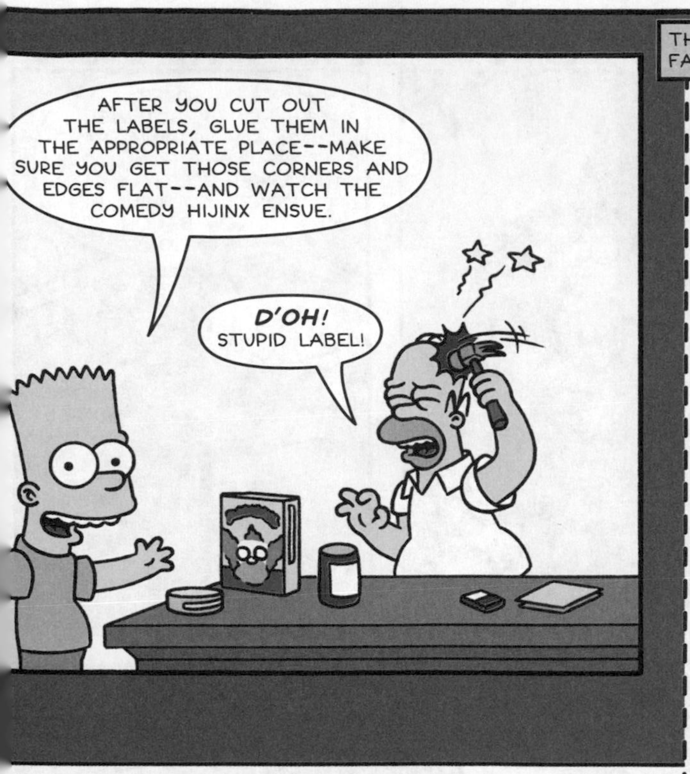
AFTER YOU CUT OUT THE LABELS, GLUE THEM IN THE APPROPRIATE PLACE--MAKE SURE YOU GET THOSE CORNERS AND EDGES FLAT--AND WATCH THE COMEDY HIJINX ENSUE.
D'OH! STUPID LABEL!

THIS ONE GOES ON YOUR FAVORITE SUGAR-FILLED CEREAL.

Nutrition Facts

Serving Size: One bowl

Amount	Cereal	with Milk
Calories	130	190
from Fat	30	50
from Head	25	45
	% Daily Value*	
Total Fat 4g	5%	3%
Saturated Fat .5g	3%	3%
Polyunsaturated Fat 1g		
Phonyunnatural Fat 1g		
Sodium 210mg	9%	11%
Potassium 45mg	1%	7%
Balonium 100mg	6%	18%
Total Carbohydrate 24g	8%	10%
Dietary Fiber 1g		
Carpet Fiber 2g		
Protein 1g		
Soylent Green 5g		
Vitamin A	10%	15%
Vitamin B12	10%	15%
Vitamin B52	10%	15%
Calcium	10%	15%
Niacin	10%	15%
Thiamin	10%	15%
Ropethemin	10%	15%
Vitamin G	10%	15%
Vitamin PG13	10%	15%
Vitamin R	10%	15%
Phosphorus	10%	15%
Magnesium	10%	15%
Gamma Rays	10%	15%
Iron	10%	15%
Copper	10%	15%
Aluminum	10%	15%
Gold	0%	0%
Riboflavin	10%	15%
Frinkinhoiven	10%	15%
Chemical X	10%	15%

*Percentages based on a 2,000 calorie diet. If intake is higher, numbers should be adjusted down, though you probably don't care about nutrition anyway, so why waste time on a fat pig like you?

STICK THIS ONE TO A SOUP CAN.

Easy Casserole Recipe

1. Heat soup contents in frying pan

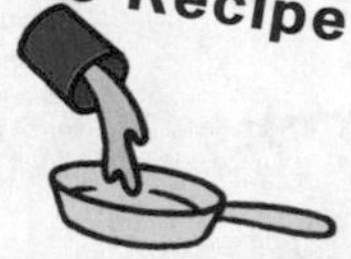

2. Add fish, poultry or beef, making sure you know which it is.

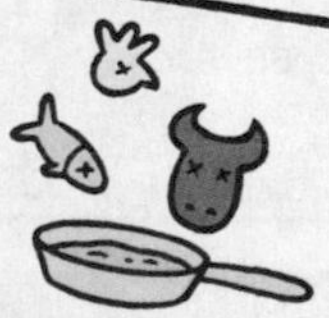

3. Mix in 2 cups white rice, some frozen vegetables, maybe a potato.

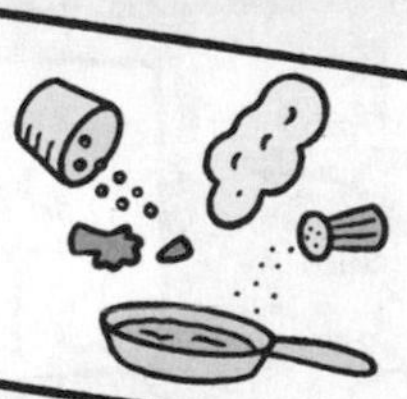

4. Simmer.

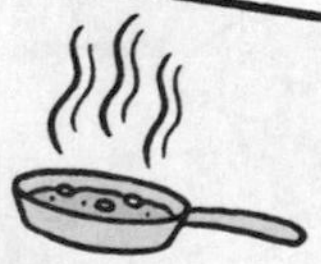

. Pour into disposal
d call for pizza
livery.

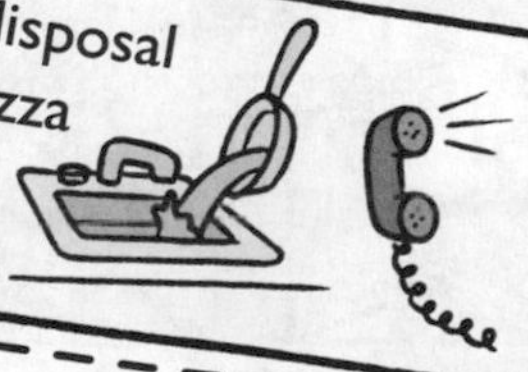

BART SIMPSON IN BART GOES TO THE MOVIES

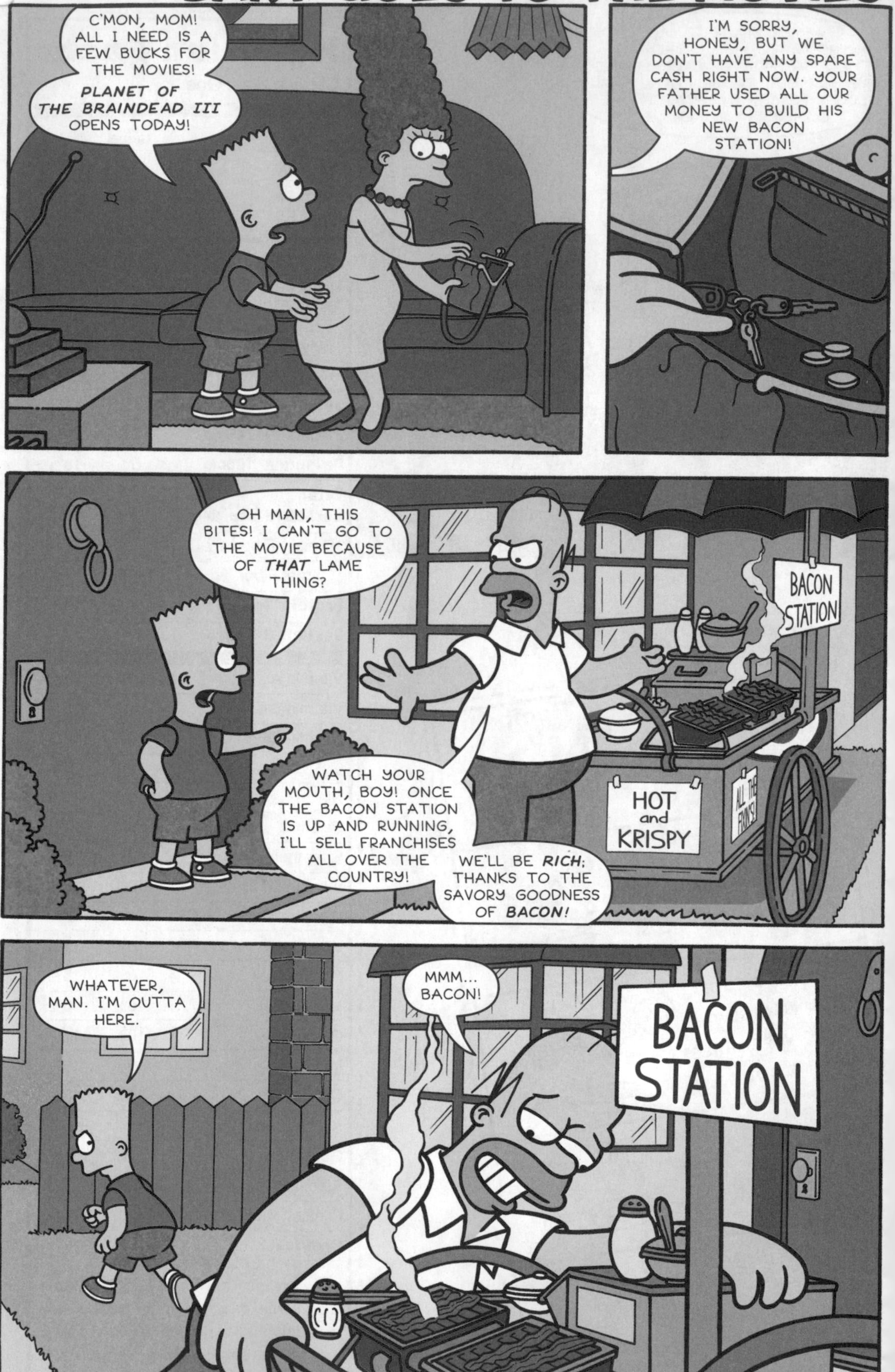
C'MON, MOM! ALL I NEED IS A FEW BUCKS FOR THE MOVIES!
PLANET OF THE BRAINDEAD III OPENS TODAY!
I'M SORRY, HONEY, BUT WE DON'T HAVE ANY SPARE CASH RIGHT NOW. YOUR FATHER USED ALL OUR MONEY TO BUILD HIS NEW BACON STATION!
OH MAN, THIS BITES! I CAN'T GO TO THE MOVIE BECAUSE OF *THAT* LAME THING?
BACON STATION
WATCH YOUR MOUTH, BOY! ONCE THE BACON STATION IS UP AND RUNNING, I'LL SELL FRANCHISES ALL OVER THE COUNTRY!
WE'LL BE *RICH*; THANKS TO THE SAVORY GOODNESS OF *BACON*!
HOT and KRISPY
WHATEVER, MAN. I'M OUTTA HERE.
MMM... BACON!
BACON STATION

BRYAN UHLENBROCK SCRIPT
MIKE DECARLO PENCILS
PHYLLIS NOVIN INKS
NATHAN HAMILL COLORS
KAREN BATES LETTERS
BILL MORRISON EDITOR

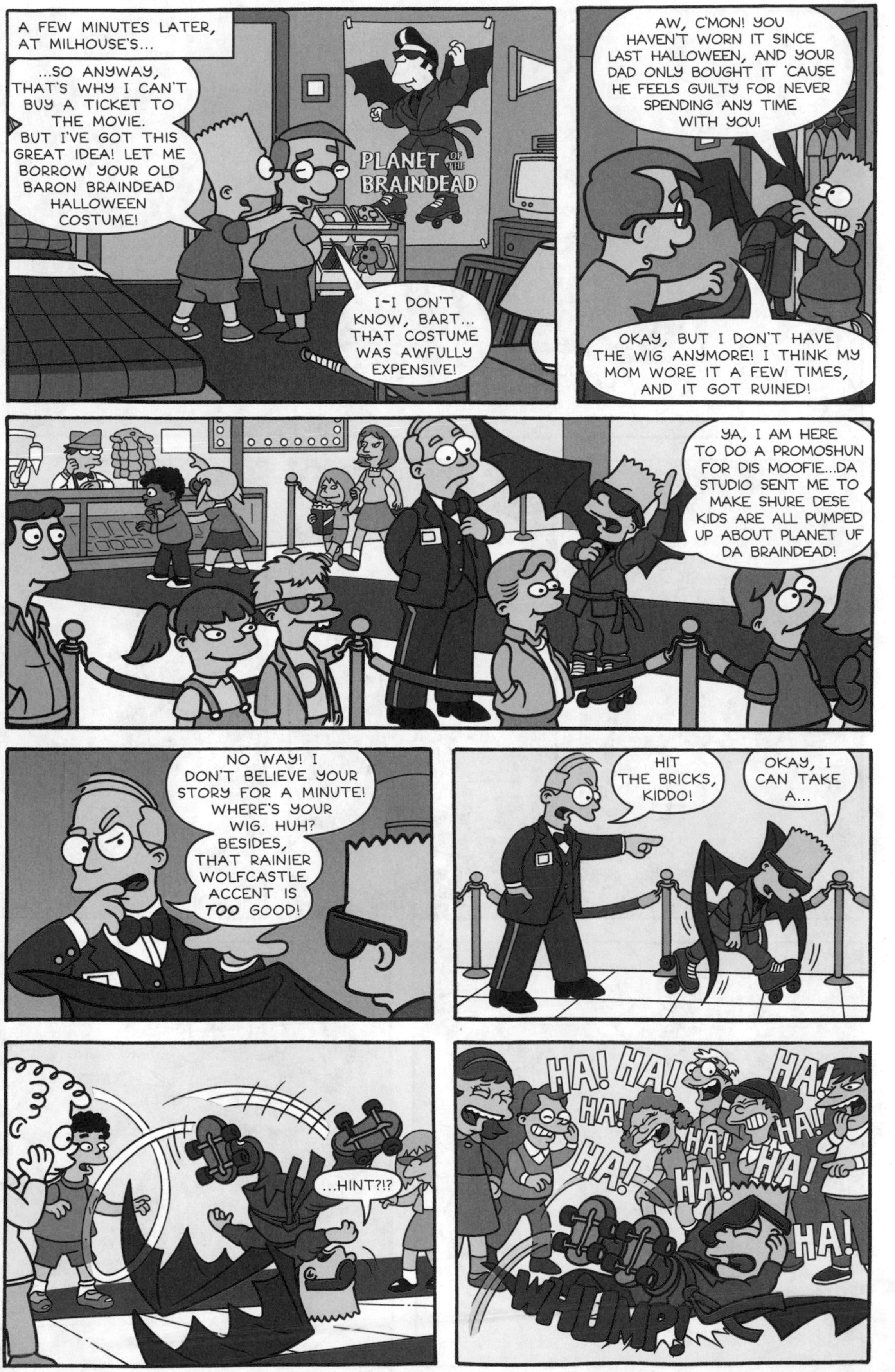

A FEW MINUTES LATER, AT MILHOUSE'S...
...SO ANYWAY, THAT'S WHY I CAN'T BUY A TICKET TO THE MOVIE. BUT I'VE GOT THIS GREAT IDEA! LET ME BORROW YOUR OLD BARON BRAINDEAD HALLOWEEN COSTUME!
PLANET OF THE BRAINDEAD
I-I DON'T KNOW, BART... THAT COSTUME WAS AWFULLY EXPENSIVE!
AW, C'MON! YOU HAVEN'T WORN IT SINCE LAST HALLOWEEN, AND YOUR DAD ONLY BOUGHT IT 'CAUSE HE FEELS GUILTY FOR NEVER SPENDING ANY TIME WITH YOU!
OKAY, BUT I DON'T HAVE THE WIG ANYMORE! I THINK MY MOM WORE IT A FEW TIMES, AND IT GOT RUINED!
YA, I AM HERE TO DO A PROMOSHUN FOR DIS MOOFIE...DA STUDIO SENT ME TO MAKE SHURE DESE KIDS ARE ALL PUMPED UP ABOUT PLANET UF DA BRAINDEAD!
NO WAY! I DON'T BELIEVE YOUR STORY FOR A MINUTE! WHERE'S YOUR WIG. HUH? BESIDES, THAT RAINIER WOLFCASTLE ACCENT IS *TOO* GOOD!
HIT THE BRICKS, KIDDO!
OKAY, I CAN TAKE A...
...HINT?!?
HA! HA! HA! HA! HA! HA! HA! HA! HA! HA!
WHUMP!

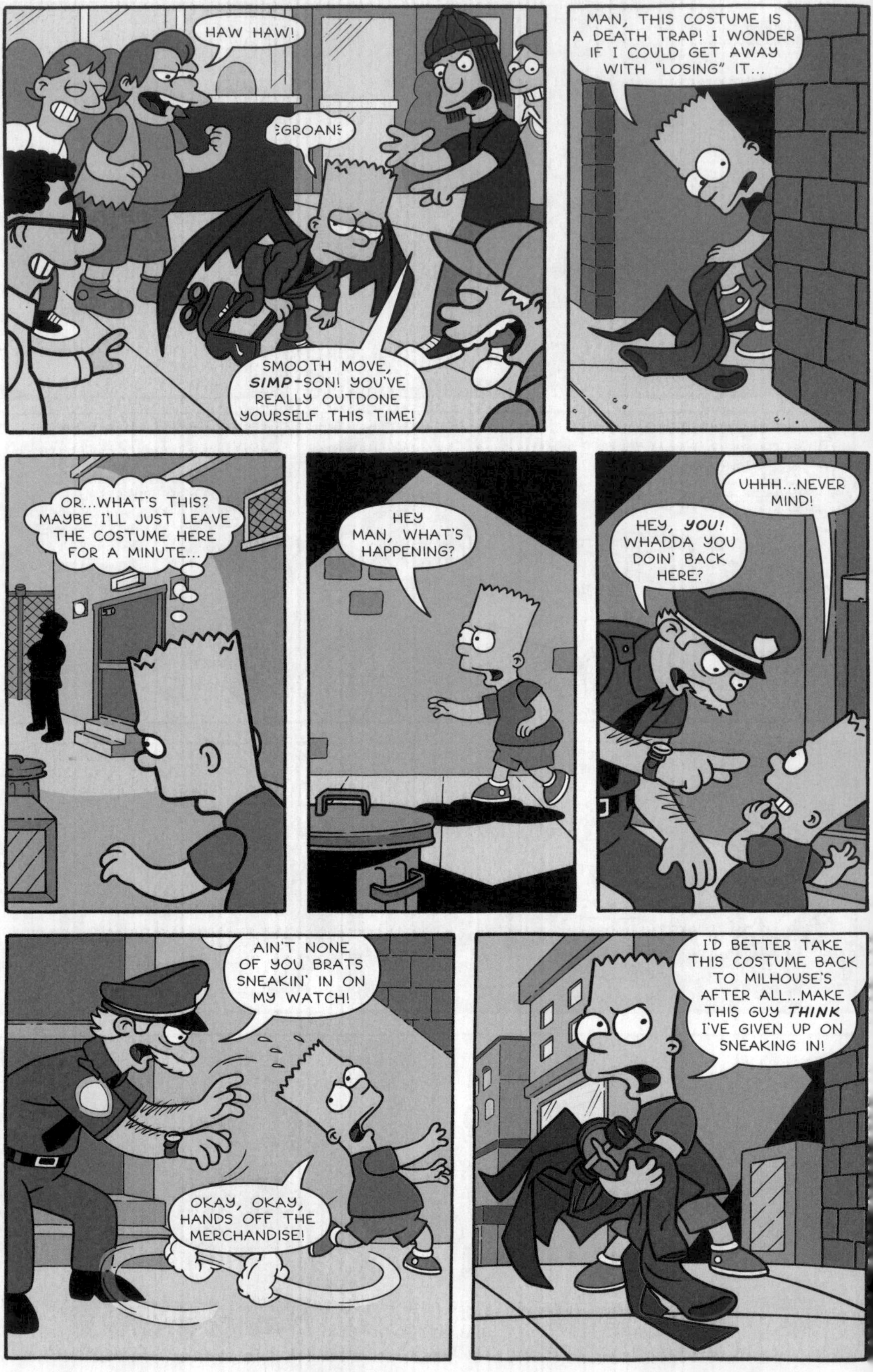
HAW HAW!
GROAN
SMOOTH MOVE, SIMP-SON! YOU'VE REALLY OUTDONE YOURSELF THIS TIME!
MAN, THIS COSTUME IS A DEATH TRAP! I WONDER IF I COULD GET AWAY WITH "LOSING" IT...
OR...WHAT'S THIS? MAYBE I'LL JUST LEAVE THE COSTUME HERE FOR A MINUTE...
HEY MAN, WHAT'S HAPPENING?
HEY, YOU! WHADDA YOU DOIN' BACK HERE?
UHHH...NEVER MIND!
AIN'T NONE OF YOU BRATS SNEAKIN' IN ON MY WATCH!
OKAY, OKAY, HANDS OFF THE MERCHANDISE!
I'D BETTER TAKE THIS COSTUME BACK TO MILHOUSE'S AFTER ALL...MAKE THIS GUY THINK I'VE GIVEN UP ON SNEAKING IN!

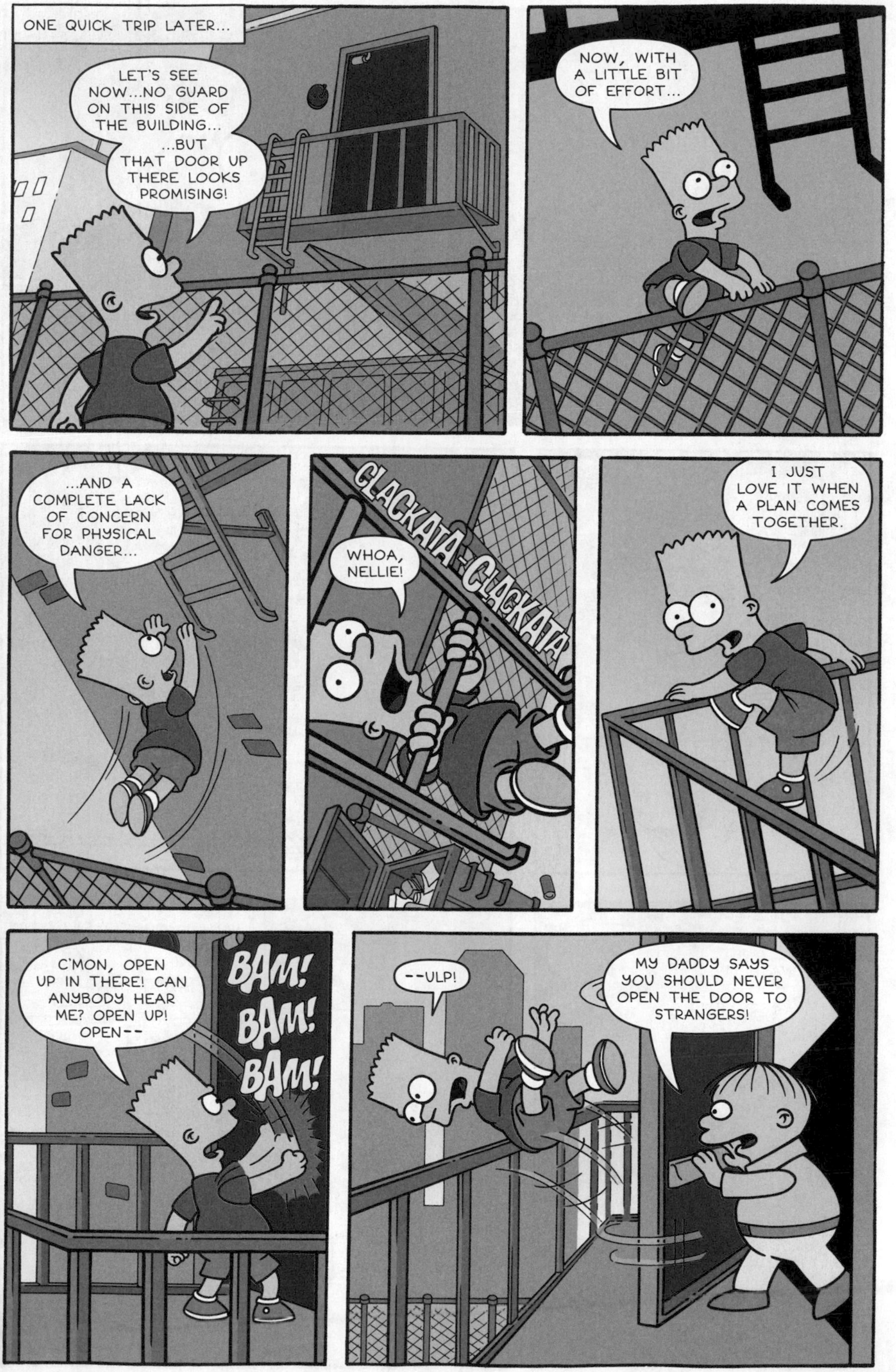
ONE QUICK TRIP LATER...
LET'S SEE NOW...NO GUARD ON THIS SIDE OF THE BUILDING...
...BUT THAT DOOR UP THERE LOOKS PROMISING!
NOW, WITH A LITTLE BIT OF EFFORT...
...AND A COMPLETE LACK OF CONCERN FOR PHYSICAL DANGER...
CLACKATA-CLACKATA-CLACKATA
WHOA, NELLIE!
I JUST LOVE IT WHEN A PLAN COMES TOGETHER.
C'MON, OPEN UP IN THERE! CAN ANYBODY HEAR ME? OPEN UP! OPEN--
BAM! BAM! BAM!
--ULP!
MY DADDY SAYS YOU SHOULD NEVER OPEN THE DOOR TO STRANGERS!

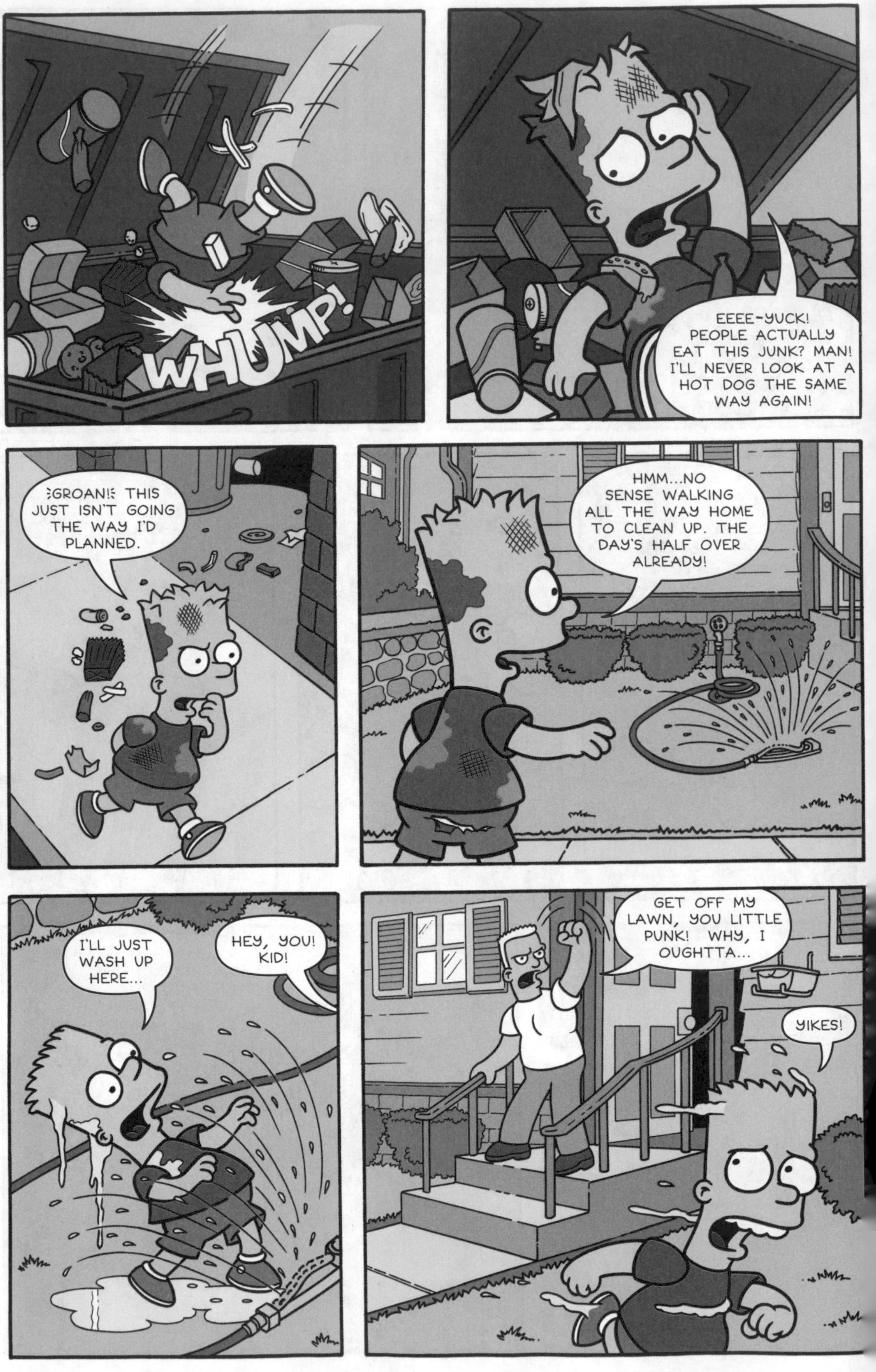
WHUMP!
EEEE-YUCK! PEOPLE ACTUALLY EAT THIS JUNK? MAN! I'LL NEVER LOOK AT A HOT DOG THE SAME WAY AGAIN!
⁝GROAN!⁝ THIS JUST ISN'T GOING THE WAY I'D PLANNED.
HMM...NO SENSE WALKING ALL THE WAY HOME TO CLEAN UP. THE DAY'S HALF OVER ALREADY!
I'LL JUST WASH UP HERE...
HEY, YOU! KID!
GET OFF MY LAWN, YOU LITTLE PUNK! WHY, I OUGHTTA...
YIKES!

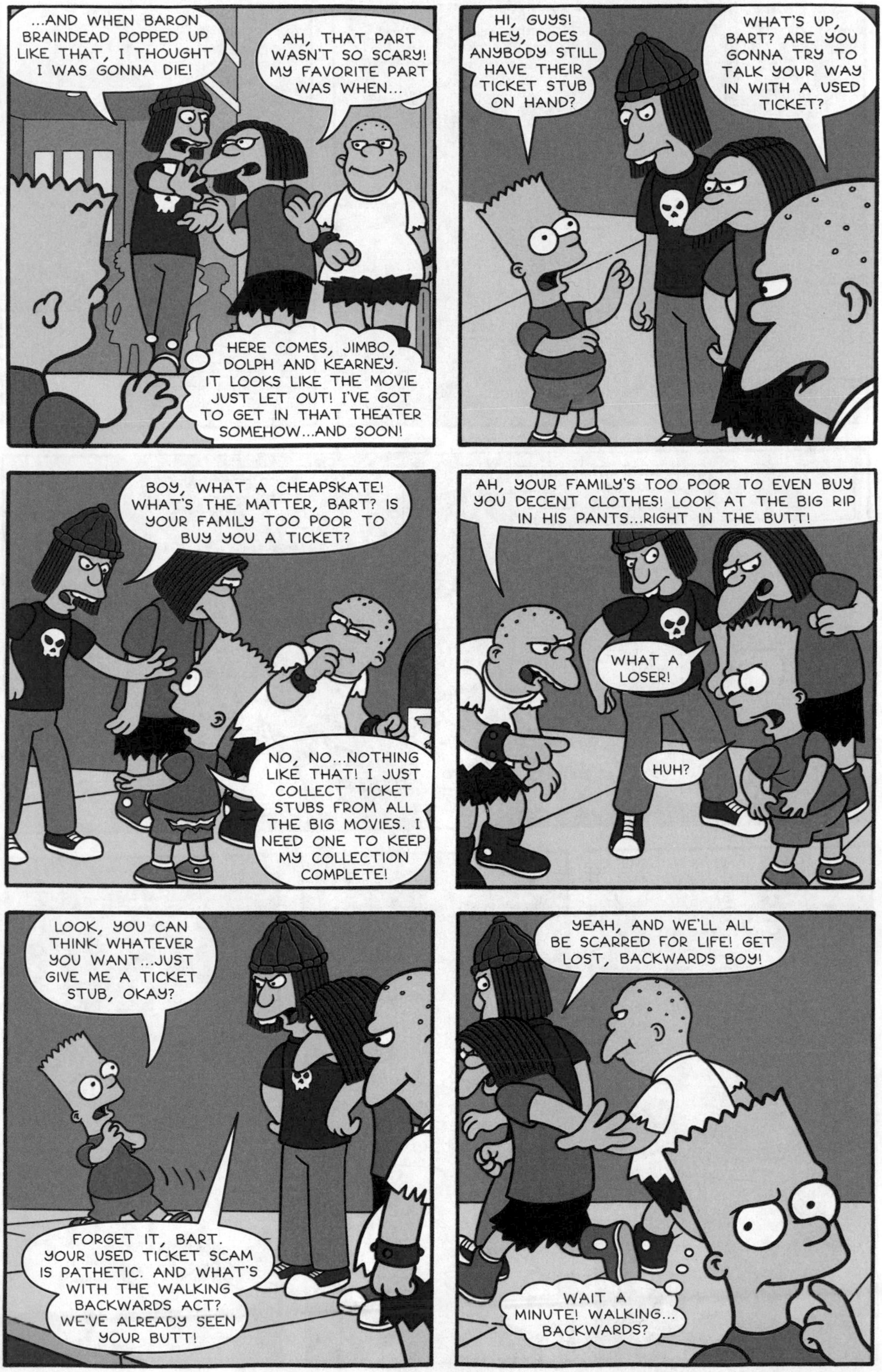
...AND WHEN BARON BRAINDEAD POPPED UP LIKE THAT, I THOUGHT I WAS GONNA DIE!
AH, THAT PART WASN'T SO SCARY! MY FAVORITE PART WAS WHEN...
HERE COMES, JIMBO, DOLPH AND KEARNEY. IT LOOKS LIKE THE MOVIE JUST LET OUT! I'VE GOT TO GET IN THAT THEATER SOMEHOW...AND SOON!
HI, GUYS! HEY, DOES ANYBODY STILL HAVE THEIR TICKET STUB ON HAND?
WHAT'S UP, BART? ARE YOU GONNA TRY TO TALK YOUR WAY IN WITH A USED TICKET?
BOY, WHAT A CHEAPSKATE! WHAT'S THE MATTER, BART? IS YOUR FAMILY TOO POOR TO BUY YOU A TICKET?
NO, NO...NOTHING LIKE THAT! I JUST COLLECT TICKET STUBS FROM ALL THE BIG MOVIES. I NEED ONE TO KEEP MY COLLECTION COMPLETE!
AH, YOUR FAMILY'S TOO POOR TO EVEN BUY YOU DECENT CLOTHES! LOOK AT THE BIG RIP IN HIS PANTS...RIGHT IN THE BUTT!
WHAT A LOSER!
HUH?
LOOK, YOU CAN THINK WHATEVER YOU WANT...JUST GIVE ME A TICKET STUB, OKAY?
FORGET IT, BART. YOUR USED TICKET SCAM IS PATHETIC. AND WHAT'S WITH THE WALKING BACKWARDS ACT? WE'VE ALREADY SEEN YOUR BUTT!
YEAH, AND WE'LL ALL BE SCARRED FOR LIFE! GET LOST, BACKWARDS BOY!
WAIT A MINUTE! WALKING... BACKWARDS?

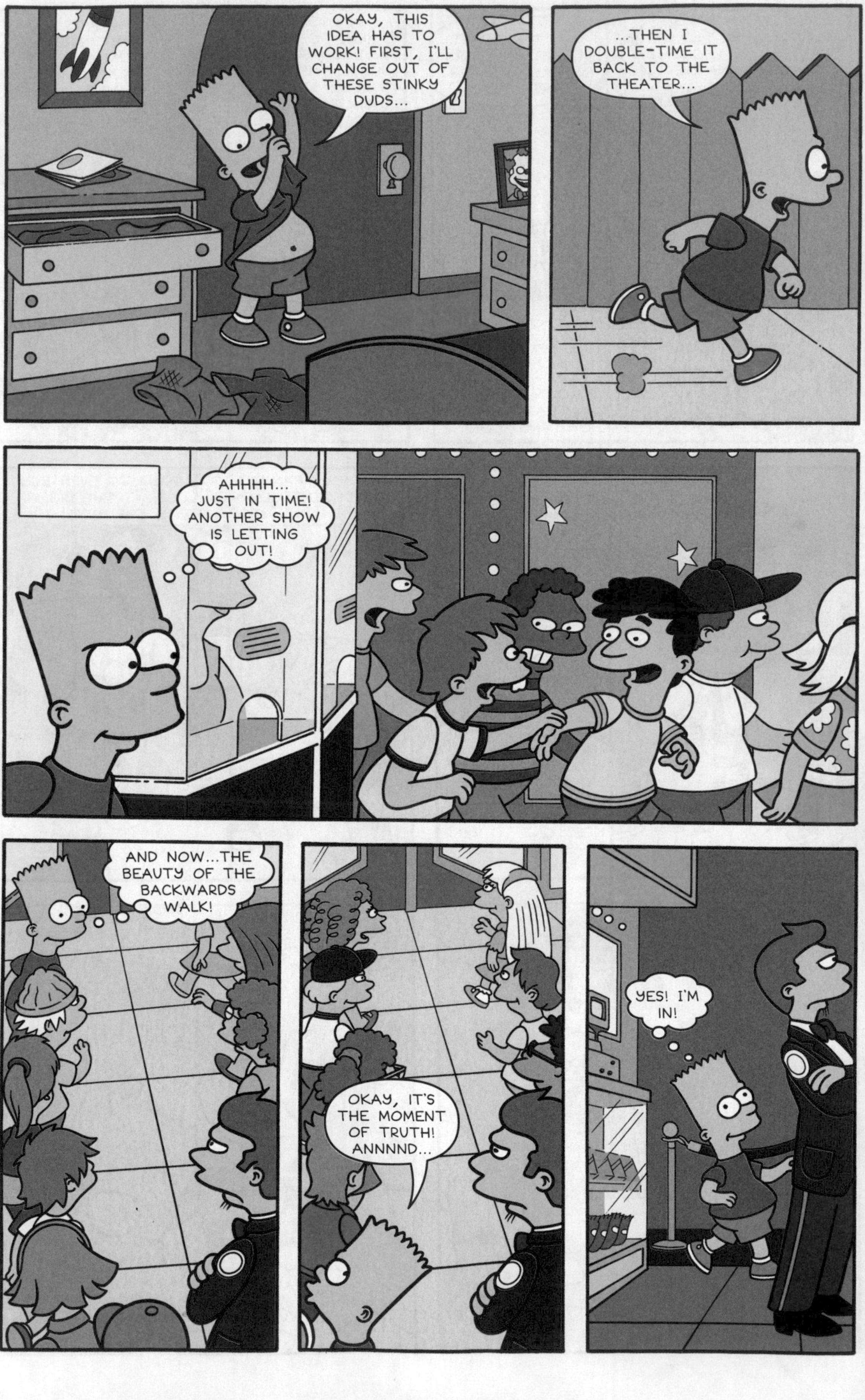
OKAY, THIS IDEA HAS TO WORK! FIRST, I'LL CHANGE OUT OF THESE STINKY DUDS...
...THEN I DOUBLE-TIME IT BACK TO THE THEATER...
AHHHH... JUST IN TIME! ANOTHER SHOW IS LETTING OUT!
AND NOW...THE BEAUTY OF THE BACKWARDS WALK!
OKAY, IT'S THE MOMENT OF TRUTH! ANNNND...
YES! I'M IN!

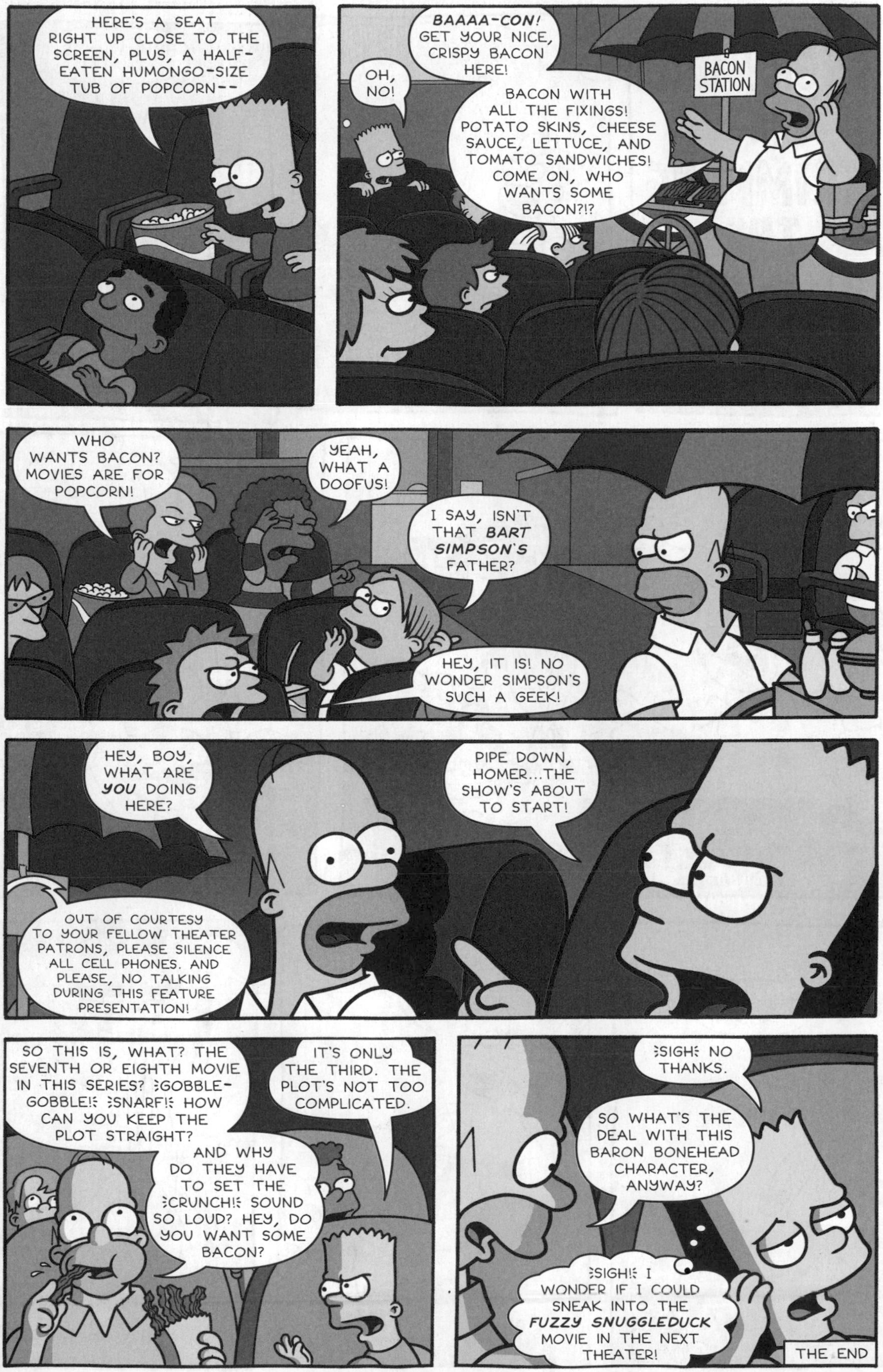
HERE'S A SEAT RIGHT UP CLOSE TO THE SCREEN, PLUS, A HALF-EATEN HUMONGO-SIZE TUB OF POPCORN--
BAAAA-CON! GET YOUR NICE, CRISPY BACON HERE!
OH, NO!
BACON STATION
BACON WITH ALL THE FIXINGS! POTATO SKINS, CHEESE SAUCE, LETTUCE, AND TOMATO SANDWICHES! COME ON, WHO WANTS SOME BACON?!?
WHO WANTS BACON? MOVIES ARE FOR POPCORN!
YEAH, WHAT A DOOFUS!
I SAY, ISN'T THAT BART SIMPSON'S FATHER?
HEY, IT IS! NO WONDER SIMPSON'S SUCH A GEEK!
HEY, BOY, WHAT ARE YOU DOING HERE?
PIPE DOWN, HOMER...THE SHOW'S ABOUT TO START!
OUT OF COURTESY TO YOUR FELLOW THEATER PATRONS, PLEASE SILENCE ALL CELL PHONES. AND PLEASE, NO TALKING DURING THIS FEATURE PRESENTATION!
SO THIS IS, WHAT? THE SEVENTH OR EIGHTH MOVIE IN THIS SERIES? GOBBLE-GOBBLE! SNARF! HOW CAN YOU KEEP THE PLOT STRAIGHT?
IT'S ONLY THE THIRD. THE PLOT'S NOT TOO COMPLICATED.
AND WHY DO THEY HAVE TO SET THE CRUNCH! SOUND SO LOUD? HEY, DO YOU WANT SOME BACON?
SIGH NO THANKS.
SO WHAT'S THE DEAL WITH THIS BARON BONEHEAD CHARACTER, ANYWAY?
SIGH! I WONDER IF I COULD SNEAK INTO THE FUZZY SNUGGLEDUCK MOVIE IN THE NEXT THEATER!
THE END

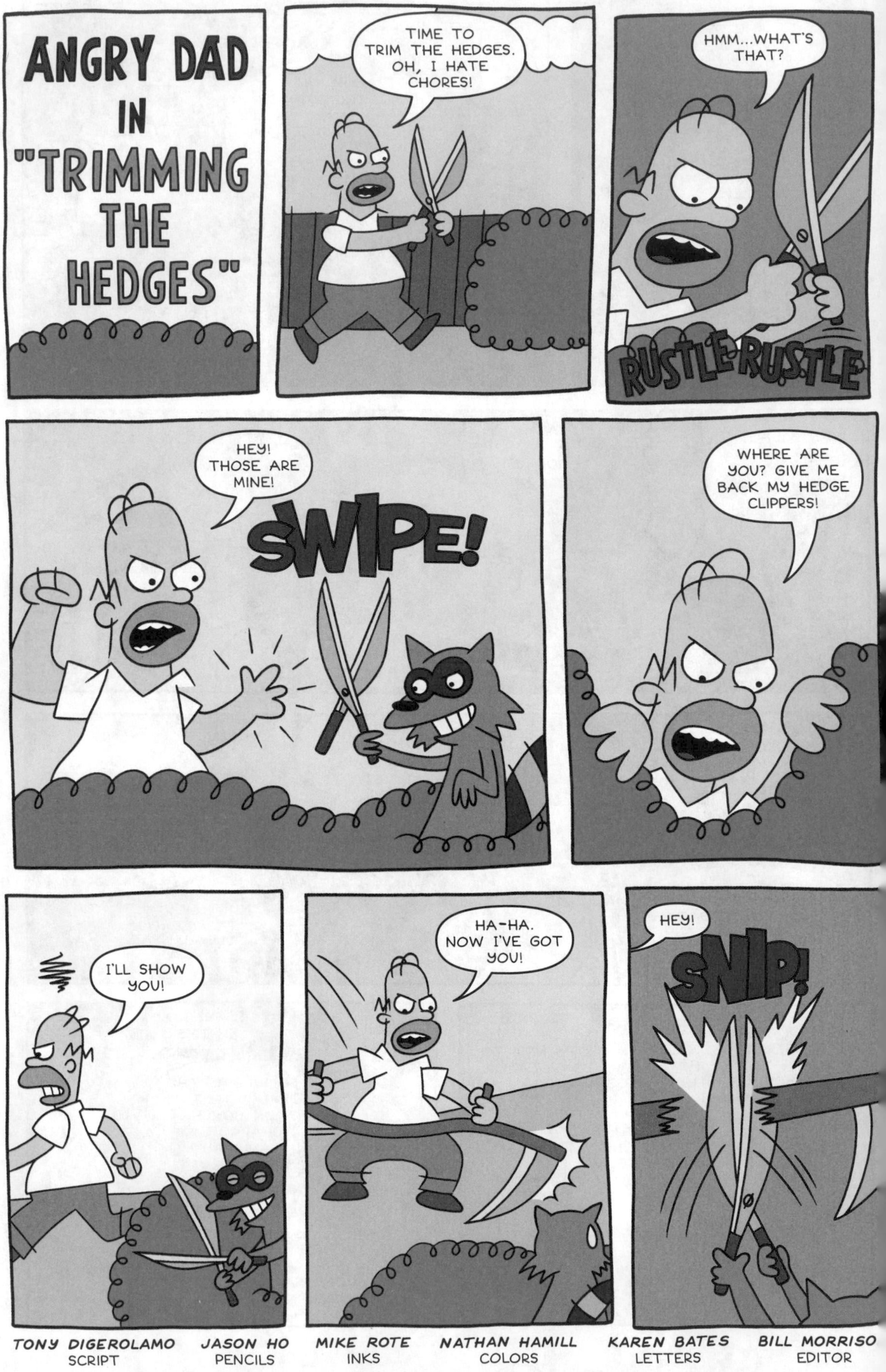
ANGRY DAD IN "TRIMMING THE HEDGES"
TIME TO TRIM THE HEDGES. OH, I HATE CHORES!
HMM...WHAT'S THAT?
RUSTLE RUSTLE
HEY! THOSE ARE MINE!
SWIPE!
WHERE ARE YOU? GIVE ME BACK MY HEDGE CLIPPERS!
I'LL SHOW YOU!
HA-HA. NOW I'VE GOT YOU!
HEY!
SNIP!

TONY DIGEROLAMO SCRIPT | *JASON HO* PENCILS | *MIKE ROTE* INKS | *NATHAN HAMILL* COLORS | *KAREN BATES* LETTERS | *BILL MORRISO* EDITOR

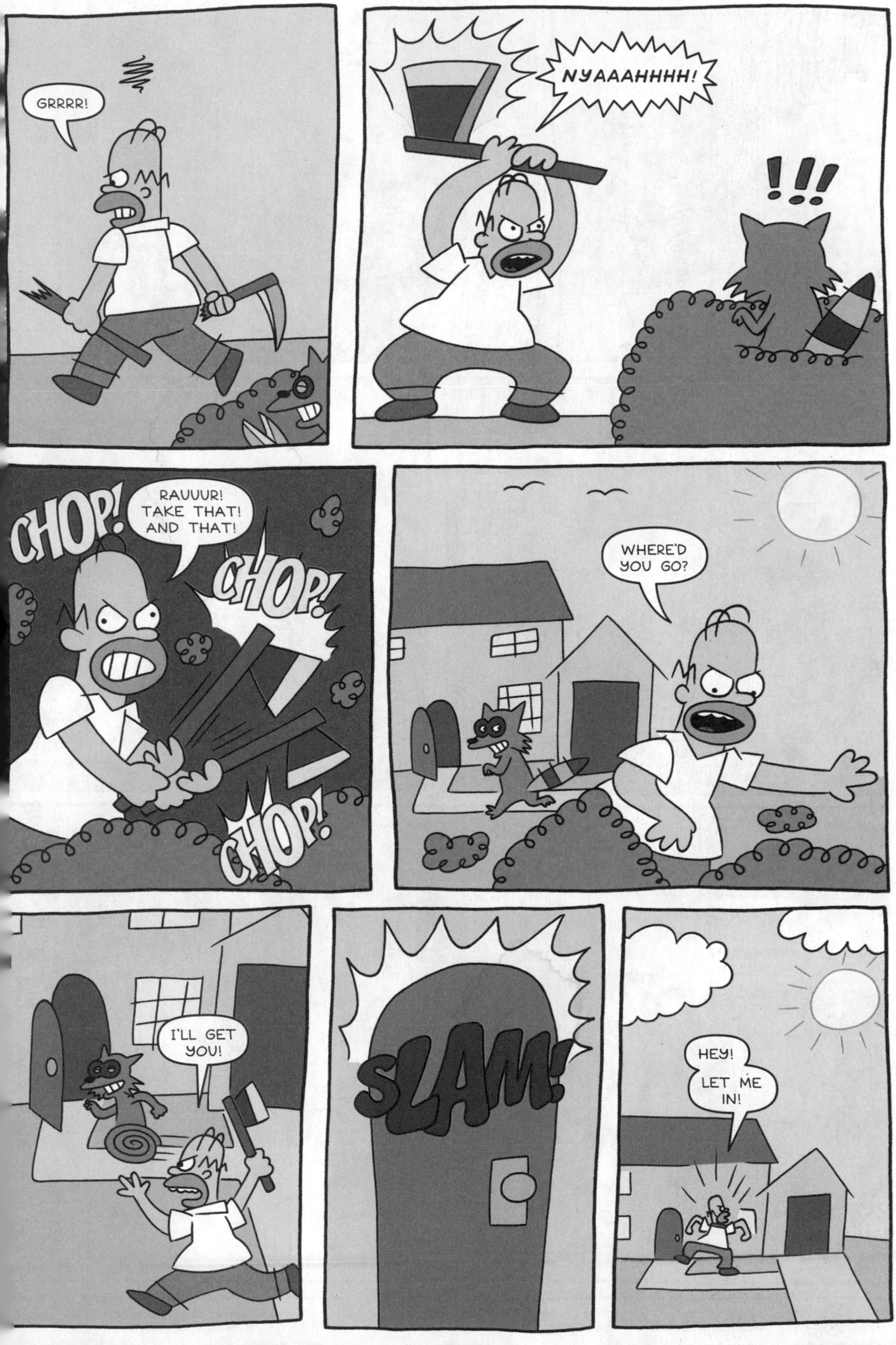

GRRRR!
NYAAAHHHH!
!!!
CHOP!
RAUUUR! TAKE THAT! AND THAT!
CHOP!
CHOP!
WHERE'D YOU GO?
I'LL GET YOU!
SLAM!
HEY! LET ME IN!

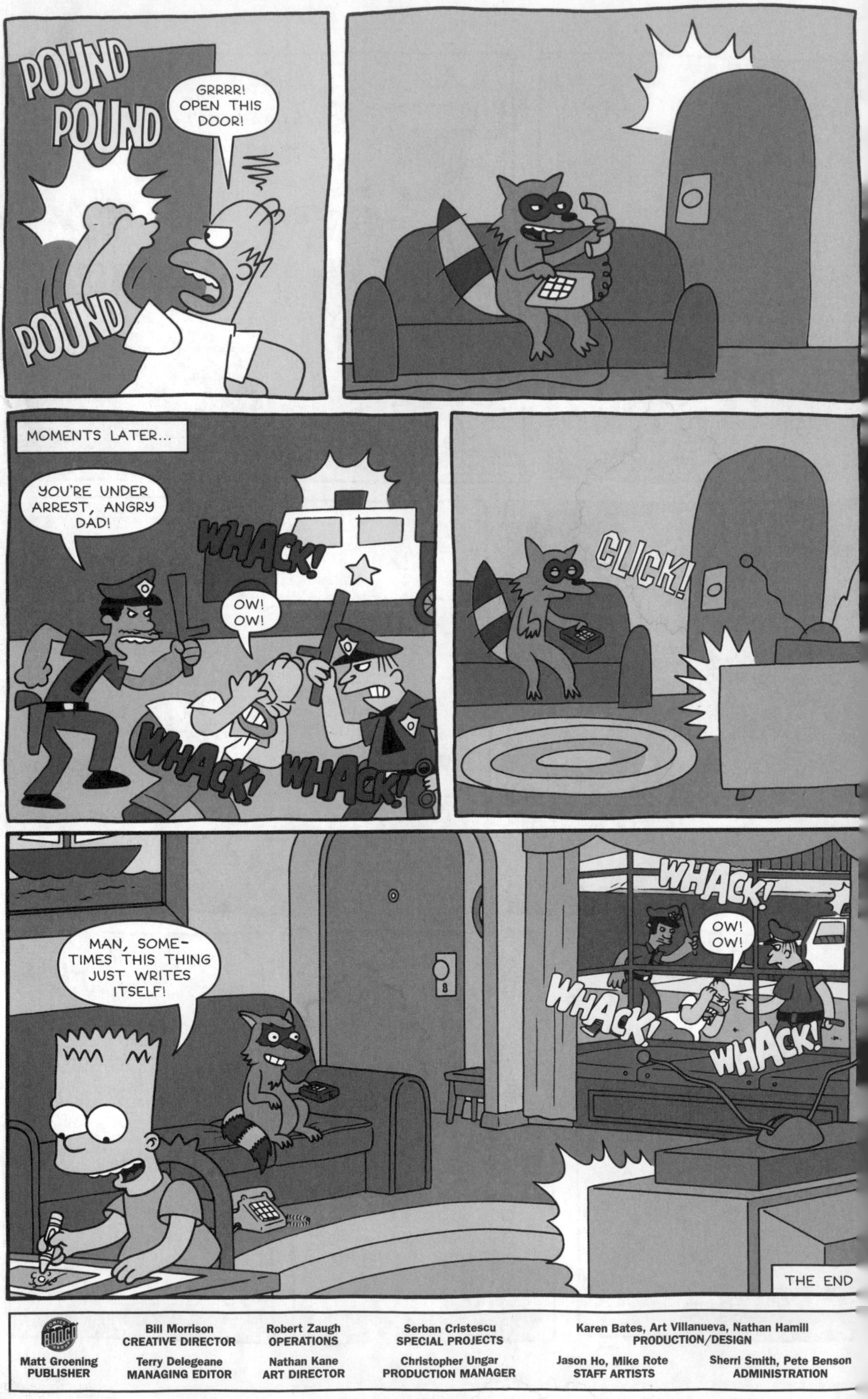

POUND
POUND
GRRRR! OPEN THIS DOOR!
POUND
MOMENTS LATER...
YOU'RE UNDER ARREST, ANGRY DAD!
WHACK!
OW! OW!
WHACK!
WHACK!
CLICK!
MAN, SOME-TIMES THIS THING JUST WRITES ITSELF!
WHACK!
OW! OW!
WHACK!
WHACK!
THE END

Matt Groening
PUBLISHER

Bill Morrison
CREATIVE DIRECTOR

Terry Delegeane
MANAGING EDITOR

Robert Zaugh
OPERATIONS

Nathan Kane
ART DIRECTOR

Serban Cristescu
SPECIAL PROJECTS

Christopher Ungar
PRODUCTION MANAGER

Karen Bates, Art Villanueva, Nathan Hamill
PRODUCTION/DESIGN

Jason Ho, Mike Rote
STAFF ARTISTS

Sherri Smith, Pete Benson
ADMINISTRATION